ELIZABETHAN
QUINTET

By the same author
OBEDIENT MEN

ELIZABETHAN QUINTET

by

DENIS MEADOWS

LONGMANS, GREEN AND CO
LONDON · NEW YORK · TORONTO

LONGMANS, GREEN AND CO LTD
6 & 7 CLIFFORD STREET LONDON W I
BOSTON HOUSE STRAND STREET CAPE TOWN
531 LITTLE COLLINS STREET MELBOURNE

LONGMANS, GREEN AND CO INC
55 FIFTH AVENUE NEW YORK 3

LONGMANS, GREEN AND CO
20 CRANFIELD ROAD TORONTO 16

ORIENT LONGMANS PRIVATE LTD
CALCUTTA BOMBAY MADRAS
DELHI VIJAYAWADA DACCA

First Published 1956

PRINTED IN GREAT BRITAIN
BY WESTERN PRINTING SERVICES LTD. BRISTOL

To
My Wife

CONTENTS

		Page
Introduction		ix
I.	Sir Francis Walsingham, the English Machiavelli	1
II.	Robert Persons, the Seditious Jesuit	91
III.	John Dee, the Queen's Astrologer	176
IV.	Mary Frith, the Roaring Girl	238
V.	Sir John Harington, the Merry Poet	264

CONTENTS

Introduction

I. Out of ...

II. Robert ..., the ... death.

III. John ...

IV. Man ... and Francisco ...

V. ...

INTRODUCTION

THE coronation of Queen Elizabeth II of England was an event in which tradition, pageantry, and the deep-felt if often inarticulate emotions of Englishmen enabled them to forget for a few carefree days their post-war problems of currency, overseas trade, housing, the high cost of living, and, worst of all, the spectre of atomic warfare. Some of the more vocal optimists were moved to express a conviction that their country was on the threshold of a second Elizabethan Age. Would that it were so. One cannot believe it would not be a good thing for the whole community of English-speaking nations, as well as for the peace of the world.

The modern American is the spiritual heir of the Elizabethan Englishman in his energy and his optimism. From our worried fifties of the twentieth century we look back at the first Elizabethans and marvel at their energy of mind and body and the intensity of their living. When we examine that energy more closely we see that an immense optimism underlay it. It is strange that this should be so. Had we been living in the early years of Elizabeth I's reign and given heed to the state of the nation outside the queen's court, the more solid London businesses, the big houses, and the small coterie of what

ix

our age calls intellectuals, there would have been many
things to disturb us. We should not have discerned too
legible a promise of the years full of creative achievement
that lay ahead and that were to enrich the English-speaking world before a mood of pessimism overwhelmed
it and foretold the triumph of Puritanism.

The old certitudes of medieval Christendom had gone;
so had the comfortable mental security of a geocentric
universe. The Escorial loomed up, a threat to England
and the new Protestant North similar to the threat of
Eastern Communism today. Diseases were widespread,
the dreaded bubonic plague, as well as the new 'disease o'
France', syphilis, which had about four centuries to run
before medicine would begin to catch up with it. The
Elizabethan English, like their modern descendants, had
the new poor on their hands, not the patient, disciplined
middle class plodding along under its burden of taxes,
but a seething, restless army of desperate men and women
thronging the roads and carrying disease, vice and turbulence to small towns and hamlets that were almost
unpoliced and defenceless.

> 'Hark! hark! the dogs do bark;
>   The beggars are coming to town,'

was more than a nursery rhyme jingle. It was a sinister
warning.

Religion? The organized, institutional religion that an
earlier age had taken for granted added darker shadows to
the picture. The Smithfield fires were a recent memory,
not just something in the history books. The English

Papists had become the underdog. Ordinary good-natured, easy-going Englishmen looked on while saints like Cuthbert Mayne, Campion and Southwell found release from atrocious torture in an obscene death. Only the choicer spirits—a Philip Sidney, a Ralegh, a John Harington—disliked religious persecution.

No; when we look at the seamy side of Elizabethan life, there does not appear to have been much reason for so much optimism and for the outburst of creative energy in the English Renaissance. Yet the energy and the optimism were certainly there. They are, I think, summed up and symbolized in the figure of Sir Walter Ralegh, the last and perhaps the greatest of the Eliza-bethans. Already we can trace in him a vein of that Puritanism which engulfed the English race in the seven-teenth century. Ralegh has a whole literature to himself, although not all his panegyrists or his detractors have plumbed the depths of his fascinating and complex char-acter. The five Elizabethans in this book are lesser figures than Ralegh, but all five in their diverse ways exemplify the hopeful, tireless energy of their period.

Sir Francis Walsingham, like Shakespeare, is some-times spoken of as though we knew nothing about his character and idiosyncrasies. Much has been lost, it is true, but enough is left for us to recall the swarthy Secretary of State, an English Machiavelli in his official life, and in private a devout Christian of the new Cal-vinistic school, an affectionate husband and father, a scholar, and a lover of books, trees, and gardens. Above all, he was a great patriot, struggling against ill-health,

family worries, poverty, in a lifelong devotion to his
England. Politics and religion are inextricably mingled
in his public life, as in the public lives of most sixteenth-
century figures. For our age his English patriotism makes
a stronger appeal than the bleak religious creed he held so
tenaciously.

For those who see Walsingham as the hero of this
group of five, Father Robert Persons will appear as the
villain. He had a good deal in common with Sir Francis,
his opponent and political enemy. Swarthy and saturnine,
strong-willed, obstinate in his opinions, cosmopolitan in
his culture, he was at bottom as ineradicably English as
the queen's Principal Secretary. The charges of treason-
mongering and treachery have been flung at Persons so
long that some of the mud has stuck, He suffers, also,
when a too-easy contrast is drawn between him and his
saintly, charming companion and fellow-Jesuit, Edmund
Campion. As with Walsingham, when we have studied
the available material, some obscurity remains. In the
case of Father Persons, however, we may hope that one
day an adequate biography will be written. A great deal
of unpublished material exists, much of it in the archives
of the English Jesuits. The Catholics of England, including Persons' own brethren, the fathers of the Society
of Jesus, have fought shy of this controversial figure in
their history. I venture to think that a case can be made
out for Robert Persons if we will think ourselves back
into his age and his set of loyalties.

The other three members of my quintet are not
political figures, unless in Dr. John Dee, philosopher,

scientist and astrologer, we choose to see the germ of Victorian imperialism. In his energy and his versatility Dr. Dee was a true man of the Renaissance. That he was part, but only part, charlatan, is possibly true. Along with many charlatans of the non-political kind, he seems to have been a likeable human being. He made himself a good deal of a nuisance, to put it mildly, to Mrs. Dee at one point in his career, but he won and held the favour of Queen Elizabeth and was well regarded by Sir Walter Ralegh. You had to be more than charlatan to do that.

With Mistress Mary Frith, less respectfully known as Moll Cutpurse, we leave the region of high politics, divinity, philosophy, and alchemy. We now associate with a gangster, but a gangster with style, flair, humanity, not the cold, ruthless, and unhumorous modern kind. Mary had the big-scale gangster's gift for organization and government, but appears to have ruled by winning affection and loyalty rather than by inspiring terror. Doubtless, brought up as she was in a decorous and God-fearing way, she must often have heard that crime doesn't pay, in whatever guise the Elizabethans put the axiom. She refused to believe it, and went on to support her unbelief by a lifetime of profitable wrong-doing and a respectable death from natural causes at the ripe old age, for those days, of seventy-five. The earnest Puritan and incorruptible statesman, Walsingham, would have shuddered to find himself grouped with Moll Cutpurse. So, in his way, would the Reverend Robert Persons, professed father of the Society of Jesus, although one can picture him as being kind, patient, and gentle with her had she

been of the old Faith, in his confessional, where he shed
his sarcasm and his Hispaniolated politics and was simply
the minister of the sacrament of forgiveness. I think, too,
he would afterwards have sent her by discreet messengers
kindly letters of spiritual direction to keep her on the
straight path, signing himself, as to his other friends,
'Yours wholly ever, R.P.'

The fifth member of my quintet is Sir John Harington,
'that saucy poet', as his godmother, Queen Elizabeth I,
called him in one of her moments of unvindictive anger.
In him we see the Elizabethan energy and optimism at
war with the temperament of the dilettante. The supreme
object of all Harington's schemes and efforts was to live
without working. He was a sinecure hunter, a climber
on to band wagons which would, he hoped, carry him
forward to nominal jobs with large incomes. Pursuing
this object he used an amount of energy and produced a
volume of work in his fifty-one years of life that would
be remarkable were it the achievement of one of our
grand old men of letters who go on writing in their
eighties and nineties.

With three centuries of Puritanism in our blood, and
the dismal gospel of work for work's sake preached to
us in our childhood, we ought by rights to despise John
Harington. No one but a curmudgeon would do so. If
he had the defects of his qualities, he also had his peculiar
virtues. Like Mary Frith, he was a late Elizabethan and
he lived on into the seventeenth century, that age of
civil war, embittered controversy, and brutality exercised in the name of religion. Yet his character seems to

skip a century, so as to blossom forth in some of the more admirable traits of the eighteenth century—its suavity and tolerance, its robust and Rabelaisian sense of fun, and a growing kindliness towards man and beast that gave promise of steady increase until the dictators led us back to the barbarism from which we started.

I

SIR FRANCIS WALSINGHAM
THE ENGLISH MACHIAVELLI

SIR FRANCIS WALSINGHAM, from his picture in the
National Portrait Gallery, gazes out on twentieth-
century London with a slightly puzzled expression.
Disillusionment is there also, and less of the harshness
one might expect from studying him only as statesman
and secret service chief. There is no record of the
painter's name, nor do we know anything of the circumstances of the Secretary's sitting for his portrait. Perhaps it is not too far-fetched to imagine the sittings taking
place amid the rural domesticity of Barn Elms in one of
the periods when the queen's Principal Secretary—
Foreign Secretary he would be nowadays, or Secretary of
State, in Washington, D.C.—retired to his pleasant
home in Surrey to guard his family from the summer on-
set of the plague or to nurse his own shattered health.

On the other hand, the artist may have painted in the
library or one of the parlours of the dignified house in
Sything (the modern Seething) Lane. There is a look of
careful dressing about the Secretary, as though he had
just come from a conference with the queen at Whitehall

B   I

or had been skilfully probing the Spanish ambassador's mind in the Castilian tongue or in the Latin which was the diplomatic *lingua franca* of the times. The sombre, but rich clothing, the ruff beautifully starched by the new process which a Dutch lady had brought into England to her very great advantage, the black skull-cap all suggest the Secretary of State on one of his working days.

Could Sir Francis step down from his frame, walk along Whitehall, and drop in at No. 10 Downing Street for a chat with the Prime Minister, recently the holder of the office Walsingham once filled, the two men would find out quickly that they had in common the distinction of good tailoring—that, and devotion to a queen named Elizabeth, young, charming, and much loved by her subjects. On one point they would differ profoundly—political ethics. Sir Francis' double standard, of Christian sincerity in private life and Machiavellian finesse in international affairs, would find no place in Sir Anthony Eden's philosophy of statesmanship.

People who know something of Walsingham's career and his secret service think they see in his extant portraits an expression of guile appropriate to one whom James I called 'a very Machiavel'. He was, indeed, Machiavellian in the technique of his diplomacy and his intelligence service. In other respects he was English, one might say generically English. Although England has produced a Walsingham, a Thurloe, and, in our times, the Special Branch of Scotland Yard and a highly skilled intelligence service in time of war, the English are not a

Machiavellian people. There is a paradox here, an enigma about the island race, and that, perhaps, is what one can read in the grave features of Queen Elizabeth I's swarthy Secretary as he looks out with those brooding eyes at his modern countrymen.

The attempt to resolve the enigma and to make sense of the addition of the adjective Machiavellian to the name of so typical an Englishman has led me to the conclusion that Walsingham was a statesman and a politician —a good deal of the former, not much of the latter— with a singular inner integrity. In that he stands out from the ruck of his contemporaries in public life, who, if we were to judge from their own protestations, were harassed bearers of stainless Excelsior flags through oceans of corruption, self-seeking, and insincerity, other people's, be it understood.

They never, like the first Elizabeth's Principal Secretary, admit to doing things in public life they would shun as private citizens. They never own up to accepting the Spanish dictum, 'Tell a lie, and find a truth'; they act on it, but raise shocked eyebrows at its formulation. Unless they are Communists, an otherwise humourless and irritating breed, they never plead guilty to doing evil for the sake of a fancied good. Not too many of them, given the chance, would achieve the same record for financial honesty and the lavish spending of their own money for the efficiency of a government department. Moreover, through the greater part of a long career of public service, Walsingham had to see his warnings disregarded, and his anti-Spanish policy, which he always expounded with a

John Bullish frankness, given the brush-off in the queen's chamber and the Privy Council. Of course, when the crash came and invasion was imminent, he was expected to help. We have seen that happen in our own time.

After victory had been won, thanks to a combination of English seamanship and more especially English gunnery, Spanish bureaucratic ineptitude, and the vagaries of English Channel weather, labelled as Divine Providence by Protestant officialdom, Walsingham was graciously allowed to use for his queen and country the last few years of an invalid's life and such scanty funds as were not earmarked for his son-in-law's debts and the salaries of the men in civil intelligence work. Add to all this that Sir Francis Walsingham was a faithful and generous husband, and affectionate father, a man deeply religious in a creed that to us moderns is emotionally unintelligible, a scholar and lover of learning conspicuous even in the heyday of the English Renaissance, and something of a pioneer in the highly civilized art of landscape gardening. The sum total is more than the crafty Secretary and secret service organizer which is all some people discern in the anonymous painting in the National Portrait Gallery.

We know little of the ancestry and the early life of Sir Francis Walsingham. A few facts enable us to guess at formative influences and help us to understand Sir Francis in his maturity. The family name is thought to have some connection with the little town of Walsingham in Norfolk, a famous medieval shrine of the Blessed Virgin, now revived by the competing efforts of Catholics and High Anglicans. Francis would have had no use for the medieval Slipper Chapel held by the Catholics, for the Italianate shrine of the Anglicans, or even for the authentic holy well, now, I believe, in the hands of the Quaker Gurneys. He was a true-blue Protestant, of the evangelical left wing of the English Church, a loyal Anglican, of the Articles rather than the Collects—but sympathetic to the group men were beginning to call Puritans. Had he been able to see what the Puritans would do to the English crown within sixty years of his own death, Walsingham might have veered more to his queen's middle-of-the-road Anglicanism.

The date of Francis Walsingham's birth is given by the books as 1530, with a question mark after it. Anyhow, he was so near a contemporary of the queen that when she was young, lively, and charming, he was a rising— and soberly well-dressed—young statesman. Perhaps that explains in part the lifelong bond between them, that survived clashes of temperament, divergence on policy, and Elizabeth's hearty dislike of the Calvinist faction in the Church of which she was the Supreme Governess on earth. We do not know for certain where Francis was born. He may have been a Londoner, born in the parish of St. Mary Aldermanbury, or so near the capital as makes little difference—on his father's newly acquired property in the vicinity of Chislehurst.

The father, William, was a lawyer, who appears to have worked for Thomas Cromwell and to have served as a legal and financial expert when Cardinal Wolsey's estate was wound up after his death. Where the senior

Walsingham stood in matters of religion in that troubled age we do not know. Probably he watched the growth of Henry VIII's *via media* and trimmed his sails accordingly. He died in the year Henry married Anne Boleyn in time to give the child she was carrying legitimacy (except in Catholic eyes).

Young Francis studied in King's College, Cambridge, and began his law studies in Gray's Inn. During his period of exile he attended lectures on law in the University of Padua. Law was in the family tradition, and the youth probably had the type of mind to make a success at it. It seems certain that he had been brought up a Protestant rather than a schismatic Catholic or a moderate Anglican, for soon after Queen Mary's accession, and when the Smithfield fires began to be kindled for die-hard Protestants, Walsingham, then a young man of some twenty-three years, voluntarily exiled himself rather than conform. One wonders if any of his five sisters went into exile with him or stayed quietly at home making the appropriate gestures. The majority of English people seemed to think that less than Paris was worth a Mass. While young Walsingham was trying to resume his interrupted legal studies, and imbibing Genevan Calvinism at the source, the clever young careerist, William Cecil, some ten years Walsingham's senior, had shed crocodile tears over his own apostasy for Mary Tudor's edification and haunted her court, we are told, with an outsize pair of rosary beads jingling in his hands. English Catholics, who have generally excoriated Walsingham for his persecution of the seminary priests, should bear in mind this fidelity to conscience, similar in quality to that of Cuthbert Mayne, Campion, Bryant, Southwell, and the other English martyrs innocent of the treason Walsingham attributed to the Papists. In fairness we must admit that two great English contemporaries, Cardinal Allen and Robert Persons, made his distrust of the mission priests appear logical.

We may regret that during this period of continental exile young Walsingham did not come under Lutheran rather than Calvinist influences. Candles and vestments, a crucifix, and the doctrine of consubstantiation softened somewhat the underlying Manichean spirit of the new religion. It was a good thing the young Princess Elizabeth had been indoctrinated with the milder form of Protestantism by her stepmother Katherine Parr. Most of the Marian exiles, unfortunately, went all out for the Genevan doctrine. Walsingham, however, the young Gray's Inn student fleeing the Marian persecution, found what he needed in Calvin's rigidly logical system of theology. It was legalistic and, on its own premises, highly rational. That Walsingham was a lawyer doubtless helped to predispose him to Calvinism. To our age it appears as one of the gloomiest creeds ever excogitated by men, but perhaps our sixteenth-century ancestors, of more robust fibre, could look contentedly on a human race of whom the majority were predestined to eternal punishment. Only a few unfortunates who were convinced they were a part of that majority seemed to have been much affected in their emotions.

When Walsingham's five years of exile came to an end

and he went back to England soon after Queen Elizabeth's accession, he was no sour Puritan of the dreary, kill-joy type satirized by seventeenth-century royalists. He had mixed with lawyers, scholars, writers, men of affairs, as well as Calvinist divines and clergymen. On the foundation of his classical and legal studies he had built a fabric of humane learning that puts him definitely in the class of scholarly statesmen. He had mastered several modern languages, and we know that he spoke them fluently and accurately, for his colleagues on the Privy Council always called on him to act as interpreter when they wished to be particularly beastly or particularly nice to some important foreigner. It is not too fanciful to surmise that the queen and her foreign secretary would sometimes carry on their official discussions in one or other of the languages, dead and living, which they spoke in addition to English. In one of their periodical squabbles on foreign policy when, in his frank way, the Secretary had argued against the queen's conciliatory attitude towards Spain, she, regarding him as a warmonger, had ended the discussion by chasing him from her presence. As she hurled one of her slippers at his face she cried, '*Point de guerre! point de guerre!*'

If, early in the public career which began soon after his return to England, Mr. Francis Walsingham, Member of Parliament for Banbury, displayed a certain severity of manner and aspect, it was temperamental rather than an effect of his theology. He was a saturnine man, capable of biting sarcasm on occasion, as was his political enemy, Father Persons. Like Father Persons, too, he

could charm with unexpected flashes of tenderness and
generosity, and one of his characteristic virtues was
loyalty.

Some of the sternness, the impatience with bunglers,
fools, and incompetents, the sudden terrifying bursts of
angry violence in dealing with political suspects and possible traitors, may have been due to the malady which
plagued him, apparently, all through his adult life. We
do not know precisely what it was or when it started.
Diagnoses of four centuries ago were seldom reliable, and
often not even intelligible. The trouble reads like an
acute form of stone and, whatever it was, it caused frequent and at time excruciating bouts of pain. Father
Persons describes it as an incurable malady of the testicles,
but clerical gossip of the English Catholic exiles must be
taken with a grain of salt. Anything wrong with people's
sexual functions must have been much more horrendous
before the days of salvarsan and penicillin. The Jesuit
controversialist was thinking in terms of a Divine visitation on the persecutor of the Catholic mission priests.

The tittle-tattle of the clerics in exile went to great
lengths of vindictive prurience at times. Anyone who
cares to read through Cardinal Allen's extensive correspondence in English and Latin will be shocked by that
saintly ecclesiastic's acceptance and repetition of a scab-
rous story, obviously unprovable, of the perverse sexual
relations between the queen and Sir Walter Ralegh. If
stories of this kind reached Walsingham's ears from
Douai and Rome—there were always stool-pigeons
among the exiles—it helps to explain his bitterness

against the spawn of the seminaries, as he called the usually heroic and blameless members of the Catholic underground.

Public service had become the accepted career for male Walsinghams by the time Francis was born. His grandfather was sheriff of Kent; his father, William, was in local government in Kent and in London, being one of the under-sheriffs of the city some time after the birth of his son. An uncle, Sir Edmund, became Lieutenant of the Tower. One of the duties of this post was the supervision of official questioning of suspects, in plain language, torture to make prisoners talk. Possibly the Lieutenant's nephew became familiarized with his uncle's inquisitorial methods, for we find him later on not averse from ordering a 'taste of the rack'—though often the mere threat of it sufficed—when he was dealing with an obstinate or strong-willed suspect. Probably he thought no more of it than a modern Frenchman does of a *juge d'instruction's* quizzing, or Walsingham's present-day countrymen do of those suave gentlemen from Scotland Yard who figure in crime plays and movies. The Walsinghams were no sadists. Sir Francis never ordered the rack when he could gain his object by a bit of verbal hectoring or even a good shaking, which he would sometimes administer with his own hands when he was annoyed or was suffering more cruelly than usual from his malady. Of Uncle Edmund one is glad to hear that he refused to have the rack wound as tightly as the Lord Chancellor wanted it when Anne Askew was being questioned. Unhappily his refusal did not save the pathetic female enthusiast. Lord Wriothesley had superior authority and it is said that he pushed one of the mechanics aside and himself gave an extra turn to the winch. If Francis Walsingham, then a young student, heard about the incident, one trusts that family loyalty, as well as humanity, made him side with Uncle Edmund against the Lord Chancellor.

With his taking his seat in Parliament as member for Banbury in the winter of 1558 we may say that Francis' career of public service began almost as soon he set foot in his own country again after his five years' exile. Banbury was a 'safe' seat; so was Lyme Regis, for which he sat about ten years later when his real life's work, diplomacy and secret intelligence, began. In a sense all constituencies were safe seats under the Tudors—for the right people, that is to say. There is no record of the young Parliament man taking any part in debates. We cannot picture Walsingham as a spellbinder, nor a weaver of graceful compliments to the crown, despite his loyalty to it on principle as well as to the brilliant woman who then wore it. He was too much the intellectual and the scholar for popular oratory or for courtiers' antics. He was the sort of M.P. who is more valuable in committees of legal experts than on the floor of the House.

Towards the end of Elizabeth's first decade as queen Walsingham began the work for which he showed a special genius, secret service in defence of the English crown and English national independence. He built up a political English secret service system which was unrivalled until John Thurloe developed his vast organization under Oliver Cromwell's dictatorship. The techniques of these two great Secretaries seem to have been very similar and they were both highly efficient. The chief difference is that the rather dour, genuinely Puritan Elizabethan did it out of his own pocket, while the Lord Protector's bland, smiling little lawyer, a bandwagon Puritan, received a fantastically large annual appropriation of public money.

The formidable, but badly mismanaged Catholic rising of the north in 1569 and the Ridolfi Plot, a mixture of subtlety and ineptitude, came about the time when Walsingham began to work in close collaboration with Lord Treasurer Cecil, the Old Fox, as the Catholics called him later on. He had recognized Walsingham's special talents and encouraged him to systematize the collection of secret data from correspondents in English pay, that is, on Walsingham's private salary list. We read that the year before the rising took place Walsingham was able to supply the Lord Treasurer with lists of all English suspects entering Italy.

The rising of the north, in 1569, might, with better management and more co-operation on the part of the leaders, have been successful. Had it been, the course of English history would have been different. How? I do not think it easy to answer. The idea that the failure was just a case of the English Catholics missing the bus is oversimplified. The deposition of Elizabeth, Mary of Scotland married to the Duke of Norfolk and put on the throne of England, the Catholic Faith—still the faith of more than half the country, says Mr. Belloc—re-estab-

lished, England once more in official allegiance to the
Papacy? All that as the product of the military strength
of the northern earls, the loyalty of Catholics to their
traditional faith, and some help from an expeditionary
force sent by the Duke of Alva? Possibly. On the other
hand, England might have been plagued with a dis-
astrous state of religious warfare. But Norfolk and the
northern earls worked at cross purposes, the Duke of
Alva was worried as to what France would do if his back
were turned to help the northern earls, and the English
Catholics were at this time weary of squabbles and persecution and mostly ready to go part of the way towards
the Elizabethan compromise until the missionary priests
and the Jesuits came along to re-animate their fervour
with a breath of the new spirit from the little north
Italian town of Trento. It had all started with a scheme
for marrying the Duke of Norfolk to the Queen of Scots,
but this was revealed to the English authorities.

The duke lacked the moral courage to make a frank
confession of the whole thing to Elizabeth and fled to
his estate in Norfolk, feigning illness. The royal favourite,
Leicester, and the queen's faithful Treasurer, William
Cecil, although they loathed each other, had organized a
committee to go into the subject. The Duke of Norfolk
was a nominal Protestant and can have had little enthusiasm for the religious, or perhaps one should say
ecclesiastical, aspect of the scheme. He was a drifter,
however. Lacking the fundamental loyalty of Robert
Dudley, Earl of Leicester, and the political wisdom of
Cecil, he waded into waters too deep for one of his

mental and moral qualities. He played into the hands of
Guerau, the intriguing Spanish ambassador, made contact with the Duke of Alva, and became the figurehead
in a tortuous plot which included the seizure of the
Queen of Scots, now a 'guest' but actually a prisoner of
her cousin of England, Queen Elizabeth. The latter
acted with a vigour and promptness that give the lie to
the picture of her as a mere catspaw of her Treasurer.
She ordered Norfolk to London, clapped him into the
Tower, and put his chief southern supporters under
house arrest. Mary, Queen of Scots, was hastily moved
south to Coventry. The northern earls were ordered to
London, but refused to obey. They had missed the tide
and were caught between the queen's energy and the
religious fervour of their Catholic followers. They let
the rebellion take its course. The earls of Warwick and
Hunsdon, the latter a cousin of Elizabeth, marched to
the north with the royal forces. By the end of the year
the rising had been crushed.

The government leaders had acted promptly and, by
our standards, ruthlessly. Numbers of rebel soldiers,
who after all were mostly dependents of the earls and had
to follow their masters, were hanged from gibbets and
trees in all the towns and villages of the disaffected area.
As anticlimax to the tragedy, after everything was over
(1570), the reigning pope, the Dominican Pius V, afterwards canonized, issued his famous Bull, *Regnans in
excelsis*, stigmatizing Elizabeth as bastard and usurper,
and inviting Christian rulers to dethrone her. All this
Elizabeth and her ministers might have laughed off, but

when the pontiff went on to release all her Catholic subjects from their allegiance, Rome had declared war against
the Tudor crown. William Cecil, the opportunist, and
his intelligence chief, the sincere Protestant Walsingham,
would henceforth regard all Catholics as potential
enemies. Elizabeth herself, scholarly, tolerant, a woman
of the world, probably a good deal of a pagan and agnostic
at heart, found herself willy-nilly in alliance with the
fanatical left wing of her ecclesiastical establishment. To
the end of her life she kept candles and crucifix, a
decorous ritual, and those 'rags of Popery,' surplices, in
her private chapel. In moments of irritation against her
faithful 'Moor', Mr. Secretary Walsingham, she could
think of nothing more cutting to say than that he was fit
only to be a protector of heretics—in this case the
Puritans, whom she heartily disliked.

There is little doubt that Cecil regarded the Duke of
Norfolk as a danger to the queen and to the whole Tudor
set-up, but the original marriage scheme had not in itself been treasonable. Cecil, however, be his private
ideas about political assassination what they may, would
not just murder the duke in the casual Renaissance
fashion, even had he been able to get away with it. The
Treasurer, all his contemporaries agree, was an adept at
'throwing the stone so as the hand be not seen'. In this
case, Norfolk settled his own fate by his folly.

In the summer following the suppression of the
northern rising, the duke had won the queen's forgiveness and been released. At this moment Signor Ridolfi
comes on the scene. That Norfolk ever dreamed for a

moment of taking part in a murder conspiracy against Elizabeth seems very unlikely, but his association with Ridolfi was damning in English eyes. One is intrigued by the figure of the wealthy Italian business man, a financial tycoon in Elizabethan London. Why did he meddle in such perilous affairs? Why did he pit his Italian brain against the bland, shrewd Treasurer, William Cecil, and his assistant Walsingham? Was it from motives of religious zeal, or were there big financial stakes tied in the plot? Or was it just from Italian love of intrigue for its own sake, the desire to be and show oneself *furbo*—slick, clever, smart? Norfolk himself was a naturally open and rather stupid man. The Italian banker, on the other hand, was a mixture of subtlety and childish indiscretion. He plotted cleverly, and then fulminated garrulously against Elizabeth to all and sundry. He was in the end no match for Cecil, who had efficient and well-paid informers keeping their ear to the ground. Walsingham was told to see what he could ferret out of the Florentine man of business.

He kept Ridolfi in mild custody for a short time and cross-examined him, but did not produce the brilliant results we might have expected. In fact, the Italian seems to have got the better of it at first. Apparently his only connection with any conspiracy was that all the suspects owed him money. He displayed the notes of hand to back up his story. One can picture the Italian shrug of the shoulders and the tolerant smile with which he confessed to his maladroit action as a business man. Walsingham was convinced of his honesty and let him go, as one sinned against but not sinning. The queen, however, got nearer the truth by her female intuition than did Walsingham by his lawyer's cross-examining. She maintained that there was more to Ridolfi than met the eye and that the examination had not got to the bottom of things.

The crowning follies of the plotters were the dispatch of money from Norfolk to Mary Stuart and a cipher letter sent from the continent by Ridolfi to the duke. The money was intercepted, and so was the letter.

The outcome of the Ridolfi Plot was that the unlucky duke was tried for treason, found guilty, and executed. He did not go to his death until the spring of 1572. The queen had a struggle with her own feelings about it. If the more perceptive among the English caught a glimpse of the hand that threw the stone, at least everything was done with due form of law, and that, even in Tudor England, counted for a great deal. William Cecil doubtless felt more comfortable in his mind. He was fifty years old, a venerable age in that era, and a member of the House of Lords under the title of Burghley, and he would be glad to think that his English queen and the Anglican *via media* now had a fair chance of survival. I think, however, that it is less than just of Hilaire Belloc to read into Cecil's mind *only* the desire to safeguard the fortunes of the 'new' men who had made a good thing out of buying or leasing monastic property from the crown. After all, those fortunes had been exempted from seizure or reprisal when England was officially restored to Papal allegiance under Queen Mary. It was one

c

of the necessary conditions Mary and her husband Philip of Spain had to accept as a prerequisite for England's return to Catholic unity. Why, other things being equal, could not the same arrangement have been made for Elizabeth, if she had married a Catholic prince from France, or her half-sister's widower, Philip II?

This speculation about the motives hidden in the bosom of the Old Fox involves a point I should like to make about Francis Walsingham. James VI of Scotland, England's James I, called him 'a very Machiavel', and we know that Walsingham used some very shady agents in his lifelong work for the queen's safety and England's independence. There was Mr. Phelippes, a genius in his own line, but a man with a questionable record and, presumably, few loyalties except to the queen and Mr. Secretary.

At some time in the development of his secret service Walsingham took under his wing Thomas Phillips or Phelippes. This man, a little, sandy-haired fellow, appears and disappears mysteriously like a wizard's familiar, which indeed was his position in the Secretary's following. There are hints of a disreputable past and some kind of trouble with the law from which Walsingham rescued him. Whether from gratitude or because of the hold his employer had over him, Phelippes served him loyally for many years, while ostensibly holding down a job in the Customs House. He finally disappears from English history with a sinecure in the royal household.

Phelippes must have had a good education, for we

know he was an excellent linguist, a master of the
classical languages and several living ones. However, his
special value to his new master lay in his ability, amount-
ing to genius, as a forger and a maker and breaker of
codes. He could copy any handwriting beyond the
powers of detection in those days, devise cryptograms
with great cunning, and, above all, break other people's
codes with ease and sureness. A minor accomplishment,
but very useful to a man in his position, was his knack of
opening and deciphering sealed letters without disturbing the seal. He foraged happily through the diplomatic
pouches, the secret papers of conspirators, and the
letters passing to and from the colonies of Catholic
exiles. How the dignified Spanish noblemen and the
clever, shrewd 'mounseers', surrounded by secretaries
and amanuenses, would have raged had they known that
their top secret papers in unbreakable ciphers were being
quietly opened, deciphered, transcribed, and sent on
their way again by the little, unimpressive Customs House
executive who had given their baggage and their hordes
of retainers diplomatic courtesies when they landed in
the foggy island peopled by simple-minded barbarians!
So far as we can restore the picture of the elusive Mr.
Thomas Phelippes from the teasing bits of evidence, he
was a genuine artist. He seems to have mingled freely
with Catholics and Protestants, unmoved by theological
passions; we hear nothing of the wenchings and carousals
of the age, and he was satisfied with a modest com-
petence all his life. It is more than probable that after
sleepless nights on a fine piece of forgery or a tough

job with a secret document on its way from the Spanish
embassy to the Escorial, Mr. Phelippes sat back and
gazed at his work as an artist gazed at a finished painting
or sculpture, or a poet feasts eyes and ears on the beauty
which his magic has created out of a few dozen signs and
symbols.

There were less admirable people on the payroll of
the Puritan statesman, such as the execrable Sledd, an
ex-seminarist who had become a government stool-
pigeon, a vicious, quarrelsome fellow who made up for
his early years of celibacy by haunting the London stews.
There he combined business with pleasure by picking up
bits of information from the sleeping partners of men
who had friends or relatives imprisoned in the Tower.
Then there was the fallen Venetian priest who kept up
the externals of his vocation and specialized in the theft
of Papal documents. Add to these, cut-throat adven-
turers of assorted nationalities, venal members of
foreign embassy households, apostate Catholics spying
on their brethren in Paris, Rome, Louvain and Douai.
and a host of minor camp followers, jailbirds earning
their freedom, valets and ladies' maid in English pay, and
probably, a certain number of counter-spies, because we
hear little or nothing of failures in the organization
directed from the well-run Puritan household in Seething
Lane, the rural retreat in Kent, or, later on, the country
house at Barnes. Yes, Walsingham had enrolled a number
of bad hats in the service of the Virgin Queen and her
England. He knowingly and as a matter of policy paid
bad men and women to work for him, because only

bad people would do the kind of work necessary. Nevertheless, Walsingham would not himself have worked for a bad superior. If he worked so long and so loyally with William Cecil, Lord Burghley, his associate and chief, it was because he held that shrewd statesman to be a good patriot and a sincere Protestant. Walsingham himself was both, but he knew a good deal about those who were neither.

Modern Catholics, happy and assured in their faith, find it hard to think themselves back into the minds of those 'apostates' who were born when the Renaissance popes ruled and who grew to adult life before the Tridentine reforms had purified what was left of medieval Christendom. It is quite conceivable that Cecil's Protestantism was as genuine as his rosary-jingling under Queen Mary was spurious, and we lack conclusive evidence that his chief motive in all that he did for the new Church of England was concern for the revenue from monastic estates. Those estates had, in most cases, to be bought from the crown, either for cash or for services rendered. Mr. Belloc's use of the word 'loot' is so repetitious that the unwary reader forms a picture of a glorious free-for-all wherein the English go-getters helped themselves to what they wanted. That was not at all the Tudor monarchs' way with their loving subjects.

Let us concede, however, that Lord Burghley's reformed faith, like his Marian Catholicism, was doubtfully sincere. There was no doubt at all about Walsingham's. He was an earnest Calvinist, a scholarly student of the Bible, a reader of theology, and a man whose family life is a touching record of affection and fidelity shadowed by tragedy—the loss of an elder daughter and of a much esteemed son-in-law, husband of the younger daughter. Something should be said about the Calvinism of Walsingham and his contemporaries. It is the fashion nowadays to poke fun at it and leave it at that—predestination—the bulk of the human race except the elect, happy me and my friends, in virtue of God's inscrutable Decrees, all going to an eternal hell that even devout Catholics of our time by-pass with asseverations of the fact that while they have to believe in it as a state of being and a place, they don't have to believe that any specific human being ever went there.

Calvinism was indeed all that we say about it, but it was something more to those sixteenth-century converts to it. They saw, like the young John Henry Newman, two individual and vastly significant beings, two foci of existence, God the Creator, and man—John Henry or Francis—the finite, contingent creature. Only those two and the relation between them truly mattered. Man prayed to and sought to touch, happily and confidently or in fear and trembling, that Supreme Being directly and without other mediator than the Incarnate Saviour who had assumed our depraved nature to save those few whom His Father had chosen. Religion—personal religion, as later Protestants called it—was no longer an affair of a mediating priesthood, of sacraments, of a daily vicarious Sacrifice of the Mass, and a corporate act of prayer called the Divine Office. Baptism, indeed, remained supremely important, but the Lord's Supper had faded into a mere symbol. When the Jesuits came along with their own freedom from choir duties, their preaching of the higher spirituality outside the cloister, people nicknamed them the Puritans of Popery. For all their stress on unity and loyalty, there was a new note of individualism in Ignatian piety, and people sensed something in common between it and the spirit of John Calvin.

There is another facet of Walsingham's Calvinism that should be considered in relation to his methods as secret service chief. Those unworthy tools, the two-faced apostates, the suborned informers, the forgers and spies, the ex-clerics spending the Secretary's money in the brothels of Bankside or London Bridge, were undoubtedly not of the elect, or their election would have borne fruits of righteousness. They were predestined to damnation in any case. Why, then, not use them against the machinations of Rome and Spain and for the security of the queen, who was a Protestant, even if a rather tepid one? The argument would not sound right on the lips of a present-day statesman, the British Foreign Secretary, let us say, or an American Secretary of State, but I can see its validity for a sincere Calvinist four centuries ago. Walsingham himself asserts candidly in letters that have been preserved his belief that statesmen, to be faithful to their duties, must use means that are not permissible to the private citizen. How many contemporary politicians working on the same assumption would assert it so categorically? The answer is, I suppose, Communists, and they only in the hearing of their own elect.

In 1570, the year of the Bull *Regnans in excelsis*, begins
the record of more active persecution of English Catholics which, with ups and downs, such as the relative
quiescence under the Puritan dictatorship, lasted, with
diminishing intensity, until 1829. For any English
Catholic who can perceive the elements that are admirable in Walsingham it is sad to contemplate his anti-
Catholicism. Yet anti-Catholic he certainly was,
although he could on occasion confer amicably and with
more than diplomatic correctness with Spanish and
French Catholics. We know, too, of one occasion, anyhow, when he showed himself gracious and tolerant
towards one of the hated 'spawn of the seminaries'. A
young priest, trained in Dr. Allen's school for martyrs
and with the chrism of ordination still fresh on his hands,
landed in England and was promptly picked up by the
pursuivants and taken to London. It must have been a
disturbing experience for that young man, however
much he had prayed for the martyr's crown in the devout
peace of his seminary, to be taken to that London house,
not so far from the Tower with its racks and dungeons,
and led into the presence of the swarthy, frowning
Secretary, the persecuting ogre of seminary meditations.
A few minutes' conversation seems to have convinced
Walsingham that the youth was ignorant of politics—
Dr. Allen, whatever he was up to himself, rigidly banned
politics from the college—and as innocent of treason as
Frances Walsingham, the Secretary's baby daughter.
Where was the young man's home, the Secretary asked.
Oxfordshire, near the city of Oxford. Very well, then,

let him go to his parent's house and stay there peaceably, bound only by the laws of the queen's realm—ah, yes, and one slight condition of this act of grace—he must call on a certain reverend doctor of divinity, an Oxford professor and a friend of the Secretary, for a quiet talk about the points of difference between their two faiths. One would like to know the subsequent history of that young priest. Did he leave the realm again—he could hardly have gone ahead with his intended ministry at that time—make a retreat at Rheims or Rome and return to England to face the rack, the gibbet, and the quartering block? Or did he succumb to the kindness, sincere or feigned, of the formidable Secretary and the arguments of the Oxford D.D., forsake his vocation and take service with Walsingham? Good Catholics will grieve to think that this may have happened, but there must have been such cases in Walsingham's career.

In the late summer or early fall of 1570 Walsingham was given a task which officially launched him on a diplomatic career. It was an assignment after his own heart. He was to assist Elizabeth's ambassador at the French court, Sir Henry Norris, in working for the full toleration of the Huguenots. This was one of those sixteenth-century moves in European diplomacy wherein religion and politics are so intertwined that it is impossible for later ages to untangle them. The minds of Elizabeth and her Treasurer, Lord Burghley, were motivated by the concept of the balance of power which has moulded English foreign policy so constantly since the loss of the French territories. Burghley certainly wished to give the

Protestant cause a helping hand whenever and wherever he could. His motives? Merely mercenary, say Mr. Belloc and his followers; the Old Fox wanted to make sure of the fortunes of the 'new' men at court. I think William Cecil was a wiser statesman and a better patriot than that. To him, as to his fellow Councillors, especially Walsingham, Spain was the enemy and the menace.

The impact of Spanish power on Englishmen's thoughts and emotions was not unlike the effect of Soviet imperialism on our minds today. France, it is true, was, like Spain, a Catholic country. Her reigning monarch was officially the Most Christian King (*Christianissimus Rex*) and she had the same mission to spread the Faith and destroy heresy. France, however, except under the influence of some rare amalgam of mysticism and active zeal, like Peter the Hermit, St. Bernard, or Joan of Arc, has a knack of wearing her Catholicism with a difference, living and letting live where those outside the Catholic Church are concerned. So it was in the fifteen hundreds in the case of the young, active, and zealous body of Calvinistic Protestants rapidly getting to a position of vast influence in the country. There were civil wars, but they did not wear the semblance of crusades. There were times when it must have seemed certain that the wavering influence of the French crown and the Gallic-minded church hierarchy, even when reinforced by the ultramontane spirit of Trent, could not stand up much longer against the powerful Huguenot minority. All in all, then, France in the eyes of Queen Elizabeth and many of her servants was a desirable ally in the cold war with Spain, a war that was not so cold in the Caribbean, where 'No peace below the Line' was accepted by both parties and caused hardly a ripple in European chancelleries.

Walsingham knew and said, in season and out of season, that the contest would become a hot war. The queen and Lord Burghley may have known it, but they disliked hearing it said. Perhaps the combined might of big, powerful France and little, active, enterprising England would act as a check on the King of Spain. Philip II, though a bureaucrat, was no fool, nor was he the insensate bigot of 'Westward Ho!' and the Victorian imagination. Moreover, he was related to Elizabeth by his marriage to her half-sister, and earlier in the story would not have been averse from a match with the young queen, bastard or no bastard in orthodox eyes. The shocked horror and disapproval with which he received the Bull of Deposition could hardly have been greater had he been a Protestant.

That Walsingham opposed the temporizing policy of the queen and Burghley, does credit, I think, to his sincerity, although the others may have had the greater political wisdom. The Secretary, however, was no warmonger, nor have we any proof that he was very intent on land-grabbing in the half of the globe which the Spanish Pope Alexander VI had earmarked for Spanish exploitation. The struggle with Spain as he saw it was primarily, although not exclusively, a religious one. The Huguenots were destined, he believed, to a paramount position in France. They, with England, would be the spearhead of a movement for a Protestant federation which would in time establish its hegemony in northern Europe—a kind of Monroe Doctrine for the region of the Reformed Faith. Oliver Cromwell had the same dream. He made the mistake of cherishing it when Spain was already in decline and France was the true threat. Cromwell was bemused by his own earnest Protestantism. Walsingham, equally religious, had better judgment and a surer feeling for European realities.

One pictures Walsingham setting out on his journey just as the English Channel was coming to the season of its ugly moods. His state of mind was probably a mixture of elation and dismay, elation at helping the Protestant cause in France, dismay at the prospect of a cross-Channel trip at a time of year that defeated Julius Caesar's pertinacity. The middle-aged diplomat seems to have been a fastidious man, and he cannot have relished the smells, noises, and violent motion of a sailing ship in the Narrow Seas. I doubt if he was a good sailor. His tastes were those of a confirmed landsman—quiet, intellectual talk with London divines and men of affairs, domestic life in rural Kent and Surrey, laying out gardens and seeing to the planting of fruit trees. Once in Paris, however, he got to work quickly and apparently with some success, for he went back to London with assurances from King Charles IX of freedom for the French Protestants. By the time winter set in the project of a royal marriage was afoot, between Queen Elizabeth and Henri, Duke of Anjou, the king's brother. This scheme and the hope of inducing the French to help

the Dutch Protestants against their Spanish masters
called for tactful handling. Norris was recalled and replaced by Walsingham, who now had to make a December crossing to take up his new post. The marriage
scheme was temporarily eclipsed. The king died, and
his brother the duke had to take his place. Walsingham,
however, stayed on as ambassador. Another marriage
scheme would soon be brewing, Anglo-French relations
were now very important, and the queen must have seen
that Walsingham was well qualified to deal with them.
It is unlikely she would have left him in Paris had she not
trusted his ability, unless we accept Mr. Belloc's view
that William Cecil, not Queen Elizabeth, ruled England
and made all major decisions.

The sojourn in Paris had two important results for
Walsingham. One concerned his religious life, the other
his domestic relations. When he had been at his post for
less than two years he witnessed the St. Bartholomew
massacre or, at least, as much of that event as could be
witnessed from the not too complete security of the
English embassy. The heinous blood-letting, caused by
a mingling of ruthless political chicanery and popular
bigotry, has served controversialists as ammunition for
nearly four centuries and they formerly kept the total
of victims at an incredibly high figure. Less heated
and more scholarly research has made the thing a bit less
spectacular, but it is bad enough in all conscience. To
Walsingham's staff and the crowd of English subjects
seeking protection within the embassy building the Paris
mob raging up and down the city must have seemed like

all the devils of hell let loose. Presumably the ambassador was given some kind of protection by the French officials, but the hordes of furious men and women, drunk with blood lust and religious mania whipped up by the queen-mother Marie de Medicis' agents, cared nothing for diplomatic immunity and might have overpowered by sheer weight of numbers any guard the embassy had. During the hours of terror after the bells of the gloomy little church of St. Germain l'Auxerrois near the Louvre had rung the starting signal there must have been moments when some leader of a crowd of butchers and incendiaries tried to urge his followers to attack the house where the foreign heretics were given shelter by the ambassador of England. However, no violence was offered Walsingham and his guests. When the fires had died down, the corpses been buried, and the official story of a Huguenot conspiracy duly publicized, the refugees were able to leave the embassy, while a correct but angry and embittered envoy expressed his sentiments and those of his countrymen to the French court. It is unlikely that Walsingham was fooled by expressions of regret and stories of the peril to the French crown that had been averted. It is equally unlikely that Marie de Medicis cared very much. The powerful Huguenot leader, the Admiral Coligny, was dead, and the Protestants were demoralized and weakened for a long time to come. Walsingham's experiences during those last days of August, 1572, confirmed him in his suspicion and hostility towards Catholics for the rest of his life.

An indirect result of the Bartholomew Eve blood bath

in Walsingham's life is more pleasing to contemplate. He acquired a young friend who became a loyal and devoted son-in-law. Among the English refugees sheltering in the embassy during that night of terror was Philip Sidney, the young and personable son of a friend of the ambassador, Sir Henry Sidney, ex-Lord Deputy in Ireland. Young Sidney was a nephew of the Earl of Leicester, protector and patron of the Puritan wing of the established Church, and already at the age of eighteen he was attracting notice as a courtier, traveller, and scholar. A genuine friendship sprang up between the middle-aged ambassador and the young man who would live in English history as an Elizabethan Rupert Brooke, the embodiment of chivalry and all soldierly virtues. At some time or other after the massacre a marriage between Philip Sidney and Walsingham's younger daughter Frances was arranged. Frances was a little girl in 1572 and she did not marry Philip until shortly before he went to the Low Countries and received his death wound at Zutphen more than a dozen years later. From what we know of her we picture a pretty brunette, winning, lively and somewhat too precocious for her parents' peace of mind. The marriage was a typical Elizabethan 'arranged' one, but by no means a loveless one.

Walsingham remained ambassador to the French court until the spring of 1573. For some time he had been begging for recall. His health was bad and he was disappointed at the failure of his efforts to achieve the offensive and defensive alliance he had been working for. It all petered out in an exchange of diplomatic courtesies.

He had great confidence in the ability of the Prince of Orange to cause trouble for Spain, and he was eager for England and France in alliance to give all-out aid, financial and military, to the Low Countries. Elizabeth had different ideas. Her apparent hesitations and vacillations were perhaps the fruit of deeper political wisdom than her ambassador's. She loathed war for its wastefulness and futility, she hated spending money, and she was too civilized a woman to be possessed by the crusading spirit. Her policy in international affairs was one of waiting to see which way the cat would jump.

The official interviews between the queen and her ex-ambassador must often have been spirited. His zeal for a Protestant crusade against Rome in the person of its strongest supporter, Philip of Spain, and the queen's resolve to avoid war at almost any cost so long as England was independent sometimes led to as much of a quarrel as was possible between a subject and a crowned head, especially a Tudor crowned head. Moreover, Elizabeth could not stand Puritans, even when, like Walsingham, they were not the canting sort. Even to her faithful 'Spirit', Burghley, she allowed herself a sneer about his 'Brethren in Christ'.

One pictures Walsingham as always very 'correct' in his official dealings with people of rank. For all his Calvinistic hatred of Catholicism he could be friendly and even charming to representatives of Catholic powers and, like all the sympathizers with the Puritan wing, he was intensely loyal to the throne. But he had none of the graces of the professional courtier, and Elizabeth liked flattery even when she saw through it and despised it. The courtly convention, of course, was that Gloriana was always young, beautiful, alluring, but the Principal Secretary, contemplating that rather bony, haggard woman with yellowing teeth and a red wig, saw her as she was, his queen, indeed, but a fallible woman whose judgment did not hold his mind in thrall. It is worth remembering, even thus early in England's story, that the Puritans were the Parliamentarians, the 'democrats', and the regicides of a later generation. The high spot of the meetings between queen and Secretary was the occasion when she quite lost her temper. 'Jesus!' she probably exclaimed, for that and ''sdeath!' were her most usual oaths, 'you are fit only to be a protector of heretics!' However, it speaks well for both the queen and her Secretary that these quarrels left no scars. Mutual trust, and whatever affection existed between such disparate characters, survived to the end. Nine months after she had allowed Walsingham to resign his embassy, Elizabeth appointed him to the secretaryship of state jointly with Mr. Thomas Smith. About the same time he entered Parliament again, as member for Surrey. Both the secretaryship and the seat in the House of Commons he held for the rest of his life. He was now high up in the government of England, sharing at first a partnership with Cecil in the handling of foreign affairs and a good deal of domestic policy so far as it was linked with the country's overseas contacts.

Imperceptibly Walsingham took charge of all that nowadays is committed to the Foreign Secretary, for the

D

Treasurer, Lord Burghley, had more than enough to deal with at home, and was willing to allow the other full executive power in his own sphere. We have to bear in mind that the final decisions on foreign policy were made by the queen herself. Had Walsingham's will always been decisive, England would no doubt have waged a war—an offensive and preventive war—against Spain long before the Armada was sent to recover the English crown for Philip II and the English Church for the Holy See.

Lord Burghley's sympathies were pretty certainly with Walsingham's, but his policy was the queen's. Neither she nor her Lord Treasurer was greatly moved by considerations of religion when the national safety was at stake. Both of them had too often changed their church allegiance for prudential motives. To Walsingham, however, the future of Protestantism was all-important. Under the correctness of the professional diplomat lay the intense, fierce earnestness of Genevan Calvinism.

For a time it seemed that Elizabeth's and Burghley's gentler attitude towards Spain would justify itself. The efficient and uncompromising Alva was withdrawn from the Spanish Netherlands. His successor raised hopes of a more conciliatory policy towards the Dutch and a more friendly one towards England. A move that pleased Elizabeth's ministers, especially Walsingham, was the expulsion from Douai of the English College, the foundation of Dr. (afterwards Cardinal) Allen for the training of missionary priests for service in England. Allen and his seminarists made their hegira to Rheims and there went on with the work of controversy, translating the

Bible, and, above all, educating the missioners on whom chiefly depended the survival of Catholic orthodoxy in England.

These missioners were the young men—they had to be young for that life of hardship and constant peril— whom Walsingham stigmatized as the spawn of the seminaries. Had the English government and English Catholics been able to come to a working agreement as did Catholics and Protestants in France at the time of the Edict of Nantes, it is probable that religious persecution in England would have come to an end some two and a half centuries earlier than it did. Elizabeth herself expressed her aversion from opening windows into men's souls, and we know she had an immense dislike of violence and bloodshed. 'Will there never be an end to the shedding of blood?' she asked wearily towards the end of her reign as one of the later batches of Catholic martyrs went to their death. The opportunist Burghley and even the ardent Protestant Walsingham were too intelligent to alienate the large and patriotic body of English Catholics. Unhappily the Bull of St. Pius V changed all that. When the hard-pressed Catholics found themselves in the quandary presented by the notorious 'bloody question' as to the pope's deposing power, they petitioned Rome for some easing of the burden on their consciences. They were told that for the time being they need not act on the orders implicit in the Bull. 'Rebus sic stantibus'— things being as they are—was the phrase. Put bluntly, and as the Council saw it, the concession meant that English Catholics need not openly throw off their

allegiance or seek to depose their queen until they had a
fair chance of success. We can hardly blame Walsingham
and his colleagues for being suspicious of their Catholic
fellow-countrymen from 1570 onwards. The innocent,
of course, suffered with the guilty, if indeed the actions
of men like Allen and Persons can justly be considered as
guilty. Against the record of a few men, such as the
decidedly unspiritual priest John Ballard, involved in the
Babington conspiracy, we must consider the two hundred or more clerics—and some laymen—who lived,
worked, and died heroically without ever meddling in
politics.

That Walsingham, during his years in office, knew of
the heroism and the personal innocence of many of the
men his spies trailed and betrayed is certain. However,
to him they were the enemy. He had the uncompromising logic of Geneva. An Englishman was either a
faithful subject of Queen Elizabeth, denounced and
declared bastard and usurper by the Pope, or he was
faithful to the Pope who had so denounced her. That
was the Secretary's rigid Calvinistic logic. It is an irony
of English history that it was also the rigid Catholic logic
of another great Englishman of the period, Father
Robert Persons, S.J.

In the early years of his secretaryship Walsingham was
busy enlarging and perfecting his system of espionage, at
home and overseas. The house in Seething Lane was the
nerve-centre of this system, which was a grievous burden
on the Secretary's income, for he was not a rich man
compared with the Cecils and the other 'new' men about

the queen. There were secret agents in France, the Low Countries, Spain, Germany, Italy, including the Papal court, and even in Turkey. Everyone in the service seems to have been very well paid, for Walsingham was the kind of man who liked to be faithfully and zealously served and he knew that fidelity and zeal among informers, spies, and stool-pigeons must be paid for. One of his favourite slogans was that knowledge is never too dear. Many of the men and women on his payroll were, of course, scoundrels like the apostate Catholics Sledd and Giffard or go-getters of doubtful loyalty. Walsingham had a knack of judging when and where to trust the people who worked for him, and indiscretion was guarded against by timely changes of assignment or location. An agent who had worked for a longish time on a job at home and had collected valuable or very secret data would then be given a good post overseas to save him from the risks of blabbing and the temptations of bribery or corruption. Only Thomas Phelippes, the little, sandy-haired Customs officer with a shady past, was always kept near at hand and received his master's complete trust. The Secretary's London house was only a short distance from Her Majesty's Customs office and there must have been many journeys back and forth between the two.

With a touch of historical imagination one conjures up a fascinating picture. The dark-eyed, swarthy Secretary in his sombre clothes, exquisitely starched ruff and lace cuffs, and wearing the black skull-cap which gives him a rather clerical look in the portraits, sits frowning over a transcript of some letter in code or a thin sheet of cipher smuggled out of Paris, Rheims, Louvain, or Istanbul, or it might be a Papal document stolen from under the very nose of His Holiness. The lofty windows are curtained against possible eavesdroppers and the noise of the London streets. If it is summer time, there will be a pervasive spicy smell, for the housekeeper will have 'suffumigated' the rooms with burning branches of rosemary as a specific against the plague. The light of the candles on the writing table is reflected in the well-kept leather and vellum of the books that line the walls, books of theology and Biblical exegesis among them. In the circle of light on the table lies the paper over which the Secretary pores with concentrated attention. When he has decided that expert work is still needed, he hands the paper to Mr. Phelippes, perhaps with a touch of impatience. We have his own word that he was a choleric man; it showed up on days when his malady was unusually painful or the queen had been particularly trying. He assured his second wife, who was very devoted to him, that choleric men made the best husbands, and perhaps that was true for secret service chiefs also. Anyhow, Thomas Phelippes always seemed to get on with him and no doubt he carried off the elusive foreign code or the tough bit of cipher and returned in a matter of hours with a fair copy in clear English, Latin, French, or Spanish for his master's eye. Both men were at home in the various languages likely to be used.

Four years after his appointment to the secretaryship Walsingham was knighted at Windsor Castle (December

1, 1577). After the little flurries of temper between queen and minister, the one worldly-wise and opportunist, the other intransigent, Puritan, Calvinist, it must have been soothing for him to feel the ritual touch on the shoulder and hear the unmusical—but royal—voice bidding *Sir* Francis to rise. Queen Elizabeth was sparing with her knighthoods, unlike the Earls of Leicester and Essex who, out of sheer good nature or personal ambition, scattered them lavishly when in possession of deputed powers. The queen's successor, James I, sold them for hard cash, along with baronetcies, his own invention, and fetching a higher price because they were hereditary. When Elizabeth knighted commoners, as was the case with Walsingham and such men as Drake and Frobisher, it was a sign of genuine esteem or of gratitude for services to herself and her realm.

The year after the bestowal of the knighthood there was an exchange of compliments between queen and Secretary. Sir Francis presented her with a blue satin gown. It was a tactful gift, for she loved clothes and could appreciate good material. Perhaps the efficient Lady Walsingham, Ursula, thought up the gift. The queen showed her gratitude by a sizable gift of gilt plate in return. That, like the knighthood, was a mark of genuine esteem, for Elizabeth was not the woman to throw her money about freely. The knighthood cost her nothing; the recipient paid, but gilt plate had to be bought from the expensive London goldsmiths.

Perhaps the gilt plate was meant to gild the pill of a distasteful assignment. Walsingham had urged again and again, until the queen was tired of hearing about it, that help in money and soldiers should be given to the Dutch Protestants. Now, in the summer after the knighting, Walsingham was to go with Lord Cobham to the Low Countries on a diplomatic mission to Don John of Austria, the late Emperor Charles V's brilliant bastard son. The object was to patch up a peace between him and the Prince of Orange, the Dutch Protestant leader. Walsingham know of the admirable personal qualities of Don John, the victor of Lepanto, but Don John stood for Catholicism and that was the enemy. However, the mission failed, and the two English emissaries were ordered back to London. It was a diplomatic set-back, of course, but one suspects that the terribly sincere Protestant Walsingham was not displeased.

When he returned to England he seems to have felt the need to do something about his own health and the welfare of his family. Nagging at every town dweller's mind when the summer came round was the fear of the plague. Hitherto Walsingham's principal residence, as well as his official headquarters, had been the house in Seething Lane. Even in the semi-rural London of the sixteenth century, however, a town house in the summer was a position of danger and anxiety. The streets were narrow, dark, insanitary. The stench from decaying garbage, foul, stagnant water, and occasional mounds of night-soil awaiting removal, or just forgotten, was appalling. It is doubtful if it could be matched by anything in Europe today, even in the worst moments of a world war. Perfumes, pomanders, herbs and rosemary branches for fumigation, figured in the economy of all but the very poorest households. The apprehension of the recurrent plague—and the memory of the Black Death about two and a half centuries earlier—was a disturbing element in the Elizabethan consciousness.

Walsingham needed a country retreat, but one more accessible than his property at Foots Cray, in Kent. He obtained from the queen a lease of the estate of Barn Elms, a crown property in Surrey, near Barnes, now a dormitory suburb of London, but in his day a village in a pleasant, heathy country a short distance from the Thames. The situation of Barnes was a great convenience to the Secretary, with his growing burden of work, his own poor health, and his concern for the welfare of his wife and daughters. The nearby river was the quickest and most comfortable route to the royal palaces of Whitehall and Greenwich, and Barnes was not too far from Nonesuch Palace, near Guildford, another of Elizabeth's favourite residences.

In 1579 the Walsingham family moved into Barn Elms, and for the rest of his life the Secretary divided his time between his town and country homes. His first wife, a widow and the daughter of a Lord Mayor of London, had died when Walsingham was comparatively young, leaving him a stepson to look after. Some three years later he married again. This second wife, Ursula, was also a widow and brought him two stepsons, but both were accidentally killed in a gunpowder explosion soon after their mother's second marriage.

One would like to know more than history has preserved about this Ursula, Lady Walsingham. She appears to have been a woman of character, domestic, steadily affectionate rather than passionate and not so brilliant as to antagonize the queen. Elizabeth loathed the women her courtiers dared to marry, especially without her permission, but in the case of elder statesmen like Burghley and serious officials like Walsingham she was tolerant but not effusive. She occasionally received Lady Walsingham at court and herself visited Barn Elms on three occasions. The presence of the royal guest and her attendants put a strain on her Secretary's resources; he was always hard up, thanks to her parsimony about government services. Later on, he was heir, thanks to a technical oversight, to the debts of his son-in-law, Sir Philip Sidney.

Sir Francis was an affectionate father as well as a good husband. He suffered deep grief when the elder of his two daughters, Mary, died in childhood soon after the move to Barnes. The younger girl, Frances, we should describe as charming or even glamorous were she our contemporary. She was an exotic against the background of a staid, Puritan household. It seems she was what we call a handful. We know of the devotion of both parents to her, but they were worried at times. At an age when modern girls are still playing hockey and getting crushes on favourite teachers, she fell in love with a worthless young aristocrat in prison for debt. The marriage with young Philip Sidney was a great relief.

The family scene at Barn Elms forms an attractive picture of Elizabethan domestic life, at least when the

Secretary was not in pain from his malady or worried by affairs of state or money matters. He had the love of the land which crops up in many Englishmen, and he gave much care to improving the estate. The house was given a new front in the eighteenth century. In modern times it was the property of the Ranelagh Club, a pleasant haven for tea or cocktails after a session of polo, golf, or tennis.

The second world war, destroyer of too much that was gracious in English life, doomed the Club and the old home of Elizabeth I's Secretary. The building was requisitioned in the war, and now stands, a ruined shell, in a wilderness of weeds and overgrown shrubbery. The land that was once Walsingham's pride and hobby is to be used for playing fields and municipal housing. There is talk of restoring the house, but it may lead to nothing, and Barn Elms cease to exist before these words are in print.

The Beverley Brook, which in the Walsinghams' time, ran through lush growths of meadowsweet and yellow water iris, has been tamed and canalized before it reaches the open spaces of Richmond Park. Perhaps some of the may trees in the district are descendants of the hawthorns Walsingham planted. He had an affection for the English hawthorn. Did its toughness and its thorns appeal to the Calvinist in him, or was it that the Lady Ursula and young Frances loved the sweet smell of the blossom?

The old Lord-Treasurer was another lover of plants and trees, and employed the learned Mr. Gerard, herbalist and botanist, to look after the Cecil gardens in the

Strand. Presumably the Treasurer and the Secretary exchanged roots, slips, and cuttings, as is the way of all amateur gardeners, and with their interest in overseas exploration and the future of an English empire in America they probably compared notes on their success with the new American plants which Mr. Gerard first tried out in his own garden in Holborn. It is likely that they all three experimented with the new, edible tubers called potatoes. When Lord Burghley stayed at Barn Elms as a guest he indulged in the only bodily exercise of which history preserves any record in his case. Like Mr. Gladstone three centuries or so later, he loved to fell trees. His junior colleague would lend him an axe and let him loose on some of the uncleared woodland. We are told that the Lord Treasurer did not make much progress. He told Sir Francis his trees were too hard to chop. As a sardonic type of humour goes with Walsingham's complexion and temperament it may well be that he saved for his elderly—and rather sententious—friend and superior a few gnarled and windblown scrub-oaks such as we still find on Surrey commons.

There were other days when the decorous Puritan house was livened up by the presence of the younger generation—Philip Sidney and his friends—who were courtiers, men of letters, and patrons of a more colourful style of tailoring than the Secretary favoured. Walsingham was a good deal of a bibliophile and although he read deeply in theology and allowed Puritan divines to dedicate their dreary pamplets to him, his interests covered a wider range than Calvinist divinity and one is sure he could keep his end up in conversation with his son-in-law and the rest of the younger set. Spenser addresses him as a patron of the arts in a dedicatory sonnet in front of *The Faerie Queene*. One cannot imagine Walsingham's sharing in Burghley's grumble at the modest pension the queen authorized for Edmund Spenser—'All this for a song?' I imagine that a brief, grim smile would have flitted across that swarthy face. We have no record of any interest in drama, but there is a type of intellectual to whom the stage makes no appeal. Ralegh was also of that type and although he lived to see the flowering of the Elizabethan drama he took no interest whatever in it. Had Walsingham lived on into the days of Shakespeare's great plays, it is possible that as a supporter of the Puritan party in the national Church he would have stayed aloof.

Several important matters occupied his mind about the time he made Barn Elms his country home. To his worry about affairs of policy, for he worried about the queen's 'soft' attitude to Spain and to what he saw as the Hispaniolated sympathies of some of the men on the Council, were added the burdens of ill health and family sorrow. His malady, whatever it was, grew steadily worse each year, and in the early summer of 1580 his elder daughter Mary died. In comparison with the typical Elizabethan he was a reserved man, more akin to the Victorian stoics with the Public School code and the stiff upper lip. We know, however, that he was deeply grieved at Mary's death, which came at a time when there was plenty to harass him in his official life. War with

Spain he saw as inevitable, and he endured the ordeal of other English statesmen in like case—of being a voice in the wilderness of public unconcern. Unpreparedness and a trust in the national ability to muddle through are recurring features of English history.

Very much on Walsingham's mind at this time, as it had been for over a decade, was the presence in England of Mary Stuart, Queen of Scots. The pretence was still kept up that the unfortunate Scottish queen, a refugee from her turbulent subjects, was a guest of her cousin Queen Elizabeth. In fact she was, as everyone knew, a royal prisoner. Her claim to the English crown, through her grandmother Margaret Tudor, Henry VIII's sister, and her position as the cynosure of all who hoped for England's restoration to Catholic unity made her a source of constant worry and disquiet to the English queen and her Council. Round Mary Stuart, willing or unwilling, centred all the plots for making an accomplished fact of Pope Pius V's deposition of the English queen.

To Walsingham, in particular, the thought of Mary Stuart, the bosom serpent as he called her, seems to have bordered on obsession. So long as Mary of Scotland was alive, he saw Elizabeth's life as imperilled. There is no doubt that, apart from his loyalty as her subject and servant, he had an affection for the queen that survived all the insults and tongue-lashings he had to take from her. When courtiers and favourites had their faces smacked and maids of honour their ears boxed, what were a few harsh words and even a well-aimed slipper?

Above all, of course, his hopes as a sincere Protestant were centred on Elizabeth. We cannot deny that throughout the nineteen years Mary Stuart lived as her cousin's captive Walsingham wished for her death, and, during the latter part of that long captivity, worked unceasingly to bring it about. That was his idea of contributing to the future of English Protestantism.

Unless we keep in mind this preoccupation of Walsingham with the new religion of northern Europe, a great deal of his motivation and his activity will be unintelligible. Religion formed the solid base and the background of his thought and, to judge by the evidence that remains, stirred his emotions more deeply than anything else. He had none of the mysticism of medieval Catholic Europe nor the tender devoutness of a later Anglicanism, but the absorbing interest in religion was equally strong in him.

The future of Protestantism was bound up in his mind with a delicate phase of English diplomacy that cropped up several times in his official career—the French marriage schemes. Almost from his entrance into diplomatic life he had been concerned with his queen's highly political courtships. A marriage between Elizabeth and the French king's brother was mooted, but the French king died and his brother succeeded him. Then the next brother in his turn was suggested as a husband for Elizabeth.

In 1571, before he had been put in charge of the embassy in Paris, we find Walsingham sending home a report on this brother, the Duke of Alençon, and, later

of Anjou. An alliance by marriage between the Tudors
and the French royal family appealed to both parties in
their common uneasiness about Spanish power. The
matter was pushed in London by the French ambassador,
La Mothe Fénelon, an ancestor of the great Archbishop of
Cambrai. He seems to have worked with more enthusiasm than his opposite number in Paris. Walsingham's
dislike and distrust of Catholicism and his apprehensions
about a marriage between a Catholic prince and the head
of the English Church outweighed his desire to throw
something in the balance against Philip of Spain. Nothing
came of it all for a long time. The massacre of St.
Bartholomew's Eve badly strained the relations between
the French and English courts. The marriage scheme was
revived in 1578 and 'that long preserved virginity' of
Queen Elizabeth, who was now forty-five years old, was
bargained against the advantages to France of her union
with the twenty-four-year-old French prince.

The revived marriage plan raised a tremendous buzzing
of fear and disapproval among the Protestants of England.
They resented the suggestion of allowing Catholic worship, even in private, to a Catholic bridegroom. The
young prince's envoy, Jean de Simier, Elizabeth's 'little
monkey' (*singe*) stirred up scorn and hatred by his vicarious
wooing. The members of the Privy Council, with the
sole exception of the Earl of Essex, were united in oppo-
sition to the scheme. The Spanish ambassador, of course,
regarded it as a threat to his country, and when the
French prince arrived in England and Elizabeth took him
to her arms, literally as well as figuratively, the Spanish

aristocrat did his best to help on the general uproar. Old and trusted courtiers protested against the proposed marriage and were severely snubbed for their pains. Philip Sidney remonstrated very frankly by letter, but his character and reputation appear to have restrained the queen's anger in his case. Walsingham, urged on by his hatred of Catholicism and, doubtless, a Puritan dislike for the antics of the irresponsible Simier, the 'Monkey', and the young prince himself, Elizabeth's darling little 'Frog' (*grenouille*) protested in person. Seniority, high office, and the queen's genuine respect for her 'Moor' failed to save him from a terrible tongue-lashing. This was one of the occasions when the Secretary was taunted with being a protector of Puritan heretics.

Walsingham and his fellow-Councillors need not have been so alarmed by the negotiations, although they dragged on until the queen was fifty years old and the whole thing had become rather farcical. It seems certain that Elizabeth had a real affection for her little 'Frog', but it is unlikely that she ever seriously contemplated marriage with him or anyone else after her early love for Robert Dudley, Earl of Leicester, had at length been transformed into the deep friendship which lasted to the earl's death. The Anjou affair ended in an elaborate face-saving, a military adventure in Flanders nominally headed by the prince with English financial backing. Elizabeth, we may be sure, grieved to see all that good English money squandered for a gesture, but Walsingham, who cared little about money, doubtless

E

thought the bargain a good one. If the queen truly loved the bulbous-nosed, pock-marked young French prince, a marriage with him might well have changed the religious history of England.

Soon after the excitement about the French marriage scheme came the so-called Jesuit invasion of 1580. Missionary priests, seculars trained by Dr. Allen at Douai, and later at Rheims, had been working in England for more than a decade, but the first blood was not shed until the martyrdom of young Cuthbert Mayne in Cornwall on November 29, 1577. A couple of years later the energetic Oxford convert and former bursar of Balliol College, Robert Persons (or Parsons), persuaded Allen to use his influence with the Pope and the father-general of the Jesuits to let English members of the new religious order, the Company or Society of Jesus, volunteer for missionary work in their own country. The Elizabethan invasion consisted of two priests, Robert Persons himself, and his fellow-priest and subordinate, Edmund Campion, and, for a time, one or two lay-brothers. After Persons' departure in 1581 there were no Jesuits in England for some time, and it was not until Charles I was on the throne that an English Province was established and a considerable number of Jesuit priests sent to work in England. The attribution by some writers of membership in the Jesuit order to John Ballard, the conspiratorial priest of the Babington plot, is false. The hordes of Jesuits invading England, many of them, according to folklore of the time, travelling in battalions, mounted on broomsticks, were a figment of popular credulity, helped by propaganda, especially from Puritan pulpits.

Walsingham, of course, sitting in his book-lined room in Seething Lane or conferring with Mr. Phelippes in the rural quiet of Barnes, knew all about the Jesuit fathers, a new sort of friars as he calls them, their history, personality, background, and how many of them had landed in England, namely, two. In fact, thanks to his foreign intelligence service, he was well documented about them before they had left the tranquil routine of their Jesuit communities.

It would be interesting to know exactly what the Principal Secretary thought about those two men, one of them to be revered as saint and martyr, a kind of clerical Philip Sidney, even by those of his countrymen who have no love for the Church that has canonized him, the other, Persons, one of the most bitterly excoriated figures in English history. Of Walsingham's attitude to the *religion* of the two leaders of the new Catholic underground we know plenty. He was not an opportunist like Cecil, a tolerant Renaissance sceptic like his queen, nor even a moderate Protestant Anglican like the Sidneys, father and son. In all sincerity he hated the Catholic Faith. That, however, would not prevent his discerning the qualities of greatness in his opponents. He was too wise a judge of human nature and too shrewd a tactician to underrate the enemy. It does not seem unreasonable, then, to assume that he could appreciate the energy, ingenuity and courage of the two Jesuits during the year they went about their work with all the might of English law enforcement, including the Secretary's secret service, dogging their steps. No doubt he was angered at times by the failure of his men to capture the two missionaries just as the official net seemed to have been thrown about them. Perhaps Thomas Phelippes, but still more the less exalted and personally despicable agents, the Sledds and Giffards and such, had to face some of the outbursts of his irascible temper. He must have been a formidable cross-questioner, whether of an obdurate suspect or an unsuccessful agent.

In Robert Persons he had an opponent who measured up to his own qualities of subtlety, enterprise, and ingenuity. The two Jesuits' constant escapes from arrest, the covering of their tracks, the setting-up and running of a Catholic secret press, first at East Ham, then at Stonor Park, near Henley, must have been great trials to Walsingham and his assistants. Much of the priests' success was due to the loyal, courageous support of a small body of young laymen, a kind of religious *maqui-sards*. The crowning affront to the Calvinist Walsingham and his people was the fact that the leader of these young lay Catholics, the Scarlet Pimpernel of the movement, was himself a convert from Puritanism, a former disciple of the leading Puritan preacher. George Gilbert would have met a horrible fate had he fallen into the hands of the government authorities, but Persons smuggled him safely out of England and later he died in Rome wearing the habit of his beloved Jesuits.

The greatest, or, anyhow, the most spectacular achievement of the two Jesuits was the printing and distribution in the early summer of 1581 of Edmund Campion's '*Decem Rationes*',—'Ten Reasons,' for adherence to the Catholic Faith and repudiation of the new Anglican Establishment. Finally, on the morning of June 27, as the crowd of scholars, dons, tutors, visitors, lay and clerical, swarmed into St. Mary's Church for Commencement—celebrated with scholastic disputations, students' Latin disquisitions, and the like—there, neatly laid on the benches for all to read, were copies of the Oxford convert's polemical brochure. It was in Latin, but Latin was not so dead in 1581 as it is in the 1950's, and there were few in that assembly who could not read the pamphlet. Many of them must have known the author, personally or by repute. He had been *the* young tutor of his time, favourably noticed by the queen, and her favourite, Robert, Earl of Leicester. Mr. Campion would go far, said his friends, the bright young people nicknamed Campionists, who aped his speech, dress, and mannerisms. The presence of all those copies of the Romish booklet in St. Mary's Church on Commencement morning was a bombshell. It was also the last magnificent gesture, except for the poignant, heroic death at Tyburn, of Father Edmund Campion. Less than three weeks later he was captured and began the long martyrdom which ended with his hanging on a rainy morning the following December. His friend and superior, Robert Persons, was hounded out of England by a pusillanimous clique of his own co-religionists some time in the month following the Commencement Day sensation.

Of Walsingham's connection with the Jesuit mission
of Persons and Campion we have only scraps of evidence.
In the middle of July, 1581, he wrote to Burghley to
say that he had been instructed by the queen to examine
some persons charged with conspiracy against her.
'Runnagate priests from Rheims and Douay' he calls
them, and it is likely they were accidental victims of the
general search for the two Jesuit missionaries. Evidently
Walsingham was not excited about them. 'As far as I
can gather,' he says, 'I think it will prove nothing.'
There is a teasing record, lacking authentic details, of an
interview between the captured Jesuit priest and certain
highly placed persons, including the Earl of Leicester,
on July 25, after the captive had been taken to London.
A persistent rumour asserted Queen Elizabeth's presence
at this interview, which was apparently managed in a
quiet and friendly way with the idea of winning Campion
back from Roman allegiance. All manner of tempting
offers, 'pregnant hopes of preferment', we are told, were
held out as bribes to the Jesuit. It has been thought that
Walsingham, as Principal Secretary and a Privy Councillor
may have been present. This is improbable, for he was
due to set out for France the next day on a diplomatic
assignment about the royal marriage negotiations, that
prolonged courtship with Anjou. Anyhow, his sentiments about the Jesuits are expressed in a letter he wrote
from Paris somewhat later. 'I pray Her Majesty may
take profit of Campion's discovery by severely punishing
the offenders, for nothing has done more harm than the
overmuch laxity that hath been used in that behalf.'

There is no indication that he saw in Edmund Campion anything but one more unit, even though a personally guiltless one, 'cozened' by others, in the great Papal and Spanish effort for the dethronement of Elizabeth and the extirpation of the Reformed faith in England.

The diplomatic mission to France had its ironical features. Walsingham, who by this time received consistent support in his ideas and his work from the Earl of Leicester, had come to disapprove heartily of the French marriage scheme on religious grounds. A good understanding with France and, if possible, a watertight treaty with her to offset Spanish imperialism he desired and worked for. However, a Catholic consort, even so much of a *politique* as the French king's brother, he saw as something perilous. He had, of course, a much clearer sense of the extent and the vitality of Catholicism in mid-Elizabethan England than our Victorian grandparents with their naïve picture of an England full of stout, honest Protestants. All Elizabethan Protestants were stout and honest and they were gratifyingly numerous in Victorian literature. Sir Francis Walsingham knew better. Despite his feelings about the French marriage and its religious implications, he made an excellent impression on Anjou, who wrote in warm praise of him to Queen Elizabeth.

The stern Calvinist seems at times to have been pretty well concealed by the well-dressed, courteous, and polyglot ambassador. With the queen herself at this time his relations were less happy. She resented his frankness. His views on the courtship of the forty-eight-year-old virgin and the French prince about half her age were set forth with a bluntness less suggestive of a Tudor reign than of the time of the Great Rebellion, some sixty years later, when the concept and the name of 'democracy' had taken hold in England. Elizabeth rejected all of Walsingham's advice and refused to confirm his negotiations with the French.

He returned to England disheartened and disgusted, weary of missions wherein he was certain of being frustrated and humiliated. His health, too, was bad, his malady beyond hope of permanent cure. He had lost his elder child a year earlier; the younger one, Frances, needed a dowry, but her father was hard up, impoverished by spending so much on a secret service for the welfare and safety of an ungrateful queen's person and kingdom. Barn Elms, with the calm presence of the Lady Ursula, the youthful affection of Frances, the quiet Puritan household, the gardens, the new plantings, even the scrub-oaks 'too hard' for old Burghley's axe—it must all have looked very restful and soothing to the weary, invalid traveller on a smelly, broad-beamed ship pitching and rolling across the Straits of Dover in the later summer of 1581.

One would like to know what he said, and still more what he thought, when he got back to London and found that the queen wished him to set out forthwith on another diplomatic mission. The Puritans did not make use of the rich Tudor stock of blasphemous invective, but Walsingham might have felt tempted to less restraint than usual. There was trouble in Scotland this time. The young Stuart prince, whose mother, the Queen of Scots, had spent more than a dozen years as her cousin Elizabeth's 'guest' in England, was coming under Catholic influences. If that state of thing went on, the self-opinionated, pedantic James would be aligned with his mother and the Catholic plotters. There would be a Scottish entente with Spain, and when the cold war of buccaneering, seizure of shipping, and diplomatic insults, became a hot war, England would have to fight on two fronts. Someone must go to Edinburgh at once, and Walsingham was the man. It is unlikely he could speak the uncouth Scots dialect which James Stuart used, but possibly he could understand it, although less readily than Latin, French, Italian, or Spanish. However, his diplomatic finesse would help him, even north of the Tweed, and no doubt his Puritanism would recommend him to the Presbyterian Lords of the Congregation, who stood for the pro-English faction in Scotland.

The tired, harassed Secretary saw himself facing more failure and humiliation, to say nothing of the physical horrors of a journey to Scotland in his state of health and at that time of year. He knew where the real difficulty lay. The Scots were tired of promises, fine words, and platitudes about the spiritual kinship between John Knox's crude, fanatical followers and the English Gloriana, with her crucifix and candles, her foreign classics, her dancing, and her bland, Renaissance scepticism. What the Scots wanted was money, and that was something Elizabeth hated parting with, as her Principal Secretary know to his cost. He went to great lengths to

beg off the new assignment. He told a friend that he
never faced any job in his life with greater repugnance.
The Spanish ambassador, who, though a grandee, was a
great picker-up of gossip, said that Walsingham refused
to go, and on his knees before the queen swore by the
Body, Blood, and Soul of God that he would not go even
under pain of hanging, for he would rather be hanged in
England than elsewhere. The phrasing of the oath has a
very un-Puritan ring, but it doubtless mirrors Walsingham's feelings about the mission. However, the queen
was adamant, and her 'Moor' set out for Scotland, but
had to travel very slowly because of his wretched health.
He spent a month in Edinburgh. It is unlikely he enjoyed
the northern capital, with its mixture of squalor and
magnificence, its narrow, stinking streets, and its tall,
dark buildings from whose upper windows the servant
wenches emptied the chamber pots on the heads of careless wayfarers below with a perfunctory warning of
'Gardy loo!' ('*Gardez l'eau!*').

Walsingham worked hard to counter the Catholicizing
influence of the Earl of Arran and seems to have gained
the ear and the friendly feeling of James, who gave him a
ring with a fine diamond in it when the English delega-
tion was due to set out on its return journey through the
quagmires that served as roads to the south. The Earl of
Arran managed to have a piece of cut quartz substituted
for the diamond before the English party started Londonwards. The earl appears to be the only person on either
side who reaped any benefit from the mission.

On the first day of December following Walsingham's

thankless mission to Edinburgh, the martyr Edmund
Campion was hanged at Tyburn, protesting to the end his
loyalty to Queen Elizabeth and his disavowal of any plans,
deeds or thoughts against her throne. One last gleam of
his wit shone out from the gloom of his surroundings.
When a hectoring parson or official, hearing him recite
the Latin prayers he had known from his noviceship days,
bade him pray in English, the Jesuit gently replied that
he prayed to his God in a language He well understood.
The sanctity of the man whose broken, tortured body
had to be helped up the ladder, conquered the brutal,
horror-hungry London mob. They insisted on his hanging until he was mercifully dead. The final obscene
details of the sentence—castration, disembowelling,
plucking out of the heart—were executed on the lifeless
corpse.

More than probably Walsingham heard an eyewitness's
account of the martyrdom. Spies and secret agents, the
plain-clothes men of the period, haunted the Catholic
hangings, shadowing men suspected of being in conspiracies on behalf of Spain or the Queen of Scots. I
think it improbable there was any softening of the
Secretary's stern expression or that any unwonted
gentleness showed in those brooding eyes, which to
visitors often suggested a poet rather than a Privy
Councillor. To him Dr. Allen's missionary priests, the
'spawn of the seminaries', and Jesuits, a new-fangled
order of friars cooked up out of old monastic rules and
the ideas from Loyola's Spanish brain, were all potential
traitors. The Bull *Regnans in excelsis* had dissolved all

Catholic allegiance. If the Papists refrained from subversive action, well, it was only because the Privy Council
had the whip hand at the moment or because Philip of
Spain was not yet ready. Thus Walsingham saw it. The
English Catholics themselves knew only too well the
quandary in which they had been put, and they could
think of nothing better than silence with which to
oppose the 'Bloody question' of the Pope's deposing
power.

For the next few years Walsingham was very busy about
conspiracies, real and imaginary. Most of them were
focussed on Mary Stuart and most had some kind of tie-
up with a projected Spanish invasion. They ran the
whole way from merely seeking to organize pressure
groups that would restore the Stuart queen to her Scots
throne with right of succession to the English crown if
Elizabeth died without issue, get the hated, little 'Old
Fox' out of office, and obtain freedom for Catholic
worship, right on to plans for Elizabeth's assassination,
and, of course, Burghley's, a full-scale Spanish invasion,
the re-establishment of the Catholic Church as in Mary's
reign, and, presumably, measures of repression against
the new heresies. Secret data about an alleged plot of
this kind had been offered Walsingham, for a stiff price,
when he was in Paris in the summer of 1581. He had not
been greatly impressed. The sale of such 'information'
was a notorious form of confidence trick tried out by
expatriate Englishmen, often apostate Catholics, living
on their wits in foreign cities.

The French marriage scheme had at length fizzled out

before the daffodils at Barn Elms were braving the March winds of 1582. In the following year the poor little 'Frog' died. One suspects that the queen felt his death keenly at the time and soon forgot him. Her Principal Secretary, we may be sure, was wholly glad when God's immutable decrees had consigned Anjou's soul to whatever state it had been predestined.

In the fall of 1583 (September 21) Walsingham's surviving daughter, Frances, beautiful, precocious, and yet steadfast—there is evidence for all these qualities—was married to her father's young friend and refugee of the Bartholomew Eve night of terror, Philip Sidney, who had recently been knighted. He may have met his future bride in the crowded English embassy while the murders were going on in Paris that evening, but she was a child of four then, an age unlikely to make a romantic appeal to a youth of seventeen. Now he was an experienced courtier, soldier and man of letters, aged twenty-eight, and she a mature young woman of sixteen. The marriage, like most good Elizabethan marriages, was an 'arranged' one. There was a certain amount of bargaining, not without hints of saturnine humour, between the Principal Secretary and the old pro-consul Sir Henry Sidney, who had governed Ireland more successfully and less brutally than most Lord Deputies and was now governing Wales.

Young Sidney had but recently got over his violent passion, whether merely Platonic or adulterous we do not know, for the glamorous Penelope Devereux, who had married the loutish Lord Rich. Whatever the morality of Philip's love affair with Penelope, it brought him no happiness. However, it inspired some great sonnets, the greatest of them all the final one of renunciation—'Leave me, O Love, which reachest but to dust.'

The wedding had to take place without the Secretary's presence. He had been sent off unwillingly, in miserable health and spirits, on that embassage to young James of Scotland. If we had no other evidence of the good relations between father-in-law and son-in-law we should know that Walsingham approved of his daughter's husband by the suggestion he made that the newly married couple should have 'their diet, if they will take it, with him and in his house'. Such a design for living was regarded with as much dubiety in Tudor times as in our own day, but it is good to know that the double household at Barn Elms and in London was a singularly happy one. The mother-in-law was a great success with the brilliant newcomer, who refers to her affectionately as 'my best mother'.

Walsingham's main preoccupation at this time was the future of Mary, Queen of Scots. To him and to Lord Burghley her death was a consummation not only to be wished but to be worked for, consistently with the various degrees of moral scruple affecting the two statesmen. Both men, of course, could expect ruin and probably death in the event of a successful Spanish invasion. Philip II, indeed, had been fooled by that skilful throwing of the stone so as the hand be not seen, and we find him stipulating for mercy to the Lord Treasurer as a friend of Spain. We cannot think, however, that the English Catholics would have let the Treasurer get away with the kind of about-face that had saved him under Queen Mary. Undoubtedly he would have tried it. He was a man with little or no capacity for religious emotion. It seems credible, therefore, that he saw Mary Stuart's possible accession chiefly as a threat to the existing political order, with which was tied up the future welfare of the Cecils. Young Robert, the hunchback second son, was already being trained to follow in his father's footsteps.

Sir Francis Walsingham's name, of course, had a high priority on the list of those who could expect sentence of death if Catholicism, backed by Spanish arms, triumphed in England. He was a true 'black Protestant', hating the old Faith of his fathers, bitter persecutor of the young men from Douai, Rheims, and the English College. It is just to say that there would have been no crocodile tears of repentance in his case, no jingling rosary beads, no willingness to find Barn Elms, Seething Lane, and the Principal Secretaryship worth a mass. He would have gone to his death scowling and defiant, praying to his Calvinist God in Greek, Latin, or French, consoled, as were the early martyrs mentioned by Tertullian, by the thought of what God had in store for these persecutors of His elect.

From what we know of Walsingham's character and record we may reasonably hold that he was, in his dour fashion, vastly more an idealist than Burghley. The restoration of Catholicism in England would be, for him, the victory of error, the return to the dark ages,

a sad maiming of that 'pure' religion which had struggled
to its birth in the mind of an Augustinian monk in
Germany and grown to its full stature, and a greater
purity of Christian belief, in the brain of a French
lawyer. God moved in a mysterious manner in orthodox
Calvinism, with fearful results in human emotions and
conduct. Nevertheless, I would sooner stand in the
shoes of Francis Walsingham than those of William
Cecil, Lord Burghley, at the Day of Judgment.

The Babington Plot of 1585–6 came as a godsend to
Burghley and Walsingham. Now they had something in
their hands which, properly used, would enable them to
destroy Mary Stuart and inflict a grievous blow on
Catholicism in England. There is no doubt that the two
of them nursed the Babington Plot as Burghley's son,
Robert Cecil, did the Gunpowder Plot, in the next
reign.

The Babington conspiracy was a confused affair,
grandiose and well financed, uncertain of its objectives,
and maladroit in its methods. It takes its name from
Anthony Babington, a wealthy young Catholic, well
educated and coming of a good family in Staffordshire.
He had been apprenticed to aristocratic life by serving
as a page to the Earl of Shrewsbury, the Queen of Scots'
kindly keeper, for a time. Apparently Babington was
very much of an idealist. He had been one of George
Gilbert's young men, who gave their money, risked
their lives, and faced the rack and the horrors of Tyburn
in order to help the missionary priests. On a visit to
Paris he had met Thomas Morgan, the Queen of Scots'

agent at the French court, and he was also introduced to Don Bernardino de Mendoza, the Spanish ambassador who had been expelled from England when his dabbling in conspiracy was too brazen and could no longer be winked at.

Babington was a romantic young man, a Quixote of English Catholicism. The thought of the charming, devout Queen of Scots, whom he himself knew, languishing as the enforced 'guest' of her heretic cousin, moved him deeply. Like all romantics, he saw what he wished to see, which, of course, did not include the suspicions surrounding Darnley's murder or the more than suspicion that the runaway Protestant marriage with Bothwell involved a not unwilling bride.

Apologists for Babington have contended that his own scheme never included Elizabeth's deposition, still less her murder. A Spanish invasion simultaneously with a Catholic rising in England would have enabled the plotters to free Mary Stuart, put her back on the throne of Scotland, get rid of Burghley, Walsingham and their supporters, and compel Elizabeth to recognize her Stuart cousin as next in succession. How the Spaniards, having been got into England, were to be got out again, was another trifle that a romantic could overlook. In the later stages of the conspiracy a certain Poley or Pooley, an apostate Catholic, worked actively for Walsingham, and seems to have acted as an *agent-provocateur*, urging on the conspirators to include the murder of the queen as part of their plan. One is sorry to learn that this Poley was a personal servant of Sir Philip Sidney.

F

King Philip of Spain was very helpful. He supplied the conspirators with a hundred thousand crowns and the suggestion for sparing Burghley as a friend of Spain. One surmises that Philip's ideas for the future of England differed from Babington's. The direction of the conspiracy, however, soon passed out of the hands of the young dreamer. Its true evil genius was John Ballard. He was a priest, but he did not exercise his priestly functions nor associate with the missionaries as his brethren in a common vocation. He was a born intriguer, with none of Babington's romantic ideals. The evidence is that he was convivial, a good deal of a show-off, and either incurably optimistic or lacking in a sense of reality, for he promised the harassed English Catholics at home all sorts of powerful foreign aid while assuring those in exile there would be a formidable and well organized rising within the country. Neither promise had any foundation.

The conspiracy in which Ballard was now so energetic had one very serious weakness—that the queen's Principal Secretary and head of the secret service was in it from the beginning. Luck or, as he would have said, Providence, had put in his way a useful but not wholly reliable stool-pigeon. This was Gilbert Giffard, a renegade Catholic who could pass himself off as a faithful son of the Church. He had started life as a student for the priesthood and had received minor orders. Then he switched to underground political work. Whether he began with the idea of selling out his own side we do not know. We do know, however, that Mary Stuart's agent sent him to England to see about a courier service between the captive queen and her friends overseas. Giffard was a poor choice for this task. He was arrested as soon as he landed in England and volunteered to act as stooge for the English secret service. He was not the only Catholic who accepted the Secretary's thirty pieces of silver. Walsingham held him in contempt, but used him. Like so many earnest Puritans, the Secretary despised these apostates from Rome.

The handling of the affair after Giffard's arrest is a good example of Walsingham's secret organization at work and will serve to illustrate his methods. Mary had been cut off from overseas news for more than a year. Gilbert Giffard had come to reopen her letter service for her. She was, of course, delighted. Well, then, decided the Principal Secretary, let the fellow reorganize the courier service, but with a difference. Unknown to the correspondents the line would run through the Secretary's hands, and those of his cipher and forgery expert, Thomas Phelippes. All the details were worked out thoroughly. The Queen of Scots had already been taken from the Earl of Shrewsbury's easy-going surveillance and given as custodian Sir Amyas Paulet. He was a strict Puritan, incorruptible, immune to bribery and to Mary's charm; also, he was very anti-Catholic.

After the scheme for using Giffard had been decided on, Mary was moved, under protest, from Tutbury Castle, in Staffordshire, to Chartley, a moated house about twelve miles away. Walsingham then prepared a trap for her. Although the Puritan knight Sir Amyas

was so stern a guardian compared to the good-natured
Earl of Shrewsbury, Mary suddenly found that contact
with the outside world had become easy. This ought
to have made her suspicious, but it did not. She had a
childlike trust in all the tricks of the letter-smugglers—
false-bottomed trunks, hollow-heeled shoes, and so on.
Walsingham knew this; he also knew all the tricks. The
one she used, planned by Walsingham or by the furtive
little Mr. Phelippes, and passed on to her by the ex-
cleric Giffard, depended on beer. No self-respecting
Briton in Tudor times drank water if he could help it, and
it must be remembered that tea and coffee were still
unknown in England. Accordingly, the regular supply
of beer for the Queen of Scots' household was a major
item in the domestic economy of Chartley. A Burton
brewer was given the contract, and one of his carriers
regularly delivered the full barrels and took away the
empties. The brewer was brought into the scheme,
probably through Giffard's agency. In the early stages
he may have thought that he was working for the Queen
of Scots.

Mary's letters from abroad went into England with
diplomatic immunity—in the French ambassador's
official mail. In terms of modern protocol, this sounds
monstrous, but everyone did it then, and the aggrieved
government would interfere or not as it thought more
to its own interest. In this case it feigned ignorance.
The French ambassador handed Mary's letters to Giffard,
who in turn passed them on to Walsingham. Meanwhile Giffard travelled slowly back to Chartley, allow-

ing time for Mr. Phelippes to work at the decoding.
When the packet of letters, seemingly in its pristine
integrity, came into Sir Amyas' hands he gave them back
to Giffard, who passed them to the brewer. Finally, they
reached Mary in a little waterproof bag that could be
slipped through the bung-hole of a beer-keg. Her out-
going mail, of course, left Chartley in like manner in
one of the empties.

Early in this tortuous business Sir Amyas Paulet introduced an extra safeguard into the procedure. Like the
strict Calvinist he was, he mistrusted depraved human
nature, especially that of a renegade Papist. The brewer
was a safer bet than the ex-cleric. Accordingly he was
taken into the knight's confidence to the extent of
knowing whose side he was working for. He was to
hand the letters he had received from Giffard back again
to Paulet, who made sure the young go-between had not
tampered with them. The brewer was nicknamed the
'Honest Man' by Walsingham's people. He did very
well out of his contract. He was paid for his beer, paid
by Mary for his work as her secret postman, paid by
Walsingham for the same services. We do not know
whether he managed to divert to his own pocket some
of the money he was meant to pass on to Giffard, but
history does record a final touch of irony; the price of
beer went up before the job was over.

Walsingham's elaborate double-cross was in full operation early in 1586. His satisfaction increased as Mary
Stuart became more deeply involved. Almost as soon
as the original letters, from friends overseas or from

Babington and his associates at home, reached Mary, the decoded transcripts were on Walsingham's writing table. Thomas Phelippes worked fast and efficiently. Then instructions for Sir Amyas Paulet would be written out and sent off. If they were especially urgent, Sir Francis would endorse them with his special symbol to make them peremptory—a small drawing of a gallows. There appears to have been mutual respect between the two Puritan knights, the one narrow, pietistic, rigidly conscientious, the other subtle, Machiavellian in his official life, and by modern standards as unscrupulous as a Communist in using any means to an end. For all his sincerity as a Calvinistic Protestant and his refusal to pay lip service to Catholicism under Mary Tudor, Walsingham was a good deal of an *Inglese Italianato*. He had picked up a good deal besides legal erudition during his sojourn at Padua in the time of exile.

All through the spring of 1586 Mary was busy with her correspondence. She kept two secretaries, French and English, on the go with her letters to and from Paris, Flanders, and the workers on the Enterprise, as the Babington plot was called. The Principal Secretary's team, Walsingham himself, the dour Sir Amyas, little, sandy-haired Mr. Phelippes, the dubious ex-seminarist Giffard, the 'Honest Man' who supplied the beer, were equally busy. In the latter part of June they had their great opportunity—or did Walsingham or Thomas Phelippes manufacture it? We do not know, and probably history will never discover the answer. Mary wrote a more or less innocuous letter to Anthony

Babington, and in his reply the young man told her of six loyal associates sworn to help him in the 'tragical execution'. Mary wrote an enthusiastic endorsement of Babington's plans.

What was that 'execution'? The murder of Queen Elizabeth, say most English historians. No, only her deposition and the removal of her evil counsellors, say Babington's apologists. The word *execution* had commonly a wider meaning in Elizabethan English than we are used to giving it. Anyhow, at this point Walsingham ordered a line of action which has enabled defenders of Mary and of Babington to question the authenticity of the whole correspondence. Sir Francis instructed Phelippes to forge a postscript to Mary's letter asking for the names of the six loyal gentlemen. For some reason or other Babington did not do so, and at the beginning of August action was taken on the basis of data gathered elsewhere. Mary was invited to a day's hunting, and accepted eagerly. Despite her forty-five years and her increasing weight she was still a keen horsewoman and hunter. While she was absent from Chartley the two secretaries were arrested and all her papers seized. A few days earlier Walsingham had arrested the first batch of suspects and they were immediately put on trial, but Mary did not know this.

One object at least Walsingham had attained. He had succeeded in thoroughly frightening the queen. Formerly he had often complained of her casual and even scoffing attitude to her Councillors' warnings of threats against her life. This time Babington's—or Ballard's—plan for assassination got hold of her imagination. Normally humane and kindly, averse from the use of torture, and hating violence, of which she had seen plenty in her early life, for once she showed a vindictiveness that seems to have shocked even her own ministers. When poor, foolish Babington and the others of the first batch to be convicted had been sentenced to death, she asked Burghley if some punishment more cruel and prolonged than the statutory one for treason could be devised in this case. Burghley replied, in mild but unconcealed reproof, that the ordinary procedure was more than enough for any criminal. Accordingly the barbarous sentence was carried out as set by law, but with all the agonizing delay that the law permitted. The London mob, brutalized as it was, shuddered with horror or with religious awe to hear the dying Babington utter the Saviour's Holy Name as the executioner's hand was already groping in his mangled body for the heart. In the subsequent executions of the rest of the prisoners sentenced, the victims were mercifully allowed to die by hanging, and the other details of butchery were omitted altogether.

Three weeks later the commission to try the Queen of Scots was appointed. Walsingham was one of the thirty-six members. At Fotheringay in the late autumn he came face to face for the first time with the woman he had worked so patiently to destroy. The bosom serpent he called her. He was impervious to her charm, for charm she had, but not beauty, and unmoved by her spirited defence at the trial until she questioned his integrity in the production of evidence. Vehemently he protested his honesty and truthfulness, but we should bear in mind that only Phelippes' copies of Babington's letter and of her reply were brought forward. Above all, we have the Secretary's own admission of the forged postscript added by Phelippes.

Mary Stuart's passion was drawn out until late the following winter, because the queen could not bring herself to sign and dispatch the death warrant. When, tardily and despairingly, she did so, she bade Secretary Davison carry the news to Walsingham, then lying ill at home. 'The grief thereof,' she added bitterly, 'will go near to kill him outright.' At length the headsman's axe ended Mary Stuart's life in the morning of February 8, 1587, and Walsingham was free to give his attention to the next phase of his lifelong struggle for England's safety—and the future of the Reformed faith. It is in this light we must regard his prolonged and tortuous scheming to bring the unfortunate Queen of Scots to the scaffold. Its motive was not personal vindictiveness. There was no reason for such an emotion in him, nor does he seem to have been the kind of man to harbour it. On the other hand, it was not romantic devotion to his own queen. It is probable that for him one lawful queen was very much like another, granting she stood for the right side—the Protestant side—in the great battle of sixteenth-century religions. In matters of Divine Right as against Parliamentary privilege it is arguable that he stood much closer to the seventeenth-century Puritans than to the Tudor and Jacobean cult of the anointed head that wears a crown. It is significant that he was the brother-in-law of Peter Wentworth, the Puritan stormy petrel of Elizabeth's Parliaments, who spent his last years in prison rather than retract his claim to a parliamentary freedom of speech that many of his colleagues looked on with horror. When Mary Stuart said, in her last moments, that she died 'for the Catholic Faith', Walsingham, if asked his judgment, would have amended her words to 'for treason', but he would have admitted that for him the Catholic Faith *was* treason. He summed up the convictions of a lifetime when he said, addressing himself to the Spaniards, 'Surely, hardly will there follow any thorough reconciliation between us unless we may be drawn to one unity of religion, for Christ and Belial can hardly agree.' It was a sentiment with which Philip of Spain would have agreed; there would have been disagreement only as to which was Christ and which Belial.

One feature of Walsingham's and Burghley's victory over the Queen of Scots and those who plotted on her behalf left the Secretary dissatisfied. By English law the property of a man convicted of treason was forfeited to the crown. These windfalls were useful as a means of rewarding faithful servants without depleting the royal treasury. Anthony Babington was a rich young man, the owner of thousands of fertile acres, the truest form of wealth in Tudor times. It would have been in order for Elizabeth, who liked to be generous to her devoted servants without dipping into her own purse, to award some at least of the confiscated property to her 'Moor', who had worked long, hard, and, at times, unscrupu-

lously by his own private standards, for her personal
safety and her crown. However, a new planet had swum
into her ken. This was Walter Ralegh, soldier, pro-
moter of American colonization, man of letters, courtier,
and connoisseur of fashionable clothes, who paid his
queen graceful compliments with the broad Devonshire
accent which he kept to his dying day. To him went most
of the Babington estates, not to the hard-working
Secretary who ran his expensive intelligence service out
of his own pocket.

It is to Walsingham's credit that he bore no malice
towards the younger man. They kept up friendly relations for the rest of Walsingham's life. They had a good
deal in common—love of learning and philosophical
speculation, dreams of a British Empire—both had picked
up the phrase from Dr. Dee—antagonism to Spanish
ambitions. There was even a vein of rather Puritan piety
under the flamboyant exterior of Ralegh's earlier days.
It comes out later in some of his poems, in the magnificent
apostrophe to Death in his 'History of the World', and
in the touching lines he wrote on the night before his
execution.

While the affairs of Mary Stuart and the misguided
young Babington and his friends were following the path
that led to the scaffold at Fotheringay and the gallows
at Tyburn, Walsingham had family sorrow added to his
burden of ill-health, financial stress, and the worries of
his official post. At the end of the summer when
Babington had been arrested came the news that
Walsingham's son-in-law, Sir Philip Sidney, had been

wounded in the Netherlands campaign. It was a bad wound, the shattering of a thigh bone by a Spanish bullet during an English attack on a provision convoy heading for the besieged town of Zutphen, but the reports were optimistic. Young Sir Philip had behaved with great fortitude and the most admirable chivalry: the story of the cup of water for the more sorely wounded private soldier passed from mouth to mouth at home. The wounded knight was passing his time writing sonnets and having them set to music. His wife, Frances, set out for Flushing to visit and nurse her husband. She was in her second pregnancy. The first child, little Elizabeth Sidney, stayed with the Walsinghams. Everyone hoped that the second child would be a boy, to carry on his father's name and reputation.

Just then the fierce equinoctial gales started raging across the North Sea and for three weeks all contact with the expeditionary force was cut off. Four days before the commissioners assembled at Fotheringay Castle for Mary Stuart's trial, the bad news reached Walsingham. His son-in-law was dead. The convalescence had been illusory; gangrene had set in, and the young man, just under thirty-two at the time, had prepared for death, devoutly, and, as he hoped, prudently, making a will in which he appointed his 'most loving wife, Dame Frances Sidney', executrix, and arranging for the payment of his debts by the sale of some family lands.

The young widow, ill with grief and with her pregnancy, was cared for by the Earl of Leicester until she was fit to sail back to England. 'Your sorrowful daughter and mine,' wrote the earl to Sir Francis, 'is wonderfully overthrown through her long care since her husband's hurt.' For a long time she was too weak to travel, and when at length she reached her parents-in-law her state was desperate. Only the Walsinghams' devoted care, including the Lady Ursula's skilful nursing, saved her. There was a terrible lying-in, and the child, the son they had all hoped for, was stillborn.

Sir Philip Sidney's corpse was brought to London and lay in state for a long time at the Ordnance headquarters, Philip's official bureau, in the Minories. Among the ironies of Walsingham's life we must reckon the magnificence of his son-in-law's funeral and his own hasty, night-time interment at St. Paul's to save his estate from expense and his family and friends from shame. For it was owing to a defect in Sir Philip's will that when the time came Sir Francis' widow could not afford to give him a becoming funeral. The lands which in good faith the dying Sidney had ordered to be sold to pay off his debts were found to be entailed, so that his executrix could not touch them. To whom could she turn? The queen had no convicted traitor's money in hand to be generous with and, moreover, she had always resented Sidney's marriage and treated his wife abominably. Leicester, a good friend, was himself hard up and had mortgaged the family plate in his queen's service. Robert Sidney, the younger brother in the famous Penshurst portrait, had made a wealthy, opportunistic marriage, but was indifferent to his relations' hardships. Years later, when Frances, twice widowed, made her third marriage, a suit against Robert was still pending.

In desperation the young widow offered to forgo her marriage jointure, such as it was, but her father combined Puritan integrity in money matters with parental affection. He produced six thousand pounds out of his own pocket, a sum approaching £100,000 in present-day values. He knew it would leave him loaded with debt and crippled by interest payments for the rest of his life, but it was, he said, a trifle on behalf of 'the gentleman who was my chief worldly comfort', and it was wrong that 'a gentleman that had lived so unspotted a reputation, and had so great care to see all men satisfied, should be so exposed to the outcry of his creditors'. Privately he wrote to Lord Burghley telling him how he had 'reduced himself to a most hard and desperate state'. The old Lord-Treasurer wrote him a letter of friendly sympathy and put the case before the queen, but we know that nothing more was done for the Principal Secretary. From his country house at Barnes he wrote to Burghley of the queen's 'unkind dealings'.

Walsingham was nearing sixty, old age for most Elizabethans. The months ahead were to be filled with physical suffering, worries public and private, and unceasing work. The malady that had troubled him for so many years had long been accepted as incurable. He had, he tells a correspondent, enriched various doctors but found no relief. Now the bouts of pain were more frequent and more intense. He often longed for death to come, and he sought in vain to resign from his responsible post. The burden of debt was a nightmare when he thought of the future of Lady Ursula and the faithful Puritan household. There was consolation in Frances' second marriage—to the handsome, brilliant young Earl of Essex, cosseted by the elderly queen and idolized by the people. Happily for himself, Walsingham did not live to see the end of that spoiled darling's career. On the other hand, he might have had a grim satisfaction could he have foreseen that his grandson, the second Earl of Essex, would command the first Parliamentarian army for the Puritans against Charles I.

For years the Principal Secretary had been the prophet of the inevitable war with Spain. Even when his health improved temporarily he had little joy of it, for the Spanish bugbear haunted him. He wrote gloomily to his friend and patron, the Earl of Leicester: 'The manner of our cold and careless proceeding here in this time of peril maketh me to take no comfort of my recovery of health, for that I see, unless it shall please God in mercy and miraculously to preserve us, we cannot long stand.' Leicester agreed with him, but the queen's dear Robin had little influence on policy now. Burghley probably agreed to a large extent in the depths of his mind, but he was keeping his own counsel. The Spaniards thought him their good friend. Other statesmen and the queen herself gave the Principal Secretary the brush-off. He was the warmonger, the voice in the wilderness, the Winston Churchill under Baldwin and Chamberlain.

Meanwhile Walsingham was incredibly busy. Messengers came and went, some openly, some secretly

after dark, to and from the house near the Tower or the
country seat near the village of Barnes. Little Mr.
Phelippes worked long hours in secret after his office in
the Custom House was closed for the night. Spies were
interviewed in several languages, diplomatic mail was
raped, top-level secret documents to and from the
Escorial were copied and decoded, morally weak or
pliant Catholic youths were corrupted by threats or
money and sent as false brethren to Allen's seminary at
Rheims and the English College in Rome. The queen's
Council was supplied with masses of confidential data,
about Spanish military and naval strength, volume of
shipping, reserves in the Spanish Netherlands, invasion
schemes.

There comes a strange hiatus in the spring before
Philip II's Armada made its attempt at invasion. We do
not know exactly what happened. Perhaps some of the
Secretary's overseas agents failed him; perhaps the Escorial's people were able to hoodwink the English secret
service, although that must have been a rare event, as
between the leaden-footed, bureaucratic Philip and the
subtle, perceptive Walsingham. For some time the
Principal Secretary was at fault. He lacked clues to
King Philip's immediate plans, and less than a fortnight
before the Spanish fleet sailed he thought the enemy
ships had put to sea, dispersed, and returned to their
bases. Then, as suddenly and inexplicably, he had all the
threads between his fingers again.

From the moment in the third week of July when the
Spanish fleet was sighted, sailing in crescent formation

up the English Channel, Walsingham and his friend and superior, Lord Burghley, both elderly men and semi-invalids, were constantly with the queen. They kept her in touch with events, grappled with problems of recruit-ment and supply, and—Walsingham anyhow—urged her to more decisive action when it was clear that English naval design, English seamanship, and the accidents of the weather would combine to defeat the Armada. Both statesmen were with Elizabeth at Tilbury when she made her famous speech, the one wherein she declares, 'I know I have the body of a weak, feeble woman, but I have the heart and strength of a king—and of a king of England too, and think foul scorn that Parma or Spain, or any other power of Europe, should dare to invade the borders of my realm.'

Walsingham would seem to have been but little moved by the queen's oratory, for we find him at this very moment complaining of royal indecision. 'Our half-doings doth breed dishonour and leaveth the disaster uncured.' Some historians have raised a doubt of Elizabeth's ever making the Tilbury speech, at least in the splendid rhetoric in which it has come down to us. Perhaps Burghley and Walsingham composed it or at least touched it up and started its circulation in London. Walsingham's double standard of morality for private and public life respectively would have allowed him to do such a thing in a good cause. Moreover, it would be an enterprise very much in line with the old Lord Treasurer's technique of throwing the stone so as the hand be not seen. By the time the speech was delivered

G

both statesmen, and the queen herself, knew well enough
that the Spanish invasion had failed, for that year at any
rate. They all three knew equally well that had the
Spaniards made a landing the hastily recruited and half-
trained English levies would not have withstood for long
the attack by Parma's veterans, the finest infantry then
under arms. However, a fillip to patriotic fervour was
desirable. The Spaniard was scotched, not killed. Also,
England's defence had to be paid for and the wounded
seen to, although, poor fellows, little was done for them
once the excitement was over.

When the autumn of that year (1588) set in, the
crippled Spanish fleet was staggering up the North Sea
in an effort to round the coasts of Scotland and Ireland
as the only hope of reaching their bases again without
molestation from the English ships, with their destructive
gunfire and their disconcerting power of manoeuvre.
Walsingham and other earnest Protestants saw the finger
of God in the outcome of the great invasion scheme. It
was indeed a victory for Elizabeth and her sailors, but
much more a triumph of the 'pure' faith over Spain and
the Papacy. Equally would Dr. Allen and Father Persons,
thoroughly English types both of them, have rejoiced at a
Spanish victory, not for joy in a foreign army of occu-
pation in their country, but as a victory for Catholicism
over the poison of the new heresies. There were, of
course, cross-currents. St. Edmund Campion had met
his death at Tyburn asserting his loyalty to his sovereign
lady and true queen Elizabeth. It is interesting to learn,
also, that the pious English seminarians in the English

College in Rome, the apple of Father Persons' eye, future martyrs many of them, broke into uncontrollable cheers when they heard that their heretical fellow-countrymen had frustrated the hopes of His Catholic Majesty of Spain and His Holiness the Pope. But, indeed, the new Pope, Sixtus V, had not been very sanguine about Philip's grandiose venture and he had an undisguised admiration for Queen Elizabeth. One wonders if the outburst of the English youths in the Roman school for martyrs—they were St. Philip Neri's *'Flores martyrum'*—was reported to Walsingham. He had good spies in the Papal city.

When the attempted invasion ended in disaster in 1588 King Philip of Spain was an old man, as age was reckoned then—sixty, Walsingham's approximate age. Like Walsingham, too, he was a semi-invalid. He was tormented by gout, and had a cataract forming on one of his eyes. His fleet of great men-o'-war had been scattered and partly destroyed; at least a quarter of the number of ships and a higher proportion of the actual tonnage had been lost. The casualties among soldiers, sailors, and the clerics who were to reconvert the schismatic and heretical English, Philip's former sub-jects, could be reckoned in thousands. The Spanish treasury had to be replenished with money borrowed at high rates of interest. Nevertheless, Philip did not give up. One of the qualities for which Englishmen like Walsingham and Ralegh, and the fire-eating Grenville, respected their enemy was his tenacity. The peril, then, was not over when the service of thanksgiving was held in the old Gothic cathedral of St. Paul and the medals were struck which told devout Protestants that their God had blown with His winds and scattered the enemy. Walsingham did not cease to expound his ideal of a Protestant federation in northern Europe and to urge continued preparedness for Spain's next effort.

The tired and sick man, however, wished that the burden of working for the queen's safety and the independence of her realm might be shifted to younger and more robust shoulders. Burghley, too, about ten years the Secretary's senior, sighed for a rest from work and responsibility. Queen Elizabeth, however, although she might gibe at Walsingham's Puritan associations and sneer at the Lord Treasurer's 'brethren in Christ', knew when she was well served. Both men stayed in office.

Walsingham survived the eventful summer and fall of 1588 less than two years. They cannot have been very happy years, despite his wife's affectionate care and his daughter's brilliant second marriage. His malady now caused him such frequent and intense pain that he often said he longed for death to come and set him free. His official labours did not grow less and he seems to have been able to delegate very little of the work to subordinates. Worst of all to one of his character was the burden of debt he had carried since the death of his first son-in-law, Sir Philip Sidney.

There were, perhaps, consolations in those last two years. At the London house, when the Secretary's health permitted, there would be the rather serious midday dinner parties. They were held at twelve o'clock rather than the increasingly popular hour of one, because twelve was the dining hour of the solid London Puritans, bankers, merchants, lawyers, some of the theological left-wing divines of the Established Church, who were Sir Francis' chosen associates when he was in town. The talk must have been largely of the clerico-political kind one connects with the period half a century later when Walsingham's grandson, whom he did not live to see, became the Puritan army's commander-in-chief. Already, when the Principal Secretary was befriending Puritans still nominally within the Church of England, they had become great organizers of committees and ballots, manipulators of votes, industrious compilers of reports and statistics. English Nonconformity was casting its shadow before.

Sir Francis' interest in every branch of literature was active to the end. The compilers of the Puritan tracts naturally looked to him as patron and were glad to put his name in their dedications. The year before he died, an abridgement of *The Acts and Monuments*, better known as Foxe's Book of Martyrs, was dedicated to the Secretary. The English-speaking world, however, is indebted to Walsingham for something that has outlived his orthodox Calvinism and the dreary literature it brought forth. I refer to his fostering the English taste for records of travel and exploration, voyages of discovery in distant seas, and the planting of overseas colonies. He gave friendly encouragement and help to Richard Hakluyt, the chaplain to the English embassy in Paris, and got him started on the research that produced the classic of exploration in our tongue, *The Principall Navigations, Voyages and Discoveries of the English Nation*. Walsingham had instructed the young cleric to 'make diligent enquirie of such things as might yield any light into our western discoverie in America'.

Hakluyt's work did not appear in its complete form until after his patron's death, but a one-volume edition appeared in 1589. There must have been some happy moments for the ailing statesman when he sat in his book-lined room in Seething Lane or in the Barn Elms library, its windows looking out on the early greenery and the flower buds of the hawthorns planted some years earlier, and opened his copy of the new folio that had just come off the press. He would have inspected the engraved map, the first one in which the name *Virginia* appears. That may have led his thoughts to the phrase invented by Dr. John Dee, the philosopher, astrologer, geographer and mathematician, with a houseful of children at Mortlake, a fussy wife, and—the Secretary may have smiled grimly—a never-decreasing burden of debts. But Dr. Dee talked of a 'British Empire', and the phrase had stuck in several people's memories, including that of Walter Ralegh, who had tried to give the dream reality. Walsingham had done what he could to encourage Ralegh in trying to build something that would challenge and, in the end, outlive Spain's hegemony in the New World.

We do not know a great deal about those months when Walsingham was approaching death. Was his mind, in the periods of respite from physical pain, calm and happy because he had the Calvinist's assurance of election? The deceits, cruelties, and chicanery of official life counted as nothing, because they were all covered up and nullified by Christ's righteousness, imputed to His elect. Or had the dying man, towards the end, doubts like those which assailed the dying Cromwell nearly seventy years later, when he piteously begged an attendant chaplain to tell him whether a soul once assured of its predestination to beatitude could possibly fall from grace? We have no such intimate record of Walsingham's death in his London house on April 6, 1590. It is a safe assumption that the dying man was comforted by the presence of the devoted Lady Ursula and very likely that of his daughter Frances, Sidney's widow and now the Earl of Essex' bride. We may, however, solace ourselves for the lack of edifying details by contemplating the authentic record of an honest civil servant in a venal and money-grubbing age (hard words for the spacious days of great Elizabeth, but history justifies them). In his will Walsingham ordered that his body should be buried 'without any such extraordinary ceremonies as usually appertain to a man serving in his place, in respect of the greatness of his debts and the mean state he left his wife and heir in'.

Evidently Lady Walsingham, whom her husband had named executrix, carried out this instruction faithfully, for the funeral took place, without pomp or ceremony, in 'Paul's church' at ten o'clock the next night. The widow lived at the Barnes house for another twelve

years and then she, too, was buried privately at night—
beside her husband—in old St. Paul's Cathedral.

Some time after the Principal Secretary's death a news
sheet telling of the event was added to the ever-growing
pile of papers on King Philip's desk in the Escorial. The
writer spoke of the sorrow felt by the English people in
the loss of a great public servant. The king read through
his correspondent's letter, then picked up a pen and
wrote a brief annotation in the margin. 'There, yes! but
it is good news here.'

Burghley wrote of the death of his colleague and
fellow-Protestant with restraint and with what sounds
like sincerity, but it is hard to know when so astute a
politician as Burghley was sincere. Perhaps that gifted
opportunist saw in the Secretary, with his uncompromising Calvinism and his refusal to climb on the Marian
band-wagon, a moral stature loftier than his own.

When we have pieced together all the shreds of evidence about Francis Walsingham the man as distinct
from Secretary Walsingham the official, we are still
baffled. Let us forget for a moment the intellectual and
artistic glories of the age and try to place Walsingham
in his period in terms of moral values. There is indeed
the 'very Machiavel' that James I speaks of; there are the
shady assistants, Thomas Phelippes, Giffard, Sledd, Poley
and their kind; there are the authorized forgeries, the
thefts of documents, the lies told to elicit truths, the
illegal 'taste of the rack' for suspects reluctant to talk,
all that was done to bring Mary Stuart to the scaffold.
However, there are many things on the credit side. We

note fidelity to a bleak and stern religion, to his country, and to a queen who gave him little enough in material rewards as compared with those who played the courtier and were less honestly outspoken. There is the worthy record of his family life, which includes his generosity as regards the offspring and the personal property of two successive widows he married in a time when married women had few rights of their own. Above all, there is the self-sacrifice on behalf of the widowed daughter and the good name of the cherished son-in-law—the taking over of Sir Philip Sidney's debts after Zutphen. Walsingham never claimed to resolve the dichotomy of his public and his private codes of ethics, and says bluntly that in the service of the state one must do things that would be intolerable in a private person; he leaves it at that; there is no attempt at self-justification.

Perhaps we get nearest the heart of this elusive man in a paragraph that sums up his thought about the relations between religion and temporal power. It is a remarkable utterance to come from the moral region that contained the queen's and Burghley's opportunism, Ralegh's go-getting, Kit Marlowe's atheism, and all the court jobbery and the greedy scramble for wealth of the lesser men about the queen. Walsingham's words, *mutatis mutandis*, might have been written by St. Ignatius Loyola when he was composing the meditations of *The Kingdom of Christ* and *The Two Standards*.

'What juster cause can a Prince that maketh profession of the Gospel have to enter into wars than when he seeth confederacies made for the rooting out of the

Gospel and religion he professeth? All creatures are created to advance God's glory; therefore, when His glory is called in question, no league nor policy can excuse it if by all means he seek not the defence of the same, yea, with the loss of life.'

II

ROBERT PERSONS
THE SEDITIOUS JESUIT

'THE seditious Jesuit'—thus his enemies, including some of his fellow-priests among the secular clergy, who also called him a Machiavelli. The abusive epithets have survived, although much else has been forgotten, including the fact that we shall falsify sixteenth-century attitudes if we see them from nineteenth or twentieth-century viewpoints.

English Catholics, even the members of Person's own Order, the Society of Jesus he loved so greatly, fight shy of this controversial figure. The English Province of the Society has in its archives a great deal of material about this fascinating Jesuit, but so far the literature of Catholicism in England lacks a biography of him. All this is quite understandable. In contrast with his fellow-Jesuit, friend and subordinate, the martyr Edmund Campion, he does indeed look something like a stage villain.

There is, I think, another reason for the unwillingness of Catholics in England to give Robert Persons his due, or, for that matter, to acknowledge his existence more than they can help. If he was indeed a traitor to his country, an Elizabethan fifth columnist deserving the scorn of all good Englishmen, then the Pope who issued the Bull of 1570, the *Regnans in excelsis*, declaring Queen Elizabeth a bastard and usurper, deposing her, inviting Christian princes to make the deposition effective, and absolving her subjects from their allegiance, must bear some of the blame. In fact, he should bear the major part. Persons was a professed father of the Society of Jesus and had taken the Jesuit's fourth vow of special obedience to the Vicar of Christ. When, therefore, this English Jesuit urged Philip of Spain and the other Catholic rulers to carry out the instructions of the Bull, he was acting as a good Jesuit and a loyal Catholic. Many writers have claimed that the Bull was ill-timed, maladroit, and based on misinformation. Catholics are somewhat unwilling to go into this aspect of the defence of Father Persons. After all, he *was* guilty of treason, if you close your eyes to the whole question of loyalty to Rome and look at him from the standpoint of modern nationalism.

Further, the Pope who issued a stupid Bull, if it was stupid, is a canonized saint, the Dominican St. Pius V. Good Catholics do not like to criticize a canonized saint, but if Father Persons' actions make him a traitor, antagonizing instead of winning over his fellow-countrymen, then the Bull was stupid and the Pope a fool. Canonization is the Church's recognition of sanctity, of heroic virtue, but it is not an endorsement of all the saint's ideas, nor does it assert his possession of political foresight or clear judgment in international affairs.

Perhaps, however, the Pope was right from a Catholic point of view, in which case English Catholics should be less reluctant to admit the logic of Father Persons' activities. Why be frightened by the word 'treason'? Cardinal Mindtzenty was convicted of 'treason' by the Communist gang that dominates Hungary. A hated opponent is always 'treasonable' in the eyes of those who have seized power and lack confidence in their moral claim to it. Cuthbert Mayne and Edmund Campion, Robert Southwell the poet, saintly in their lives and martyrs by their deaths, were all found guilty of 'treason' and executed for it. When they were taxed with the 'Bloody question' of the Pope's deposing power, they found that St. Pius' Bull had left them facing an intolerable dilemma. The concession demanded by their country's government was disloyalty to Rome; less than that, including silence, was taken as an admission of guilt. The only way out was death. Persons, had he been captured with his friend Campion, would have suffered the same fate on the same charges, long before there was any question of dealings with Spain or work for her Armada.

As to these later activities of Father Persons, we may question his judgment, but not, I think, his logic. I turn to an American ecclesiastic for a truly perceptive as well as generous assessment of Father Persons' place in the history of Elizabethan Catholicism. 'The only English Catholic churchman of the time who had the necessary courage, and with all his faults, the ability to reorganize the shattered House of God in England, was Father

Robert Parsons, the Jesuit. . . . Father Parsons understood the religious situation of his country more co-
gently than any living Catholic at that period; and it is
to be regretted that jealousy and political intrigue failed
him in his gallant attempt to save the realm to the
Church.'[1] The case of Robert Persons, S.J., deserves a
more impartial study than it usually gets.

A few words about the family name before we seek to
recall the masculine, *prepotente* figure from the Elizabethan past. 'Persons' I have written, and *Personius* he
signs himself in all his Latin letters, following the
Renaissance convention of Latinizing everything (Stonyhurst appears as *Saxumsylvense* in certain old documents,
I am told.) 'Parsons' write most of the moderns, thereby
ensuring something like the Elizabethan pronunciation.
Elizabethan English, however, a more vigorous and
forthright language than our standard or 'educated'
speech, gave to the syllable -*er* a sound more akin to the
British 'cl*er*k' or 's*er*geant.' Perhaps a good, broad
Scots 'persons' (*pairsons*) is the nearest modern equivalent.

A reader of biography likes to know at once what his
hero—or villain—looks like. We have no record of the
appearance of Robert Persons in boyhood or youth. He
came of too plebeian a stock to figure in anything similar
to the charming Penshurst picture of young Philip and
Robert Sidney. However, we have plenty of data—in
portraits and descriptions—that enable us to see in
imagination the adult Persons, priest and Jesuit. Try to

[1] Dr. Peter Guilday—*The Life and Times of John Carroll*, vol. I.

conjure up a Catholic, and Jesuit, Walsingham. It is not so
fantastic as it sounds. There was a Jesuit Walsingham of
a family related to Queen Elizabeth's Secretary of State.
Persons and Walsingham stood respectively for the two
streams or tendencies which flowed out from the Reformation. There is the strong counter-attack, the Counter-
Reformation, which Rome made when she awoke.
Humanly speaking, she awoke just in the nick of time—
from the long sleep of the later Middle Ages and from
the pagan stupor of the Renaissance Popes. The typical
and one of the most potent forces in this movement was
the new Society of Jesus, given official recognition by
Pope Paul III in the Bull *Regimini militantis ecclesiae*
(September 27, 1540), only six years before Persons'
birth. Robert Persons stands out as one of the great
personalities in the generations of Jesuit clerks-regular
who followed those *primeros padres* who were St. Ignatius
Loyola's immediate disciples.

Sir Francis Walsingham is even more typical of the
other stream, that of out-and-out Protestantism, which
in Elizabeth's reign began to be known as Puritanism.
It is strongly tinged with the Manichaean strain which
crops up throughout the history of Christianity. With it,
in this case, goes the acceptance of the Bible as the rule
of faith, the right of private judgment in interpreting it,
a suspicion of ritual, and, above all, a dislike and distrust of Rome—the Triple Tyrant, the Scarlet Woman,
the Whore of Babylon, and so forth. From this insistence on private judgment has followed the fragmentation
of northern theology. Perhaps the intellectual process

will go on until only Rome and Moscow seriously compete for the soul of modern man.

There is, then, a dramatic fitness in the resemblance between Robert Persons and Francis Walsingham. Both were swarthy, dark-featured men, 'black' men as our Elizabethan ancestors called them; both normally wore a rather formidable, saturnine expression, not wholly the product of temperament, but owing something to ill-health which hung over them all through their adult life. In the case of Walsingham there was the acutely painful form of stone (probably), of which he was never cured, while his Jesuit opponent was afflicted, perhaps from his noviceship days in Sant'Andrea, by a 'recurrent' fever. This, one presumes, was malaria, the chronic Roman fever that was the curse of the Campagna and the Papal city until modern times. We should excuse both men their occasional acerbities, Walsingham his angry cross-questionings and his shaking of suspects unwilling to talk, Persons his sarcasms and the bitter tone of much of his controversy, including some of his remarks about Queen Elizabeth. They were, after all, milder than those of his friend, the devout and scholarly Cardinal Allen.

Not only in appearance were the Jesuit and the queen's Principal Secretary very much alike. In their mental and emotional qualities, their traits of intellect and of will, they were similar. Both were clear-headed, logical, and forceful in their thinking; both equally suffered the limitation of the severely logical—they often missed the wood for the trees. Walsingham, lacking equally Burghley's opportunism and the queen's commendable aversion from war, might have plunged England into a war for which she was even more unprepared than she usually is. Father Persons, too, but for various factors, including the patriotism of most English Catholics, would have brought upon his country a foreign invasion and, added to it, the horrors of civil disturbance, another northern rising like the one ruthlessly suppressed in 1569. The bitter tone one detects at times in the Jesuit and in the protector of heretics (Puritans), as the queen once called Walsingham in one of her tantrums, is attributable to this diamond-hard logic of their minds, with due allowance made for the irritant effects of their bodily ills.

In their virtues, also, and their attractive qualities we can trace a resemblance. Each was what we should call a man's man. We cannot picture Walsingham uttering or writing the kind of flattery which Ralegh and Spenser, for both of whom he had a friendly feeling, offered Queen Elizabeth, nor is it conceivable that he gave more than a cursory glance at any of the queen's beautiful maids of honour. He was a most satisfactory husband and parent. He assured a correspondent, with a touch of the saturnine humour that is part of his personality, that choleric men make the best husbands. He knew himself to be a choleric man. Robert Persons, also, was a choleric man. We can imagine him, had he not been a religious and a celibate, being a very satisfactory husband, faithful, affectionate, but not too demonstratively so, grimly humorous about women's special idiosyncrasies. Both men had the gift of eliciting friendship from their equals,

H

loyalty and gratitude from subordinates. This means more in Walsingham's case than Persons', for the former's subordinates were, many of them, spies and counter-spies, informers, *agents provocateurs*, and other men and women whose fidelity was usually a matter of the cash nexus and little else.

Robert Persons was a Somerset man, born at Nether Stowey, a place whose name calls up associations with Wordsworth, Coleridge, and the *Lyrical Ballads*. The future Jesuit was born in 1546, thirteen years after Elizabeth Tudor's birth and a dozen years before she ascended the English throne and undid the work of her half-sister Mary, the work which Persons would try in vain to restore. Romantics and the astrologically-minded may read a special meaning into the date of Persons' birth, June 24. The Church calendar marks it as the feast of St. John the Baptist, but in secular annals it is Midsummer Day. People born on that date may be supposed to have ardent, passionate natures. Are we to find here the reason for the existence in the one person of the sarcastic, often bitter, political contro-versialist and the earnest clerk-regular—'new-fangled friar' as Walsingham called it—with a deep inner life fed by daily meditation and the Mass?

The future Jesuit's father was Henry Persons, whose wife Christiana bore him eleven children. Reputedly Henry Persons was a blacksmith, a fact sometimes quoted in the son's disfavour when an appeal to caste prejudice would help in controversy. More unscrupulous oppo-nents went further and invented a bend sinister for

Robert Persons. His true father, they said, was John Hayward, the local parson. This Hayward was one of the many clerics, the majority among the lower clergy, who had managed to swallow the various religious settlements that were made before the Anglican *via media* took its permanent form in Elizabeth's reign. Sir John Hayward —parsons of the time, like parish priests before them, were 'Sir' by courtesy only—had been an Augustinian, one of the 'black canons' in the community at Taunton. On the suppression of the religious houses he had accepted a government pension, recognized Henry VIII's supremacy over the Church, and been given the living in Somerset which made the Persons parishioners of his. It would be interesting to know how much of a Protestant he was. Had he accepted the new doctrines with fanatical sincerity, as did the Scots cleric John Knox? It is more likely he was a schismatic rather than a heretic, one of those conformists who made the required gestures, mouthed the official slogans, and inwardly held to the old beliefs, went through the communion service of Edward VI's Prayer Book in public on Sunday, and celebrated the Mass in the Sarum Rite privately, absolving and communicating those of his parishioners who shared his ideas and could be trusted.

The above is the more probable view of Hayward. He took a very friendly attitude to the Persons', Catholic at heart as a family and in some cases returning openly to orthodox practice. Henry Persons was reconciled by the young priest Briant who suffered at Tyburn with Campion. Anyhow, we know that Hayward took an interest in the boy Robert Persons and gave him his start in getting an education beyond that of the average small craftsman's child. There seem to be no other grounds for the myth of Robert's illegitimacy, and when he was a Catholic priest and a Jesuit any calumny could be put about and find acceptance in some quarters. Presumably he was the most academically inclined among the blacksmith's children, and it was natural that the local parson, ex-Augustinian canon and the most literate man in the parish, should take an interest in the lad. He arranged for the boy's admission to the elementary school at Stogursey, Stoke Courcy in later times, and, when the foundations had been laid, saw that young Persons got his three years in the free school at Taunton. After that, Hayward himself helped to pay for Persons' education. Then he drops out of sight. Devout Catholics may hope that what he did for Robert Persons will at the Day of Judgment outweigh his readiness to hew to the Party line. Earnest Protestants will doubtless feel that it damns him more irrevocably.

Persons started his university life at Oxford when he was eighteen, a comparatively mature age for those times. In 1564 he entered St. Mary's Hall for two years of logic, a blanket term for a curriculum that included not only what was kept of the medieval discipline in formal logic, but also mathematics and rhetoric, and perhaps some courses in what was then called natural philosophy, the germ of our modern studies in physics and chemistry. Latin was still the accepted language of academic life as well as of diplomacy, so the blacksmith's son from

Nether Stowey began to acquire the facility in Latin which later was to serve him so well in an international body like the Society of Jesus. Perhaps Oxford, more conservative and more Catholic-minded than Cambridge, kept up the old Italianate pronunciation which made Latin a true *lingua franca* for educated Europeans. Persons' extant letters and diaries show that he had mastered the language for comfortable, everyday use, as he did Italian also.

Two years after he had come up from Somerset the young man entered the college, Balliol, which was to include his name among those of so many famous graduates and fellows. A young man some half-dozen years senior to Persons, a don at St. John's College, was the idol of the bright young people at this time. They listened to his lectures, competed for his services as a tutor of his college, imitated his dress and mannerisms. His name was Edmund Campion, and his followers were proud of being called Campionists.

We have no evidence that the Balliol man whose father was a Somerset blacksmith had anything like a close friendship with the brilliant young tutor at St. John's. The two moved in different circles. Whatever the honest blacksmith and the ex-Austin canon turned Anglican parson could do for Robert in his early years at Oxford, it is unlikely he had enough money to keep up with the fashionable Campionists. He was undoubtedly a 'reading man', and from his later university career we get hints that he may have suffered from what our generation calls an inferiority complex. The strati-

fication of English society along lines which survived
until 1945 and are by no means dead yet had begun to
replace the hierarchical structure of medieval England.
Robert Persons was definitely not 'gentry', and perhaps
some of his contemporaries were willing to make him
feel it. The sons of 'new' men themselves, they would
be glad to bolster their self-confidence by despising a
village blacksmith's son. There may also, of course, have
been title-tattle about the ex-Augustinian. The Elizabethan gentry were men of the Renaissance, free with
slander and invective, and knowledgeable about the
vices of mankind.

Persons' own references to the Campion of Oxford
days suggest acquaintanceship and a respectful admiration.
When Queen Elizabeth made a state visit to the university, accompanied by her dear Robin, the Earl of
Leicester, and was entertained with masques, amateur
theatricals, scholastic disputations, and fulsome addresses
in Greek and Latin, the popular Edmund Campion won
the visitors' special notice and favour. He delivered one
of the flattering orations to the queen and Robert Dudley
and, in a prelection on natural philosophy, expounded
for her benefit the effect of the moon on the tides. The
young man's academic brilliance, good looks and personal charm were duly noted at the highest levels. The
earl, speaking for himself as well as his queen, gave the
college tutor a figurative pat on the back and encouraged
him to look forward to very satisfying prospects in the
queen's Church if he chose to take orders.

The new Anglican establishment had need of men like

Campion. Some of its bishops were none too pleasing in Elizabeth's eyes. She disliked their Calvinism, their uxoriousness, and their too obvious keenness to make a good thing of the episcopal office; a set of knaves she called them. The lower clergy were a mixed lot—fanatical emigrés who had taken refuge in Geneva, Utrecht, or amongst the Huguenots during Mary's reign, 'hot' Puritans all of them; there were easy-going ex-monks or friars like the parson at Nether Stowey, and half-educated louts chiefly intent on raking in their tithes and making the most of the new freedom from celibacy and church discipline. Campion was the queen's ideal of a young churchman, scholarly, well-spoken, of pleasing manners and appearance, a faithful celibate. One has the impression that he was one of those fortunate young men who are naturally chaste and to whom celibacy is practicable even without the intervention of religious motive. Doubtless the queen, a good judge of men, sensed this. She hated a licentious cleric, and barely tolerated a respectably married one. Anyhow, she marked the tutor at St. John's for future preferment. Robert Persons of Balliol looked on, an interested spectator, at the speeches, prelections and disputations, 'whereof,' he he says, 'myself was then an eye-witness, though some six or seven years behind Mr. Campion in standing and in age.'

In the spring of 1568 Persons took his B.A. degree, and before the end of October had been made a fellow of his college, of which he was soon to become dean and bursar. Meanwhile Campion, who had become a proctor and had received the Anglican diaconate, was going through an interior struggle that was to lead him to Roman obedience, the Jesuit Society, and, ultimately, torture in the Tower, and death on the gallows at Tyburn. He fled from Oxford in 1569, significantly enough on the feast of St. Peter-in-Chains (August 1). It was the year of the northern rising, the last formidable effort within the country to restore in England a Catholic throne and Papal suzerainty. The following year St. Pius V, the Dominican Pope, issued his Bull, *Regnans in excelsis*, excommunicating Elizabeth, who was declared bastard and usurper, and freeing her Catholic subjects from their allegiance. Whatever view Catholics took of the timeliness of the Bull—we know that the orthodox Philip II of Spain regarded it with horror—there was no longer any room for the old easy-going compromise of parish church on Sunday and Mass in secret, Prayer Book in public and the Sarum or the Roman rite in private. A good Catholic in England could no longer be a good Elizabethan, that is to say, in the eyes of his Protestant fellow-countrymen, a good Englishman. It was a tragic dilemma, the source of domestic griefs, many apostasies, and the supreme heroism of the English Catholic martyrs.

Whether Persons of Balliol shared the dismay of the Campionists when their darling left Oxford and exiled himself in Ireland we do not know. Probably he did not. He was too busy with his philosophy and divinity and the tutoring of younger students to help pay his own way until he was on his feet financially. In the winter of

1572 he became a Master of Arts and must have rejoiced to feel that he had got well started. By this time he had twice taken the oath which pledged his solemn recognition of the royal supremacy in the Church of England. Did he act in bad faith? Not wholly, I think. In his time and circumstances he could not choose the position of a High Anglican or an 'Anglo-Catholic,' and he must have had his doubts about the clean sweep which the Reformers wished to make of the old tradition. The early editions of the *Encyclopedia Britannica* tell us that he was 'a zealous Protestant and acute disputant'. If so, he was probably whistling to keep his courage up. The picture of him as a sincere believer in the pure faith of the Reformation, like Walsingham, is out of character. Probably his mind was in a state of unrest and uncertainty about the Papal claims, doubtful of the position of the queen's Church in some kind of invisible Catholicism. Whatever the arguments this 'acute disputant' used to keep himself in Balliol College with his feet on the road to preferment, they lasted for a couple of years only.

Despite the somewhat forbidding countenance in the extant portraits and what we know of his sarcasm and his fierceness in controversy, Robert Persons had the gift of winning and holding other men's friendship and loyalty. This was especially true in the case of younger men. Persons would seem to have been a born leader, but his leadership had the quality we see in people like Florence Nightingale, Baden-Powell, and Albert Schweitzer; it evoked deep affection, love in the Elizabethan sense. It will be seen later in its most touching form in his relation with George Gilbert of Suffolk. In Balliol College he was more than kept busy with all the pupils he could deal with, in addition to his college duties. The young students were devoted to him, and he enjoyed a steady and widespread popularity with his juniors for the next two years, but he had not the glamour of the St. John's tutor who had thrown up his brilliant prospects and disappeared from the Oxford scene.

At this time crops up what I venture to think may be the evidence of an inferiority complex. The clever and industrious young dean of his college, some twenty-five or twenty-six years of age, was popular with his juniors but could not hit it off with the other Fellows. In certain cases the friction developed into something like open enmity. It is an irony of the record that one of these cases was that of Christopher Bagshaw, himself a zealous convert to Rome later on. One would like to be able to state that the two became loving friends in the Catholic Church. They didn't. They were on opposite sides in the unhappy squabbles between Jesuits and a party of the secular clergy. So embittered were Persons' relations with his senior colleagues, not all of whom can have been so very difficult to live with, that one is forced to believe there must have been some cause for it in himself, a touch of arrogance, it may be, in the blacksmith's son in community with gentry or near-gentry. Moreover, he was a strong-willed man and, until the strict training of Jesuit obedience had moulded him to the Ignatian pattern, a self-willed one. At Balliol, then, he was a good deal of a guerrilla leader with a chip on his shoulder, not the disciplined soldier in a well-run army that he became later.

Things came to a head early in 1572. We do not know exactly what happened, whether the doubts and difficulties about religion could no longer be silenced, or whether the quarrels with his senior colleagues made his position in Balliol impossible. On February 13 he resigned his fellowship and his college positions and hurried away from Oxford to London with his brother Richard. There was a good deal of rumour-mongering, and some of the explanations that have come down to us cancel one another out. Roman doctrine, for example, is alleged, but so is Calvinism. Charges, almost certainly calumnious, that as bursar he was guilty of some kind of peculation can be matched by the assertion that he exposed or was about to expose some financial misconduct of the Master of Balliol, Dr. Squire. Even more incredible charges, hinting at some kind of sexual misbehaviour, were made, but they have the appearance of mud-slinging as part of a frame-up. Evidently Persons and his brother had reason to fear the hostile clique at the university, for they fled to Lord Buckhurst as to a friend and protector. He assured their freedom from interference in London, and Robert was able to sell a piece of land he owned in Somerset. It is unlikely it amounted to very much, but it enabled him to leave England and head for Padua, with the idea of studying medicine.

The year before Persons' hurried departure from Oxford, Campion had applied for admission to the

Society of Jesus and was now a humble novice in a
patched cassock, busy with the domestic chores and the
household brooms and brushes that figure in one of his
gaily affectionate letters. Walsingham, at the centre of
his spider web of secret service in London, knew all
about it, but it is doubtful if Persons had heard the news
yet. At the outset of his continental travels he denied
that he had submitted to Rome, but after visiting Calais
and Antwerp he came to a temporary halt in Louvain,
which at that time swarmed with English Catholic
exiles, laymen, priests, and members of religious orders.
Here Persons came in contact for the first time, so far
as we know, with the Society of Jesus in the person of
Father William Good. A sizeable number of Englishmen
had already joined the new religious order, and amongst
them Father Good was conspicuous for his success in
making English converts. He persuaded Robert Persons
to make a ten-day retreat, which he himself directed,
using the *Spiritual Exercises* and the new technique of
retreat-giving which was already becoming a tradition of
the Society less than twenty years after its founder's
death. Persons' doubts were cleared up, his difficulties
answered, and at the end of the retreat Father Good
reconciled him to the Church and sent him on his way
to Padua with his blessing. The medical studies were
duly begun in February, 1575, in the great Italian university famous for its faculties of law and medicine, but the
twenty-eight-year-old convert had glimpsed a career
other than that of general practitioner to a little colony of
Catholic expatriates. He had a vocation to the new and,

as we should call it, romantic future in the revolutionary body of Roman clerics, who had no choir duties, no fixed religious habit, little sense of nationality but an enthusiastic devotion to the Pope, whose advanced guard and shock troops they were, both in the vast, new regions overseas and in the old European countries where the Reformation was sweeping away the remains of Catholic Christendom.

The medical studies were abandoned. In April Persons set out on foot for Rome, either in a penitential spirit or because the money from his sale of land in Somerset was running out. It was an heroic venture. At the end of May, not long after the pilgrim left Padua, the summer temperatures are beginning in central Italy, and the walker was no great pedestrian. He tells us, with a touch of humour, that he managed to carry out his resolve to do the whole two hundred and fifty miles or so on foot. 'Though I was no good goer on foot, and the weather very hot, yet by God's help I made that journey without any riding.' On July 4 he was received into the novitiate house adjoining the church on the Quirinal, where now the custodian shows you the body of another devout recruit to the new Company of Jesus, the youthful St. Stanislaus Kostka of Poland. The English blacksmith's son, although not so robust as we might have expected, was more fitted for survival than the young Polish aristocrat, or, as he himself would doubtless have said, less ready for heaven. There was no English Province of the Jesuits until Stuart times, so in the house at Sant'Andrea the new novice learned to adjust himself to Roman food,

Roman habits of life, the Roman climate, and to exchange his West Country speech for Italian and the rather quaint form of Latin talked in Jesuit novice houses.

Early recruits to the Society of Jesus were attracted by the apostolic and missionary character of St. Ignatius' order. Its great work as the teaching order of the Tridentine church and its part in holding back the Protestant Reformation from the total conquest of Europe were afterthoughts, one may say, in the mind of its founder. They were tasks which the circumstances of the time and the will of the Pope assigned to the Jesuits long before the rules and constitutions were in their final form. St. Ignatius Loyola had two main activities in view at first, to reform and purify Catholic life where it still survived, and to convert the heathen millions who had not yet heard of the Christian revelation. It is noticeable that these two aspirations figure in the lives of all the early Jesuit saints and of many, like Robert Persons, who were great Jesuits but not saints. St. Francis Xavier was the model of Jesuit missionary zeal in the early days.

Persons, as a novice, first thought of the Indies. England seems not to have entered his mind as a field for his apostolic zeal until somewhat later. England was a Christian country, even if in schism, and her unity with the See of Peter had survived from the sixth century until the reign of Elizabeth's father. Her half-sister had restored the link with Rome and if now it had been severed by Anne Boleyn's daughter, well, that was a passing phase. Pius V had declared her bastard, excommunicate and usurper; the strong arm of Spain and the efforts of Catholic Englishmen, freed by the Pope from allegiance to the Tudor woman, would soon undo the mischief. Meanwhile, myriads of souls in Asia and the Indies were being lost every year because they died without baptism and the chance to profess the Christian faith. It was a spur to the zeal of fervent novices like Persons and his brethren in Sant'Andrea to reflect that millions of souls were going to hell because of the lack of missionaries. Insistence on the doctrine of Limbo for virtuous heathen and of baptism of desire, which enables modern Catholics to take a less gloomy view of the outlook for Quakers, Unitarians, Moslems, and Jews, has made for a more kindly attitude towards these separated brethren, but it leaves the modern Catholic less worried about these 'other sheep' not of the true Fold. Persons and his contemporaries took a poor view of the probable fate of most of those who died outside the Church.

The saintly—and uncompromising—Pope Pius V had died three years before Persons started his noviceship life, but the Dominican Pope's successor, Gregory XIII, though less harsh in manner, made no change in the stand Pius had taken with regard to Elizabeth. She remained officially deposed, and only the unwillingness of Philip II of Spain to back up the deposition by force prevented anything serious being done. Meanwhile the unhappy English Catholics sought some way out of the dilemma in which they had been caught. If they repudiated the *Regnans in excelsis* they were disloyal to the Pope; if they did not repudiate it they were guilty of

treason under English law. The only alleviation they
got from Rome after pathetic appeals by laymen and the
old Marian clergy was that *rebus sic stantibus* (so long as
matters stood as they were), they need not do anything
about the deposition. The queen and her Council, of
course, were not appeased by the concession that about
half her subjects were authorized to stay loyal until they
got enough foreign support to send her packing. Brother
Persons, going about his daily duties in the Roman
novitiate, cannot in fairness be expected to have taken
a qualified, still less a rebellious, attitude to the official
utterances of Christ's Vicar.

The years of classical or scientific studies, and of
philosophy, followed by years in the schoolroom, which
come between a Jesuit's first vows at the end of his
novitiate and his study of theology followed by ordination, were telescoped in the early days. There was an
urgent need of workers in every branch of the Society's
activities. Moreover, many of the neophytes who put
on the novice's patched cassock and who subdued body
and mind to routine menial tasks for two years were, like
Robert Persons, mature men, accomplished scholars,
and experienced teachers or administrators. After his
two years at Sant'Andrea Persons made his first or simple
vows, and about a year later (1578) was ordained to the
priesthood. However, he had meanwhile sat at the feet
of some excellent masters of theology in the Roman
College—Robert Bellarmine, the future cardinal and
canonized saint, Suarez, one of the greatest of post-
Reformation theologians, and Fathers Clavius and Pereira.

The newly ordained priest was now one of the five thousand or so picked men who made up the *Compañia* of Jesus, as its soldier-founder called it. The official title *Societas* had been adopted, and its enemies called the members Jesuits in derision. The new priest was too able and too useful a man to be left long in routine work as mission preacher, confessor, or catechist, and was soon appointed to be the English penitentiary at St. Peter's. It was an important position for a new priest, and a convert from the English schism at that. He became the official spiritual director and confessor to the growing colony of English Catholic exiles in Rome. Not only did he preach to them in their own language, hear their confessions and give them absolution and guidance, a part of his work in which he was deeply earnest, kindly, and understanding, but he also listened to their fears and hopes for the persecuted Church in England, discussed their worldly problems, and, when they were hard up, collected money for them or found them jobs in the service of the Pope or the King of Spain. All through his later career of adventure and peril, international intrigue, and administrative tasks, this readiness to give a helping hand to those who were down and out remained a characteristic of the man. That, and his gifts of tenderness and wisdom as a director of souls, ought to be kept in mind when we look at the forbidding portrait of the dark-faced cleric with the sarcastic mouth who worked for the success of the Spanish Armada.

Thoughts of his own country as a field for his zeal came to Father Persons about this time. His dream of the Indies received no encouragement from superiors, possibly because of the bodily strength and toughness needed in the Far East. Perhaps he was already a victim to the fever which troubled him at intervals. A malarial mosquito entering a noviceship window before it was closed against the pestilent night air may already have done its work. Anyhow, we find him and Campion, now a professor in a Jesuit college in Bohemia, exchanging letters in which they voice their hopes of a new outlet for their missionary fervour. The blood bath of English Catholics, provoked by Pius V's Bull, had begun with the execution, according to the ghastly sentence for treason in those days, of Cuthbert Mayne, a young secular priest working in Cornwall (November 29, 1577). The horrible details of death for treason were well known to the young men who prepared themselves under Dr. William Allen at Douai and Rheims and, later, under the Jesuits, in the English College in Rome. Despite the horrors, the stream of volunteers kept flowing. Dr. Allen was never short of recruits, only of money to feed and clothe them and send them to their probable Calvary in England. Between the year of St. Ignatius' death (1556) and the time when Father Persons was getting into his stride as penitentiary some seventy Englishmen had joined the Jesuit Society. It was to be expected that these ardent and idealistic young men, with the example of Allen's seminary priests before them, should yearn to share their work and peril and their chance of the glory of martyrdom. The emotion is similar to that which sent thousands of their countrymen in a later age to death in Flanders in the early years of the first world war. With the sixteenth-century Jesuits the motive was more compelling because of religious certitudes.

At the beginning of April, 1579, Father Campion arrived in Rome, called by superiors from his teaching work. His younger colleague, Robert Persons, had been at work to win for members of the Society the privilege of risking torture and death alongside the seminary priests in England. Persons was a friend of Dr. Allen, the Douay founder. Both men had the same enthusiasm for the reconversion of England. Both, also, had the same idea as to how it should be achieved—by foreign invasion, with a simultaneous rising of Catholics within the country. They cherished this dream through most of their active lives, but both seem to have died in the conviction that Edmund Campion had chosen the better way. It is only fair to point out that the first attack on English schism and heresy was religious and non-violent. The venture was made more difficult and given an appearance of duplicity in English eyes by a remarkable piece of ineptitude on the part of Papal and Spanish officialdom. Persons and Campion and the others who were risking their lives did not know of this until much later.

The negotiations for the inclusion of Jesuits in the work of the English Mission had been slowed down for a time by bureaucratic snags. Difficulties were raised at headquarters. In a mere forty years of existence a religious order, even a revolutionary one like the Society of Jesus, can develop a great deal of cautiousness. How could a

Jesuit observant of his rule keep up his daily religious duties—morning meditation, spiritual readings, examinations of conscience, statutory prayers for benefactors and special intentions—on the English Mission? Interior recollection, so important in a body that had given up choir and chapter house, would be very hard for clerks-regular who roamed the country in disguise, living in rich men's houses or public inns, mixing as putative laymen, soldiers, merchants, and what-not, with heretics, worldlings, lechers, meeting female penitents or disciples without the safeguard of a *socius'* or companion's presence. The earnest, devout, but very conservative father-general, Everard Mercurian, a Fleming, went forward with a slowness that must have been trying to enthusiasts like the two Oxford converts.

At length the affair gained momentum. A whole cavalcade was planned for the assault on English heresy—secular priests, Jesuits, including a lay brother, servants, even poor old Dr. Goldwell, the Marian bishop of St. Asaph. Before the journey to the sea was completed the bishop had to cry off on account of weakness and ill-health. No prelate was appointed in his place. Both the assignment of an elderly, ailing and rather timorous man and the failure to replace him were mistakes. The absence of a missionary bishop led to trouble a few years later.

The Jesuit part in the venture consisted of the two priests, Edmund Campion and Robert Persons, with Ralph Emerson, a lay brother. The latter was a little, insignificant man with a big heart and great strength of character. He suffered much in prison afterwards and spent the last years of his life abroad, totally paralysed as a result of what he had gone through in English prisons. Father Campion, as senior in age and in the Society, was appointed superior. However, he begged the general to revise this arrangement and make him subordinate to his junior colleague. Perhaps this was the humility of a saint or perhaps he thought Persons' zeal was more under control by prudence and worldly caution and that this would make for safety in times of danger. Events proved him right, but did not deprive the Church of a martyr.

Meanwhile Father Campion, waiting in Rome for the expedition to set out, was able to satisfy his desire of religious friendships and acts of piety. He wrote enthusiastic letters about the forthcoming missionary journey. They were intercepted by the English Machiavel's ubiquitous agents. In the book-lined room in Seething Lane the Principal Secretary read them or copies of them and laid his plans to deal with what to him was a treasonable conspiracy. Unfortunately for the Jesuits, Walsingham had been, in Elizabethan phrase, beforehand with them. He knew, as they did not at the outset of their venture, of a piece of Papal maladroitness which damned them in English official eyes.

Probably Persons and Campion, the latter almost certainly, paid a farewell visit to Father Philip Neri, the elderly Florentine priest who had founded his community of Oratorians at Santa Maria in Vallicella, the New Church as it was called. Father Philip loved the English Mission and its idealistic young men. When he met the seminarians from the English College in the streets of Rome he would doff his hat and greet the embarrassed youths with '*Salvete, flores martyrum*' ('Hail, flowers of the martyrs'). The old-music-loving and fun-loving Oratorian saint would have found a congenial spirit in Father Campion. With Father Roberto, perhaps, the saint would have been somewhat more formal and ceremonious. Persons, after all, was a religious superior, and one suspects that with the consciousness of a more plebeian background he may have been less forthcoming than Campion. But we must not picture him as a stuffed shirt or a church bureaucrat. There is evidence of deep emotional intensity at certain crises in his life. One cannot believe that he would remain unmoved when the old saint at the Chiesa Nuova gave him the parting accolade, the brotherly embrace in token of farewell and blessing.

The northward trek to the Channel ports was a leisurely affair, full of discomfort and, at times, danger. It had its amusing interludes, as when, in the Protestant cantons of Switzerland, the travellers disputed with the new religionists and sought to entangle the venerable heresiarch Beza in the meshes of scholastic logic. The old scholar, with black gown and patriarchical beard, received the visitors courteously but sidestepped an argument with them. The indiscreet zeal of some of the party made the neighbourhood too hot for them and they hastened away from Geneva into French territory.

During a stay at Rheims in the course of this journey they received the piece of news which had already reached Secretary Walsingham's ears. It was a cause of great distress to the Jesuits. Dr. Nicholas Sanders, another brilliant Oxford convert, a theologian and a controversialist who had a fund of sarcasm, had been sent to Ireland as Papal nuncio with the object of stirring up and canalizing Irish discontent at English tyranny into a movement on behalf of the persecuted Church. Nowadays we should call it Irish nationalism. Walsingham and the other Councillors called it treason, fomenting rebellion among the queen's Irish subjects. The nuncio was to receive Papal and Spanish military support. It was a grave matter for Fathers Persons and Campion. The English government could not fail to regard the two ventures, in Ireland and England, as part of a single planned enterprise. They apparently were not, for neither the Jesuits nor the unfortunate nuncio, who eventually died of hardship and exposure in the wilds of Ireland, knew of the deplorable timing of the two expeditions. As often happens in bureaucracies, the Papal right hand did not know what the left hand was doing.

The arrival at Calais in the early summer of 1580 brought the travellers within sight of the English cliffs, and of new hardships, constant peril, and the chance of torture and an agonizing death. At the same time it was a relief to be done with the wearisome journey across the continent. Persons had been away from England for six years, Campion somewhat longer, and any apprehension about re-entering the country was mingled with the joy of homecoming. Despite his sojourns in Italy and Bohemia, Campion was ineradicably English. So, in a different mould, was Persons, for all his cosmopolite training and his Ultramontane sentiments. One suspects that he might have said, with a later Oxford convert, W. G. Ward, that although his heart was Roman, his stomach was English. Indeed, his enemies later on referred to him as 'a Jesuit beyonde the seas, yet an English man'.

As a matter of prudence the Jesuit priests crossed the Channel separately, of course in disguise. Father Persons, as superior, sailed first and his companion was to wait in France until he had news of the other's safe arrival. On June 12 a military officer landed at Dover. He wore 'a suit of buff laid with gold lace, with hat and feathers suited to the same'. He was dark-featured, brisk in manner, a man used to command, although polite and friendly in his bearing, perhaps with a touch of bravado pardonable in a good Protestant who had been risking life and limb in the service of the Huguenots, or the Dutch Calvinists in arms against the King of Spain. The customs officials, and the pursuivants hanging about the port to keep an eye open for the subversive 'Jebusites' wanted by the queen's Principal Secretary, were very courteous and helpful to the demobilized English officer. He was able to make arrangements for an equally smooth procedure for another English traveller, his friend, a jeweller coming to England to deal in divers precious gems. The conceit had pleased Father Campion, who, in return for rack and rope, if that were God's Will, offered his dear countrymen the pearl of great price, the Catholic Faith.

With an impudence worthy of a Hitchcock film, Father Persons, as soon as he reached London, made his first contact behind the Elizabethan iron curtain. He visited the Marshalsea Prison, a jail famous in the history of Catholic recusants, for a call on Thomas Pounde, a Hampshire squire who deserves a place in the roll of English eccentrics. He had been a courtier, a merely nominal Papist who 'conformed', and something of a favourite with the queen, who admired his skill as a dancer, until the day when, pride going before a fall, the squire of Belmont slipped and fell while essaying an encore of a difficult step, and the queen, parodying the formula of conferring knighthood, adjured him, 'Rise, Sir Ox.' '*Sic transit gloria mundi,*' said the humiliated country gentleman as he hurried out of hearing of his queen's loud, mannish laughter and the titters of her courtiers.

Forthwith he was confessed and shriven, became an ascetic and a *dévot*. He was now imprisoned, not too rigorously, however, for refusing to attend the Anglican services. By the grapevine methods of prisoners he had received news of the Jesuit mission and was full of zeal to help the two priests. He easily arranged for a quiet, private talk with his visitor. The braided and befeathered army captain left the Marshalsea with directions for getting in touch with young George Gilbert, another courageous and devoted layman, who had gathered together a band of followers, fervent Catholics like himself, young, well-born, well-to-do, unmarried, sworn to help the English missionary priests with money, equipment, servants, personal attendance at the risk of their own liberty and life if necessary. Gilbert was a Suffolk man and a former disciple of Dr. Edward Dering, a fine preacher and one of the most distinguished clerics of the Puritan left wing of the Church of England. Gilbert had been reconciled to the Catholic Church in Rome by Father Persons while he was a penitentiary at St. Peter's. The young convert aspired to membership in the Society to which his friend and spiritual father belonged. The friendship and the quasi-paternal affection of the learned, busy, shrewd, and intriguing Jesuit for the generous, good-natured, devout and perhaps slightly priggish young man is one of the most delightful instances of Robert Persons' genius for human relations.

For some weeks after the officer from the Low Countries had been joined in London by his friend the jeweller, the two went about town in their respective disguises, hearing confessions, saying Mass, instructing, solving cases of conscience, collecting money for needy Catholics and, most remarkable of all, preaching to large congregations. Their mission was primarily to their fellow-Catholics, aiding Dr. Allen's secular priests in the administration of the sacraments, guiding consciences troubled by the problems of conformity and recusancy that beset men torn between loyalty to their Papally deposed queen and to the Pope's uncompromising Bull. There was little or no contact with Protestants by the two Jesuits in their sacerdotal character. The sifting out of lost sheep genuinely seeking the Fold from disguised government wolves, and the initial instruction of *bona fide* enquirers was the work of George Gilbert's young men.

Further, the orders given to the two priests by the Jesuit father-general, included a prohibition of discussing politics. This, however, had been qualified by the concession that a slight exception to the rule might be made for a few persons known to be trustworthy and discreet. With the wisdom of hindsight we may regret this qualification. It is unlikely that Edmund Campion made any use of it. His references to Queen Elizabeth, where they have been recorded, are loyal and affectionate. They lack the fulsomeness of the career courtiers and the go-getters, but they might have been made by Sir Henry or Philip Sidney. To what extent Father Persons availed himself of his father-general's concession at this time we do not know. Perhaps the Stonyhurst archives will satisfy our curiosity some day. All the evidence is of strenuous and arduous missionary journeys, endless hearing of confessions, preaching, solving moral problems, helping the needy and distressed. The last-named work of mercy was always one of Robert Persons' preoccupations.

In July a conference or synod was held in Southwark, so that the two Jesuits could meet representatives of the old Marian clergy and some of the leading Catholic laymen. The meetings had to be organized with great secrecy because of the watchfulness of Secretary Walsingham's agents. The rendezvous was a house somewhere near the church of St. Mary Overy ('over the river'), now St. Saviour's, the Anglican cathedral, and within sight of the massive walls of the old priory, which the queen's father had suppressed. The assembled clerics and laymen had various thorny problems to tackle. There were questions of collaboration with the heretical government, Catholic disciplinary matters of fasting and liturgy, the embarrassing conduct of a priest, Father James Bosgrave, who, picked up by government agents, had in all good faith told them he knew no reason why a good Papist might not attend Protestant worship. Above all things, however, those harassed survivors of the Marian régime, lay and clerical, wished to meet these new, enigmatic religious who had neither cloister nor canonical choir, were independent of episcopal authority, and had come to England with disturbing Tridentine teachings about what was God's and what was Caesar's. Over them hung the shadow of the late Pope's Bull, *Regnans in excelsis*. We know next to nothing of the actual meetings. It is doubtful whether all of Robert Persons' diplomacy or Edmund Campion's obvious sincerity and his personal charm sufficed to allay the suspicions of the 'old' Catholics. The laymen were gentry and great landowners, who had seen the former mild penalty of a twelvepenny find for non-attendance at Anglican worship replaced by new and crushing exactions that would soon impoverish a faithful non-conformist. The ecclesiastics were probably only too anxious to be left in peace as pseudo-tutors, secretaries, stewards and so on in the households of their rich patrons. Some of them, perhaps, had been Vicars of Bray in their time, conforming outwardly to the various religious changes while secretly carrying out the old rites and administering the Catholic sacraments. I think it a reasonable surmise that a listener at these meetings would have detected the hostility which hounded Persons out of England soon after his companion's arrest and which later on blazed up in the Appellant controversy, wherein a Catholic clerical minority ranged itself with the state officials against the Appellants' own Ultramontane brethren and the Tridentine government-in-exile of Father Persons. However, the amenities were observed at Southwark and ended in mutual compliments and the new missioners' assurances of the strictly religious nature of their task.

In the summer heats of that year Father-general Mercurian, who had received Persons into the Society, died in Rome. It was not until late the following winter that a general congregation of the Society elected his successor, Claudio Acquaviva, a Neapolitan, young, learned, brilliant, and a born administrator, one of the great men of Jesuit history. He was an enthusiast for the English Mission and had himself volunteered to go and work in it. However, he was put in charge of the Roman Province, and on February 19, in the year after Persons and Campion had landed in England, the vote of his brethren laid on him the supreme command, a lifetime's responsibility. He was not yet forty years of age. His generalship covered the rest of Father Persons' life. This is important, for in seeking a just estimate of Father Persons we should bear two things in mind. The first is the soldierlike quality of Jesuit obedience; the second is the fact that Father-general Acquaviva was an able political strategist.

One does not know when the two Jesuits in England heard the news of Father Mercurian's death, and, in any case, they were unlikely to guess that the cautious, slow-moving Fleming would be succeeded by the young Roman Provincial who was so good a friend to the English Mission. Meanwhile, there was more than enough to keep the two Jesuits busy. The meeting with the Marian clergy and the leaders of the Catholic gentry had been a matter of courtesy and policy. Neither party was under the other's authority and there were no Catholic bishops at liberty in England to lead and govern the persecuted Church. It was an unfortunate state of things, but it was not at this time, as some writers have asserted, the fault of the Jesuits.

The two planned to spend the summer in missionary work, Persons in the west, Campion in the north. They took separate regions, not only to extend the area of their influence, but also to halve the risk of their mission's being ended by capture. Dr. Nicholas Sanders' expedition to Ireland had roused the English government to great activity in the hunt for the Jesuits. One cannot reasonably blame Burghley, Walsingham and the rest for holding that the two expeditions were connected, when they had the text of Pius V's Bull before their eyes. The surprising thing about the Jesuit mission of 1580–81 is not its short duration, but its managing to last as long as it did. Its perils and alarms, narrow escapes, and split-second feats of resourcefulness parallel the stories of underground workers in Hitler's Europe.

George Gilbert saw to it that the fathers were well equipped for their first missionary journey. Each was given two horses, a servant, two suits, books and vestments, and the sum of sixty pounds. The amount of money must be multiplied by at least ten to give some idea of its purchasing power in terms of present-day sterling. The suits comprised the disguises for the priests, sometimes as soldiers, sometimes as government officials, lawyers, physicians, even as ministers of the queen's established church. Campion, in doublet and hose, and wearing a sword, was 'ridiculous' in his own eyes, he tells us, but Persons, a more aggressive type, seems to have worn his lay attire, especially when it was a military disguise, with an air that exacted respect and service from others.

Before parting for the summer the two missioners met in a friendly layman's house in the suburban village of Hogsden, the ancestor of the drab and rather sinister borough of Hoxton. With the priests at the parting meal was the irrepressible Thomas Pounde of Belmont, who had managed to 'fix' his good-natured jailer at the Marshalsea Prison for a day's leave of absence. Mr. Pounde told his Jesuit friends that all sorts of rumours were bruited about concerning them and that it would be a good idea to leave written declarations of their aims and policy with him. In the event of the priests' capture by the Council's agents, Pounde would bring these papers to light to prove innocence of treasonable intent. This was good common sense, and Persons, as superior, approved the plan. With the promptness of a man of action he cleared the silver and crockery from one end of the table and wrote out his own apologia forthwith. It is now in the possession of the English Jesuits.

Father Campion's paper was a more elaborate composition, of which the rhetoric rises to genuine eloquence. He challenged his Protestant opponents to meet him in frank and public disputation, appealing for a safe-conduct and a fair hearing to the members of the Privy Council and to Queen Elizabeth herself. To her and of her he always spoke with respect. Unfortunately Thomas Pounde's discretion was not equal to his good sense in other respects. He was so moved by Father Campion's eloquent prose and the fearless challenge to the powers of Church and State that he must needs have some manuscript copies made and show them in the strictest confidence to a few chosen and reliable fellow-Catholics. Needless to say, the Jesuit's challenge was soon an open secret. Campion's 'Brag and Challenge' his enemies called it, and when at length they met him in oral disputation they chose the conditions, which were unjust, cruel, and tragic for him, a man broken by inhuman tortures and awaiting a horrible death.

Thomas Pounde, faithful to his arrangement with his jailer, went back to his prison, and the two Jesuits departed for three months or so of travel, missionary labour, and ever-present danger. Campion made his way northwards. Everywhere his preaching made a great impression. The memory of his eloquence lingered on through several generations, so that even at the end of the Cromwellian Protectorate men still remembered the sermons on the *Ave Maria*, the Ten Lepers, and the Last Judgment. A probable host of Father Campion in Lancashire was Sir John Southworth, who himself suffered imprisonment for his Catholicism and was the father of one of the only two priests executed under Cromwell.

Father Persons meanwhile was incredibly busy in the Midlands and the western counties, especially Northampton, Hereford, and Worcester. He said Mass, heard confessions, solved cases of conscience, preached and instructed, bringing to the harassed, wavering Catholics the fervent orthodoxy of Trent and the new Society of Jesus. One of the men he reconciled was Sir Thomas Tresham, a knight whose devotion and loyalty to his heretic queen was second only to his ardent Catholicism. His son was one of the Gunpowder Plotters in the next reign; both father and son were executed, victims of that tragic folly of desperate young laymen.

All through the summer of 1580 the Jesuit was accompanied by George Gilbert, the athletic, fair-haired young Suffolk squire who had been converted from Puritan fervour to equally zealous Catholicism. There was a difference of some ten years only in the ages of the two men, but the relation between them was rather that of father and son than older and younger brother. Father Persons' priesthood and the fact that he was godfather to his neophyte were reason enough.

The Jesuit's affection for Gilbert and his constant

K

solicitude about the young man's safety give the lie to the Persons of pseudo-history, a ruthless, inhuman Machiavelli, the 'lurking wolf' of the government proclamation of 1581. One might also draw attention to his own description of his emotion as he witnessed the fervent piety of the English Catholics who heard his Mass and listened to his preaching. 'It fills me with amazement,' he writes, 'when I behold and reflect upon the devotion which Catholics in England show by their gestures and behaviour at Mass, for they are so overpowered by such a sense of awe and reverence that when they hear the name of the Pope pronounced in the Office they beat their breast; and then the Lord's Body is elevated, they weep so abundantly as to draw tears even involuntarily from my dry and parched eyes.'

A report of his summer's activities which he wrote for the general of the Society gives some idea of the strenuous life of those months in the western shires. From dawn until late at night he was on the go, saying Mass, sometimes preaching twice in one day, sending priests to places that needed them, hearing confessions and reconciling schismatics, writing letters, helping prisoners and the distressed with alms collected from wealthier brethren. 'Daily I am asked, and daily do I beg,' says Father Persons. Throughout his life this theme crops up. During that summer of 1580 there was so much to do, he says, that he would have lost heart but for the thought of the religious objective of it all, and the consoling effect of the people's response to his ministrations.

At some time in the course of his travels he gave a

demonstration of his presence of mind. When the incident occurred he seems to have been out walking, not a favourite exercise of his, but perhaps his athletic young Suffolk friend had dragged him away from his books and papers for once. Anyhow, the two entered a roadside inn for a meal and there, staring at them from the wall, was a portrait of Robert Persons. He was, as we should say, wanted by the police. The pictures had been distributed by the Council to inns and alehouses when the pursuivants were combing the country for the pestilent Jesuit. Father Persons' action was prompt and effective. He dashed the picture from the wall with his stick and with a great show of anger called for the landlord. 'How now, sirrah,' he shouted, 'do you mean to insult your customers by having such a villain's picture in your house?' Trampling on the offensive broad-sheet he defaced it beyond possibility of recognition before the innkeeper, flustered and cowed by this choleric soldier, could explain that the 'Jebusite's' picture was there by official orders.

Perhaps it was at this time, during long days in the saddle, riding through the narrow, rutted lanes of Tudor England, that Father Persons' ideas on English ecclesiatico-politics took the form they held consistently almost to the end of his life. Taunton, an unfriendly historian of the English Jesuits, thinks this was so. The hard, uncompromising logicality of his mind, his intense loyalty to the Papacy, the obstinate nature of his character, about which even his colleagues and fellow-Jesuits agree, would have led him to a whole-hearted acceptance of the Bull of excommunciation and deposition. He would have formed the conviction that Pius V had pointed the way—Spanish invasion and a Catholic rebellion—to England's reunion with the Holy See. Perhaps the Balliol rumour of early Calvinistic tendencies was not wholly false. When we study him as he turns his thoughts to the English religious situation, we are aware of something he has in common with the heresiarch of Geneva. No one can deny Persons' mental powers, but most Catholic Englishmen, in his own time and since, thought Edmund Campion's heart better than Robert Persons' head.

Late in October the two missioners made their respective ways back to London, where they learned that the danger of their position had become greater. English ill-success in dealing with the Irish rebels, naval demonstrations by Spain, and the number of persons converted or reconciled, had stirred up the authorities to feverish activity. The Council was fulminating against the Jesuits, the pursuivants were following up every probable and improbable clue, and from the house in Seething Lane the Principal Secretary was sending out orders to his spies and secret agents. Father Persons had to plan for the winter months ahead. Travel would soon become difficult, at times impossible. London, the small, Elizabethan London, was becoming too dangerous. Father Campion and George Gilbert, both of them born enthusiasts with a strong vein of Quixotry, had to be protected. In Persons the zeal that had led him to volunteer for the Indies and then for the English Mission

was balanced by a sense of responsibility and by his
affection for the other two men. Gilbert he wanted to
smuggle out of the country as soon as he could; the
young convert wished, in any case, to become a Jesuit
and a priest. Father Campion was to be sent up north
again while the roads, which became impassable quagmires in a rainy winter, were still open.

The conservative Roman ecclesiastics who had feared
for religious observance under English Mission conditions
might have been reassured at this time. With the winter
coming on, London echoing to the hue and cry for the
two priests and their lay helper, and every government
spy and stool-pigeon eager to win the favour of Mr.
Secretary and the Council, Father Persons and his fellow-
religious took time off for an item of Jesuit practice that
had fallen due, the annual renewal of vows. For two or
three days the missioners and the lay brother Ralph
Emerson shut themselves up in silence and gave their
time to religious exercises in the house of Mr. Griffiths,
a trusted layman who lived near the Middlesex village
of Uxbridge. When the short religious retreat was over,
the two Jesuits parted again. Father Campion rode
northwards. Persons was sending him up to Lancashire,
where Catholics were numerous and influential, and
safety, therefore, was greater. Campion was to write a
book in defence of the 'Challenge' to which Thomas
Pounde had given untimely publicity. Father Persons, as
superior, allotted himself the place of greater danger.
He stayed in London, in lodgings near Bridewell, in
suburban villages, and occasionally, in those days of

vast, rambling premises, enormous households, and indiscriminate hospitality, in one or other of the queen's palaces.

All through the winter the hunt for Persons and Campion went on. Several priests were captured and tortured, victims of the intensive search for the more urgently wanted Jesuits. However, the faithful Lancashire Catholics took good care of Father Campion, although even this most strongly Catholic county of England provided its alarms and dramatic moments. On one occasion the government agents, by luck or cunning or somebody's treachery, followed a clue which led them to the very garden where the Jesuit was taking the air with his host and some of the household. With a safety margin of seconds only, the priest was saved by a quick-witted servant maid. With feigned indignation she gave the priest a violent shove—a 'thrutch' they call it in Lancashire—that sent him headlong into an ornamental pond. When he clambered out, effectively disguised by mud, slime, and pondweed, the pursuivants joined in the laughter against the loutish fellow who had made a pass at the virtuous maid. Then they apologized for their intrusion and went their ways.

While Campion was up north, hard at work on his controversial booklet, with only such distractions as the incident just related, Persons, lying cheek by jowl with the queen's Councillors and all the ablest priest-hunters of the capital, launched the most audacious of his enterprises. This was the secret printing press. All the circumstances of this venture have a very modern flavour to them. The ever-present threat of arrest, torture, and a judicial frame-up ending in death, the need for mobility, the dangers from weak friends and disguised enemies, the problems of getting raw materials and equipment, the stratagems to put the authorities off the scent, and, finally, the hazardous task of distributing the product, all read like a chronicle of the resistance movement under Hitler.

Once again, as at their arrival in England, the Jesuits were indebted to their lay helpers, George Gilbert's young men. Gilbert himself largely financed the press, but its work would have been impossible without technical help from another of the men of the Catholic underground. Stephen Brinkley, learned, competent, zealous, a man of fortitude who was captured, racked, baffled his inquisitors, and escaped to the continent, is one of those Elizabethans who appear on the stage of English Catholic history, impress us by their personality and their doings and then vanish teasingly from the records. He knew all about paper, founts of type, the processes of printing and binding, and, essential if he was to dodge Walsingham's drag-net of secret service, how to find and enlist loyal helpers. He became production manager, technical expert, and personnel chief to the press. He gathered together seven Catholic printers willing to work at so dangerous a job. Whether the open-handed Gilbert paid unusually high wages we do not know, but, whether or not, Brinkley chose his men with good judgment. They had to be men of loyalty, fortitude, and strong nerves as well as skill in their craft.

In the middle of winter the press was set up in a rented house called Greenstreet, at East Ham, then a village about five miles out of town. The landlord was told that 'seven young gentlemen' were going to occupy his house, and so Brinkley's seven Catholic workmen were dressed for the part and appeared in public on horse-back. They soon ran into various kinds of trouble. The local parson and the churchwardens threatened to become a nuisance or worse when the seven young gentlemen failed to appear at any of the Anglican services as required by law. It was impossible not to arouse suspicions of the work going on in the house, and the suspicions grew stronger when a large quantity of paper was bought and delivered at the place. Finally the unfortunate servant of Brinkley's was caught and racked, but betrayed nothing. Father Persons and George Gilbert went into hiding for a day. Next morning the priest sent his servant ahead to have a look around. The man did not return by nightfall. This was disturbing, as the man's father was a Protestant minister. Although the fellow showed up the next day, confidence had been undermined. Despite these various alarms and the state of tension in the East Ham household, the first booklet came off the press without mishap. *Some Reasons why Catholics should not go to Church* was its title. It was Father Persons' challenge to those who sought a compromise by secret Catholic worship and public attendance at the Church of England. The title page gave 'Doway' as the place of publication, but Norton, the government expert, soon tore away this camouflage.

Two Protestant clergymen were prompt with replies
to the Jesuit. The one that attracted the greater notice,
*An Answer to a Seditious Pamphlet lately cast about by a
Jesuit* was written by the ecclesiastical left-winger
Charke, a protégé of the Lord-Treasurer. Another
pamphlet came from one Hanmer, a less dour kind of
parson, 'much given', we are told, 'to banqueting and
drinking and jesting and scoffing'. Copies of the Catholic
pamphlets were to be found in shops and houses, of
Protestants as well as known Papists. In fact it became
part of the method of distribution to see that those secret
publications were found in Protestant hands, for, later,
when their possession was made a statutory offence, this
strategy bred confusion in official quarters.

The printing, publishing, and distributing of Father
Persons' work under the nerve-racking conditions of the
press at East Ham was a triumph of audacity and planning,
whatever its religious effect. The neighbourhood, however, had grown too hot to hold Stephen Brinkley and his
printers any longer. Hospitality was offered generously
—room for the press, board, books and service for the
staff and the priest and Gilbert when they chose to be
there, at Henley Park, the house of Francis Browne,
brother of Viscount Montague. After a time there was a
second removal, to a house in a wood belonging to Dame
Cecilia Stonor.

Father Persons set to work on a reply to Charke and
Hanmer, and rushed the manuscript of this *Censure* to the
newly organized press so quickly that it was in print
within a week. Again 'Doway' appeared on the title

page. The Council, of course, simmered with indignation, knowing the press was somewhere close at hand. Parliament had already debated special action against the two Jesuits. Campion they referred to as a 'wandering vagrant' and Persons as a 'lurking wolf'.

Soon Persons was at work attacking a certain John Nichols, a renegade seminarist turned informer and government stooge. Nichols had recanted his Catholicism in print and had turned over to the authorities information, some of it spurious, about the English students in the colleges at Rheims and Rome. When Persons had finished with Nichols, the ex-seminarist was pretty well discredited in the eyes of fair-minded readers. There was alarm in official circles. A bill to cope with the 'Jesuit poison' was drawn up. On March 18 it received the queen's signature and became law as an 'Act to retain Her Majesty's subjects in due obedience'. Already English Catholic subjects studying abroad had been ordered home. Priests and Jesuits had been warned to leave the country, but now harsher measures were passed. The fines for non-attendance at Anglican worship were raised, and, worse still, reconciliation with Rome and receiving absolution were made treason. One may remark at this point that Lord Burghley was always in favour of relying chiefly on financial pressure in the battle against the Catholics. He was by nature a mild man, but he was also a realist, and he knew that no body of people can be squeezed for ever and survive as an organization. Queen Elizabeth herself was habitually averse from violence and bloodshed. She thought banishment an adequate way to deal with the Roman missionary priests, and we have the record of that despairing cry of later years, 'Will there never be an end to the shedding of blood?' Her faithful Parliament, however, and the solid citizenry of London were an obstinate race, who became increasingly Puritan as time when on. The Puritans were crying out for fire and slaughter against the Catholics even when they themselves were feeling the chilly breeze of royal and official disfavour.

The hard-pressed English Catholics went on struggling to find a way between the horns of the dilemma made for them by the Bull of Deposition. A secular priest issued a pamphlet, anonymously, to claim that Catholics might in good conscience concede the merely outward gesture of conformity, attendance at Anglican worship. Father Persons quickly answered him in a brochure dedicated, whether seriously or with an undercurrent of satire we do not know, to the queen herself. Then there was talk of getting the queen's putative suitor, the Duke of Anjou, to intercede for his fellow-Catholics in England. He refused to interfere, as he was to refuse later in the year to make any effort to save Campion from the horrors of Tyburn. A meeting of Catholic gentry at the Throgmorton family seat discussed offering a large sum of money to the crown to purchase toleration. It was a case of belling the cat. No one would undertake to be the emissary.

Father Persons meanwhile was going ahead with the work of the secret press, hurrying back and forth between his work in town—preaching, hearing confessions, giving spiritual direction, collecting and distributing alms, letter-writing—and the industrious little group with Stephen Brinkley in their hideout up the River Thames. In London the Jesuit was helped in his work by a young secular priest, Alexander Briant, who had been a pupil and friend in Balliol days.

Briant already had the makings of a saint. He was selfless, prayerful, gentle both to friends and enemies, yet of more than human fortitude. He had reconciled Persons' father to the Church. Early one morning Father Persons went back to town to find that a former servant had betrayed his friend to the government officers. His lodgings had been ransacked, books and papers carried away, and, worst of all, Mr. Briant, lodging nearby, had been arrested. He was ferociously racked for information about the secret press, but could not be made to reveal his friend's whereabouts. The operation of the press went on.[1]

The hiding place in the wood by the river was a good one. The trees were thickly planted, and the building was easily reached—or left in a hurry—by way of the river. At Easter-time Persons received, by a trusty messenger from the north, the manuscript of Campion's

[1] Alexander Briant was given the privilege of admission to the Society of Jesus during his imprisonment. He is, therefore, reckoned as a Jesuit martyr. At the time of his arrest he was still a secular priest. The title 'Father' was not used for secular priests until modern times. As in France and Italy at the present day, it was applied only to members of religious orders.

book, the *Decem Rationes*—'Ten Reasons' for Catholicism as against Anglican claims. The production of this book was to be the crowning achievement of the press. Father Persons read through the manuscript. The numerous quotations bothered him. Opponents would, in the spirit of the times, pounce on every slightest verbal error or misquotation and claim a victory in dialectics. The author had checked all his quotations, but all must be rechecked, decided the prudent superior. One of George Gilbert's faithful band came to the rescue. Young Thomas Fitzherbert had lately been converted. None but his Catholic friends knew of him as a Papist. He could come and go in comparative safety, and in various libraries in town he laboriously checked all Father Campion's quotations. Then, as the may blossom was passing its prime and the trees about the secret press were forming a denser screen, the author himself came down and joined his colleagues. The news of young Briant's apprehension, cruel sufferings, and unbreakable spirit moved both his Jesuit friends deeply. 'We talked nearly a whole night on what we should do,' says Father Persons, 'if we fell into their hands, which really happened to him [Campion] afterwards.'

The production of the book, to be ready for Commemoration at Oxford (late June), went ahead despite suspicions and alarms, risks from wandering agents of the Lord Treasurer and Sir Francis Walsingham, sorrow over the fate of Mr. Briant, and practical difficulties about type and paper supplies. Campion had a prevision of the end that awaited him in spite of all his companion's prudence and managerial ability. 'I cannot long escape the hands of the heretics,' said Father Edmund, 'the enemy have so many eyes, so many tongues, so many scouts and crafts. I am in apparel to myself very ridiculous; I often change my name also. I read letters sometimes myself that in the first front tells news that Campion is taken. . . . Threatening edicts come forth against us daily . . . I find many neglecting their own security to have only care of my safety.'

At length the books were all printed and bound, and nothing was left but the dangerous task of distribution. In a secret letter to one of the Italian Jesuits Father Persons describes the stratagem of slipping copies into Protestant houses, shops, and street stalls, even into the royal Court, for the greater bewilderment of the pursuivants when they started a round-up of owners of the illicit volumes.

On the morning of June 27 all the very important persons, members of the nobility and gentry, distinguished foreigners, dons, and college tutors, flocked into St. Mary's Church to hear the speeches and academic exercises of Commemoration, and there, on all the seats and benches, were copies—some four hundred of them— of the much-wanted Father Campion's *Ten Reasons* against belonging to the established Church of England. It must have been a tremendously sensational occasion. The little book was in Latin, but all those people could read Latin, and one surmises that they paid scant attention to the speeches and disputations.

The two Jesuits, doubtless, and the courageous priest

Hartley who planted the books in the church were 'lurking' in some place where reliable friends could bring them news of the event. Father Persons' satisfaction in the outcome was enhanced by the fact that he had just got George Gilbert safely out of England. He had a great affection for that loyal and open-handed young convert and had been intolerably worried about his safety. Gilbert, he tells us, 'because so hateful to the heretics (especially as he had once been one of them) that they searched for him everywhere, and threatened to put him to a cruel death if they could catch him. Now, although he cared little for this, yet since I saw that he could work no longer and stay in England without plain peril of his life, and that we had more trouble and anxiety protecting him than ourselves, I at last persuaded him to leave all things and cross over the sea, to keep himself for happier times.'

The time had come round again for the renewal of vows, the simple ceremony by which the Jesuit, although permanently vowed to his triple sacrifice, reiterates year by year until his final vows the oblation he made at the end of his two years of novitiate. After the short time in retreat given to meditation, penance, confession and communion, the two priests parted on a country roadside near Oxford. Persons was to go back to his underground life in the heart of London, Campion to go north again. Before they separated, after the accolade or farewell embrace allowed by the Jesuit rule, they exchanged hats. It was an accepted pledge of loyalty and affection between male friends among those less inhibited Elizabethans. Perhaps there was a touch of playfulness on the superior's part. Campion, 'ridiculous' to himself in Tudor male finery, had to accept Father Persons' befeathered military headgear for some less flamboyant kind of hat. I think that Father Persons, despite the solitude in the midst of perils which he, a man habituated to community life, would now endure without his beloved George Gilbert, was relieved to see Campion ride away on the first lap of his journey northwards. Father Edmund, the idealist, the Quixote, the aspirant to martyrdom, would be safer in the remote, Catholic north.

Father Persons, heading towards London, was overtaken by two riders. Father Campion and Brother Emerson had retraced their steps. Campion had one last request to make; he had just thought of it. Could he call at Lyford, a moated house in Berkshire, just for a few days? Lyford was a centre of Catholic piety. Mrs. Yates sheltered eight homeless Bridgettine nuns; she had resident priests, and there was Mass nearly all the time. Persons, responsible for his colleague's safety, had qualms about it. Finally he gave way. Edmund Campion was irresistible. The superior downed his own fears and scruples by putting the priest, at his own suggestion, under obedience to Ralph Emerson, the diminutive lay brother with the big heart. Then the two priests parted company again, and as they sat their horses and gazed backwards each saw his brother in religion for the last time on this earth.

The parting was on a Tuesday (July 11). By the follow-

ing Sunday evening Campion was a prisoner in the hands
of the law. He had gone to Lyford, ministered to the
pious females, obeyed Brother Emerson as to his departure, and made his way to Oxford. But his pulpit
eloquence—for he seems to have been a Jesuit Chryso-
stom—had bewitched his friends. They sent some of
their men-folk galloping after him and talked him into
going back again, for just one more Mass and sermon.
He did so, and was betrayed by one Eliot, Judas Eliot
as the Catholics called him thereafter. The fellow seems
to have stumbled on Father Campion by accident at
Sunday Mass.

Persons, only a short distance away, heard of the
catastrophe and wanted to hurry back to meet his friend
at a crossroads as he was taken Londonwards. His lay
friends prevented him from doing this, but his servant,
not known by sight to the officers, rode out and managed
to exchange signs of friendship and sympathy with the
prisoner.

Then began Campion's prolonged Way of the Cross,
starting with cajolery and friendly offers made by the
Earls of Leicester and Bedford, and, according to an
unproved rumour, by the queen herself, proceeding to
indescribable rackings and other tortures, and ending at
Tyburn gallows on a stormy December 1. But Persons
was over in France before the execution and had to wait
for an eyewitness's account until young Henry Walpole,
converted when some drops of the martyr's blood
splashed on him, crossed the Channel.

Some weeks after Campion's capture the secret press,

L

with its manager Brinkley and the seven faithful printers, fell into government hands. One of the printers, William Carter, eventually suffered death at Tyburn, but Brinkley, after tortures on the rack and weary months in prison, made his way to France and rejoined his friend Father Persons, whose *Christian Directory* he helped to bring out.

After Campion's arrest Persons made his way southwards. We can trace his progress to the house of a Mr. Shelley, Michal Grove, in Sussex. There he was present at a meeting of laymen and Marian clerics, probably in early August just after his friend Campion had endured his first tortures in the Tower. The fierceness of the persecution, the harsh new penalties for recusancy, the intensity of the hunt for priests and Jesuits, had tried Catholic endurance to the limit. Many of those present, possibly a majority in the end, urged Father Persons' withdrawal. Some went further; they said that if he did not go of his own will, they themselves would give him up to the government. This foreshadowed the tragic policy of a section of the Appellants who, later on, tried to buy a measure of toleration for their brethren by going into partnership with a cynical, persecuting government against the rest of their fellow-workers.

Father Persons spent that winter (1581–82) in a house of the Society of Jesus in Rouen. The most romantic, and the most hazardous, episode of his Jesuit career was over, but he was only thirty-five and for nearly thirty years more he was to lead a life of almost unbelievable activity, as writer, controversialist, founder of colleges, and partaker in the intricate European politics of the Counter-Reformation.

We do not know for certain what were his ideas as he travelled about England. If he was already committed to the hope of a foreign invasion and the forcible reconciliation of his country to the Papacy, it is unlikely he said much to his fellow-Jesuit about it. Edmund Campion lived and died an Elizabethan Englishman of the best type—not that of the go-getters and careerists whose sycophancy nauseates the modern reader. His patriotism, like that of such men as Sir Philip Sidney, was an amalgam of affection for the country of his birth and a personal, somewhat romantic, loyalty to Queen Elizabeth. His sovereign lady he calls her, in contrast to the epithets hurled at her by Cardinal Allen at the time of the Spanish Armada. Yet Allen, the solid Lancashire Catholic, and Persons, the west-country blacksmith's son, were not less English in temperament and idiosyncrasies than Campion. Persons, indeed, had he lived a couple of centuries later, would have fitted perfectly into the community of 'gentlemen of Stonyhurst', the group of ex-Jesuits—the Society was suppressed in 1773—restored in 1814—driven back to England by the French Revolution and settling down to a life that was part country squire, part missionary priest and schoolmaster. The Society of Jesus, however, like the Catholic Church herself, is an international body. This sense of universality was, I think, always very strong in the consciousness of Robert Persons after that ten days' spiritual retreat in

Louvain and his submission to Rome. When he was
driven out of England after Campion's arrest he was of
necessity an internationalist, despite the typically
British bull-headedness which a shrewd Flemish father-
provincial had picked out as one of his faults. He lived
in communities of foreigners, with Latin, French,
Italian, and, later, Spanish, as his everyday media of
intercourse with his brethren.

Persons had in Dr. Allen a friend who had long been
committed to the idea of a rebellion together with a
Spanish invasion as the means to restore England to the
Holy See. Of the two friends, Persons was the more
dominant, but presumably each reacted on the other.
By the late winter after Campion's martyrdom Father
Persons' mind was busy with an invasion scheme in the
intervals of his writing, for he was still carrying on the
controversy with the two Anglican divines, the Puritan
Charke and the worldly Hanmer. He also wrote a book
on the anti-Catholic campaign in England, *De Persecu-
tione Anglicana*, and, more important for posterity, he
composed the first part of what was originally called 'The
Book of Resolution', which we know in its final form as
The Christian Directory, one of the classics of spirituality
in English. He also found time, and collected the funds,
to establish a boys' school for the sons of Catholic exiles,
at Eu, in Normandy.

The invasion scheme, to which all this work as author
was the background, was concerned with Scotland. The
young Stuart king was coming under Catholic influences,
chiefly that of the Duke of Lennox, and now was the time

to strike a blow for the Queen of Scots' liberation and England's restoration to Roman unity by an invasion over the Border. Thus it appeared to many of the exiles. The Jesuit father-general sent Father Creighton, a Scotsman who had joined the Society, as emissary to King James, but with orders to visit Father Persons on the way. There were conferences with the Duke of Guise, who had given Father Persons the money for the boys' school at Eu.

Father Creighton went to Scotland, but was back in Normandy in the spring, and then the three of them, the duke and the two Jesuits, went to Paris for more conferences, this time with Dr. Allen, James Beaton, the exiled Archbishop of Glasgow, and the French father-provincial. Details were gone into for the Border invasion and a rising in England at the same time. The schemers ran into snags at once. There was scepticism about the rising. Only Persons was wholly optimistic about the English Catholics' readiness to co-operate. Then it came out that Lennox wanted twenty thousand men; Persons thought eight thousand enough. The Pope and the King of Spain were expected to help. Nowadays it all sounds rather amateurish. We can explain the Jesuit's misreading of English Catholic sentiment only by assuming that he was already out of touch with the English mind, both Catholic and Anglican. Thus he would remain for the years ahead. Dr. Allen was given a leading place in the scheme. With suitable church dignity, the bishopric of Durham, for example, said Father Persons, Allen's presence would be worth a division, as we should put it. This was another fallacy.

Dr. Allen, for all his natural kindliness and good nature, his English temperament, was not acceptable to his countrymen, who regarded him as a product of the Marian régime.

When the conferences in Paris were over, Father Creighton hurried to Rome to lay the scheme before the Pope, while Father Persons made his way over the Pyrenees to win the support of Philip II. The Spanish king, having reduced Portugal to satellite status, was busy setting up his bureaucracy in Lisbon, and thither the Englishman went to meet him. The meeting has features to please the ironic student of history. The Spaniard, who by accepted standards should have all the dash, sparkle, and *élan*, was slow, cautious, enmeshed in the red tape of his own Escorial. The English blacksmith's son was ardent, impetuous, sanguine, However, in spite of these differences or perhaps because of them, Robert Persons made a favourable, and lasting, impression. It is to be kept in mind that the king and the English Jesuit were both genuinely religious men. In the intensity of their Catholic faith there was a bond of sympathy which went deeper than political agreement or social differences. Although Philip was then busy with Spanish re-armament and wanted all the money he could get for his army and navy, he was persuaded to grant a generous subsidy to the Scottish king. More delightful to record, Father Persons also cajoled him into underwriting a big annual donation for friend Allen's college at Rheims. Unfortunately for the Scottish invasion scheme the Protestant Lords of the Congregation got the upper hand in Scotland, and the young king was forcibly switched over once more to Presbyterianism, a cult for which he retained a lasting dislike.

King Philip and the Catholic exiles did not give up hope of success in an armed attack on Elizabeth's government. They had their fifth column within her kingdom, but it should be stressed that at this time, as well as later, it was a minority. The Catholic plotters had plenty to extenuate their deeds, even if we are unwilling to admit that St. Pius V's Bull of 1570 made it possible for them to act in good conscience. Their priests were tortured and butchered, their worship proscribed, while the Mass, the centre and mainspring of their spiritual life, was declared treason. If these things are too idealistic for Marx-infected realists, there were the crushing fines that had been enacted at the time of the Jesuit mission. 'This', said the Spanish ambassador, reporting to the king 'is Cecil's idea, who says that it is much safer for the queen to deprive the Catholics of their property than to take their lives.' We may assume, then, that a sizable party of young members of the Catholic gentry, in the mood of desperation which involved them in the insane Gunpowder Plot twenty years later, were willing and active co-operators in the invasion-cum-rebellion scheme. In the late summer and fall of 1583 we find Father Persons, an indefatigable traveller, hurrying back and forth across the continent on the business of the new scheme, one based this time on a naval invasion of England.

During a stay in Paris in the course of his travels he

received the news which saddened him more than anything else in his whole life, more even than Campion's
seizure and execution. On October 6 George Gilbert
had died in Rome. The young Suffolk squire had set his
heart on the priesthood and admission to the Society of
Jesus, but his knowledge of English affairs, his experiences with the two Jesuits, and his organizing ability
made him valuable in Rome, and the Pope had deter-
mined to use him for some kind of diplomatic mission.
His ardour for the obscurity and mortifications of the
Jesuit novitiate had to take second place to obedience.
Then he picked up a malignant fever, such as northerners
were constantly falling victims to in those days of the
undrained, malaria-ridden Campagna. In a few days he
was dead, but he died happily, for he was accepted as a
novice of his beloved Father Robert's Society of Jesus.
His body was buried in the novitiate church of Sant'
Andrea. Father Persons, getting the news in a letter
from one of his Italian brethren, wrote in return,
'Blessed be Jesus Christ and the Father of all mercies
for this blow also, though it is the heaviest which my
soul has ever felt at the death of any creature.'

Grieving deeply for the young man who had been his
convert, godson, benefactor, companion and sharer of
hardship and peril on the English Mission, the Jesuit went
ahead in the negotiations with the Spanish king and the
Duke of Guise. We wonder how closely Walsingham's
secret service was in touch with it all. The Principal
Secretary was paying good money to agents with anything worth the price. Sir Francis and his cunning little

Mr. Phelippes between them had nosed out and trained many a Judas among the Catholics at home and in the colonies of exiles. This time, however, catastrophe fell upon the plotters through one of their own number, Francis Throgmorton, whose frequent visits to the Spanish embassy had roused the suspicions of Walsingham's men. The young man was arrested, and although he managed to destroy some papers and send others to the Spanish ambassador, various lists of English Catholics were found in his lodgings. After prolonged torture on the rack he broke down and confessed that the names were those of men ready to take part in the rising.

And Father Persons, moving back and forth between the tranquil routine of Jesuit community life and activities like those of Richelieu's Grey Eminence in a later generation, what did he think of it all? With his genius for friendship, his sympathy for those in distress, the lasting affection he had for Father Campion and George Gilbert, he cannot have been unmoved by the sufferings and ghastly deaths of his young countrymen who stayed at home, working, scheming, plotting, to turn back the hands of the clock in England, depose a popular monarch with the help of foreign arms, and put her Scots cousin— to Englishmen a hated foreigner—on the throne.

When this scheme had failed, and the unhappy Throgmorton had gone to his death, Father Persons was busy for a time with exclusively literary work. He completed and, with the technical help of Stephen Brinkley, published his 'Book of Resolution,' now, in its final form,

The Christian Directory. This is his monument more
enduring than brass, a masterpiece of lucid, straightforward, virile writing, given to the world before
English prose had gone through its adolescent sickness
of Euphuism. One may quote a later ecclesiastic, Dean
Swift, giving testimony in *The Tatler*, to the Elizabethan
priest. '. . . The writings of Hooker, who was a country
clergyman, and of Parsons the jesuit, both in the reign
of Queen Elizabeth, are in a style that, with very few
allowances, would not offend any present reader.' To
those who know Robert Persons only as the 'seditious
Jesuit', an Elizabethan Benedict Arnold, such a paragraph as the following, from the pages of *The Christian
Directory*, may suggest another side to his character.

'God hath imparted certain sparcles of beautie unto
his creatures, thereby to drawe us to the consideration
and love of his own beautie, whereof the other is but a
shadow; even as a man finding a little issue of water, may
seeke out the fountain thereby, or happening upon a
smal vaine of gold, may thereby come to the whole mine
itself. But we, like babes, delite ourselves onlie with
the faire cover of the booke, and never doe consider
what is writen therein.' (*The Christian Directory*, Pt. 2,
chap. 4.)

In the spring of 1585 Pope Gregory XIII died. His
policy towards England had closely followed that of St.
Pius V. The conclave which met to elect a new Pope
did not come to an end until September. Their choice
was Felice Peretti, who took the title of Sixtus V. He
was a Franciscan who had come up the hard way from a

childhood of more than Franciscan poverty in a village
on the Adriatic coast. His accession cannot have been
viewed with much pleasure by Father Persons. His
Holiness was not over-friendly towards the Jesuits, he
was sceptical about Philip II's grandiose invasion schemes,
and he had a frankly expressed admiration for England's
heretic queen. Although he was committed, under
Spanish pressure, to a substantial hand-out from the
Papal treasury for the invasion scheme, he appears to
have made no secret of his opinion that it would be
money down the drain, thanks to Queen Elizabeth's
character and her popularity as a ruler, and the naval
ability of her seamen.

Mary, Queen of Scots, was executed at Fotheringay
Castle on February 8, 1587 (new style). Her death, for
which Burghley and Walsingham had worked so long
and patiently and for which her cousin Elizabeth had
signed the warrant with distress and scruples of mind,
blotted out the focus of English Catholic conspiracy and
ended all reasonable hope of a Catholic succession. Most
Catholics at home had remained loyal to their Tudor
queen from the beginning, and now even those who took
the Bull of Deposition as a guide to their consciences
mostly settled down to make the best of their lot and
wait for happier days. In the little English enclaves
overseas, in France, Spain, Flanders, the Papal States, the
dream of a forcible reconversion of England lingered on.
Dr. Allen and Father Persons had been called to Rome.
Both men were working actively for the coming invasion of England, the Jesuit in efforts to stir up the slow-

moving Philip of Spain, and the founder of seminaries in the composition of his *Admonition to the Nobility and People of England*, which was to strike a forceful propagandist blow at Elizabeth's position when the invading fleet set sail. We can see how much the exiles had lost touch with English sentiment, Catholic as well as Protestant, when we find the devout, scholarly Allen writing of Queen Elizabeth, and expecting to win his countrymen's support, in such terms as the following: '. . . a most unjust usurper and injurer of all nations, an infamous, depraved, accursed, excommunicate heretic, the very shame of her sex and princely name, the chief spectacle of sin and abomination in this our age and the only poison, calamity and destruction of our noble church and country.'

The virulence of this unfortunate broadsheet has been put down by some historians to Father Persons' account. They think he was the true begetter of the *Admonition*. Certainly, for many years his restless energy was behind most of Allen's ventures. He was fourteen years junior to Allen, but seems to have been always the dominant party in the friendship. In later years, when so many dreams had come to nothing, the elderly cardinal, ever homesick for his native land, drew away from Persons' ideas, although the friendship remained. During the preparations for invasion, however, Persons' was the controlling hand. He was very busy in 1587. He made his final vows as a Jesuit, including the special fourth vow of direct and full obedience to the Sovereign Pontiff. Those who know something of the strong corporate loyalty of Jesuits to their Society, an emotion similar to that of an earnest professional soldier or sailor, will know how much that solemn profession meant to a man of Robert Persons' temperament.

At one period of his career enemies accused him of aspiring to the cardinal's hat. I think the charge is negligible. It does not fit in with the man's intense devotion to his Order. Those who have known Jesuits forced under obedience to accept dignities in the Church, have seen how unwillingly in most cases they leave the ranks of their Society for a place in the hierarchy. The promotion which Persons would have declined for himself he worked hard to win for his friend. He saw him in his mind's eye as Papal nuncio, the medium of England's new reconciliation to Rome, and her Primate when the old order was restored. He pulled the wires successfully. On August 7 Dr. Allen was promoted to the rank he would need for his future position in England. He frankly admitted the influence that had been at work. 'Under heaven', he says, 'Father Persons made me a cardinal.'

A query occurs to us as we follow Father Persons' career through the Armada years. Mary Stuart's death planted a question-mark in the outlook of political-minded Catholics. Who would take the unfortunate Queen of Scots' place as claimant to the English crown? Her son was a poor bet for such as Persons. The Presbyterians had got hold of James Stuart again and, although he loathed them, they had cut him off successfully from all Catholic influences. Father Persons was not at a loss. Even before Mary Stuart had been beheaded, he had set to work. He was very much the white-headed boy of the Spaniards by this time, and Philip's ambassador to Rome thought very highly of his abilities. It was the ambassador who dropped the hint that set Persons to work building up the case for a Spanish grab at the crown of England. 'Right of conquest' sounded rather shoddy even to sixteenth-century ears, especially when a not-too-optimistic Vicar of Christ was involved in the enterprise. Accordingly the Jesuit got hold of the best available genealogist—there were always devoted workers ready to serve the dynamic Robert Persons—and set out the claim of the Spanish king's daughter in virtue of Lancastrian descent. It was not so fantastic as it sounds to our generation. Father Persons' contemporaries were affected by appeals to legitimacy, and he knew it. It is amusing, however, to find him later on putting forward a statement of the rights of peoples to choose and to depose their rulers that aligns him with the Presbyterian George Buchanan and—the Founding Fathers of the United States.

The Armada, with its thousands of soldiers and sailors for the invasion and its accompanying clerics for the conversion of England, sailed in the summer of 1588, speeded by the prayers of all good Spaniards, of some Italians, and a few Englishmen. I do not think many Englishmen, even Catholic exiles, prayed very heartily for its success, because when the news of the well-nigh unbelievable disaster reached Rome, the English seminarists cheered for the victory of their Protestant Lord-

Admiral and his heretic subordinates.[1] While the unhappy Armada was struggling homewards round northern Scotland and Ireland, many of its ships wrecked on unknown coasts and their crews massacred by wild clansmen, Father Persons was on his way to Spain once more.

The journey this time was for purely domestic purposes, in intention, anyhow. Philip II had shown a disposition to butt into the government and mode of life of the Jesuits in his kingdom. It was a regrettable habit of absolutist monarchs, reaching its climax in Joseph II of Austria in the eighteenth century, instrumental in the Society's suppression. All serious trouble for the Jesuits in King Philip's territories was averted. The Father-general, the wise Acquaviva, recognized his own flair for diplomacy in his English subject and sent him to steer the Catholic Majesty from meddling with the Spanish Jesuits. Father Persons achieved success by exercising an amount of tact we might not have expected from the Balliol official who had set all the other dons by the ears and quarrelled with the head of the college. Philip not only accepted the English priest's mediation and kept his royal hands off his Jesuit subjects; he made a confidant of Father Persons and let it be known to the Jesuit general that the English priest was very much *persona*

---

[1] Lord Howard of Effingham was a Protestant, definitely what at the time was called a 'hot' Protestant. Daniel O'Connell unwittingly started a modern legend that the Lord High Admiral was a Catholic. From early times there were both Catholic and Protestant branches of the Howard family.

grata at the Escorial. Father Persons remained in Spain
for nine years.

By this time no doubt Persons had become a good deal
of a cosmopolite. Englishmen who were hostile to him
called him 'Hispaniolated'. It was a term of oppro-
brium at the time, with the emotional overtones that
attach to 'Red' or 'fellow traveller' in these days. Perhaps
Persons was Hispaniolated. It would have been part of
his tactful dealing with the king and the grandees in
church and state to appear so. The swarthy, rather
stern-faced priest might easily have passed for a fellow-
countryman of his Founder. However, like Sir Walter
Ralegh and other country-bred Englishmen of the period,
he probably kept the local accent and intonation of his
native country when he spoke English. It would have
seemed incongruous to hear his voice, with the pleasant
Somerset drawl, its *s* softened to a *z* every time, in secret
conference with some expatriate English Catholic who
came to him with a foolproof plot for the deposition.
The trouble was that no one, not even Father Persons,
ever came across a plot that was Walsingham-proof.

Like Gilbert and Sullivan's hero, Persons, as his
enemies admitted, was 'yet an English man', although
'a Jesuit beyonde the seas'. A touch of the John Bull
in him comes out after the failure of the Armada, when
he was still urging invasion schemes on the slow-moving
Philip. He voiced his anger and irritation at Spanish
arrogance towards Englishmen, and Spanish official in-
difference to English sentiment and English loyalties.
The Hispaniolated Jesuit's feelings were those of the

Londoners who stoned and snowballed Philip II's followers when the king was in London with his English wife, Queen Mary. The years in Spain were by no means given exclusively to political intrigue. Indeed, we shall misread Robert Persons' mind and character if we picture him as a Richelieu or a Mazarin. Richelieu was primarily a Frenchman, a French nationalist, secondarily—and a very poor second—a churchman. Persons was, in his thoughts, ambitions, and emotions, wholly a cleric and a religious. It is a safe assumption that had the Marian settlement with the Papacy survived or had some compromise between Pope and heretical queen been made, we should know of Robert Persons only as a great Elizabethan prose writer, a skilled director of souls, and, perhaps, a great organizer and ruler in the growing Jesuit order, like Claudius Acquaviva, under whom he lived for most of his Jesuit years. The solid achievement of the nine-year sojourn in Spain was the establishment of the English seminaries there to supplement the work of Douay and Rheims. Persons had already pointed out to Cardinal Allen the need to have colleges for training English priests elsewhere than in France. The college at Valladolid was in full operation within a few years of Father Persons' arrival in Spain, and it went on educating young men for work in the British Isles after the Society had been suppressed in the eighteenth century.

Perhaps the most interesting phase of the Spanish interlude in Persons' career is the controversial battle between this 'English man beyonde the seas' and his English queen or, anyhow, her government. Philip II,

M

urged along vehemently by Father Persons and somewhat less enthusiastically by the authorities in Rome, was preparing to redress the failure of 1588 by a bigger and better invasion. Walsingham's secret service, of course, had been keeping the Privy Council well informed. King Philip's undeniable kindness and generosity to the Catholic refugees made it easy for the Lord-Treasurer and the Principal Secretary to get their spies in and out of Spain. Walsingham died in 1590, but the espionage service he had built up continued.

In the winter of 1591 a denunciation of the Spanish preparations for war was issued in the queen's name. Father Persons was specifically mentioned and duly excoriated. The following summer he had his reply written in Latin, translated into French and English, published on the continent, and smuggled into England. This *Responsio ad edictum Elizabethae* bore the pen-name of Philopater on the title page. It was a vitriolic composition, although the queen herself was treated with comparative restraint. She did not willingly agree to the proclamation, said Philopater, but was taken in by the fraud and importunity of Lord Burghley (William Cecil). Walsingham being dead, Cecil was the chief target of the Jesuit's attack. The Lord Treasurer, he said, anticipating Mr. Belloc's reading of Elizabethan politics, 'controls almost all things in England by his own judgment'. There is a thumb-nail biography of the Old Fox, very unflattering and, perhaps, not wholly authentic. He was of obscure origin, we are told, his father, David, who had served in King Henry VIII's guard, being a

tavern-keeper in Stamford. The son William 'for a time
sought part of his living by tolling the bell in St. John's
College'. This snobbish criticism of working one's way
through college was probably less than sincere coming
from a fervent Jesuit who had willingly undertaken the
menial jobs imposed on Jesuit novices for their souls'
sake.

Philopater takes a few cracks at Sir Walter Ralegh in
passing. The rumours of Ralegh's 'atheism' and the
'school of atheisme', where young men 'were taught to
spell *God* backwards' and to ridicule the Bible, had
reached Father Persons' ears, and he evidently thought
the gossip good enough for one of Elizabeth's favourites.
Perhaps he would have been kinder to Sir Walter Ralegh
could he have seen that a few years later Ralegh himself
would show great courtesy and kindness to a Jesuit
martyr, Father Cornelius, and even risk his own position
by trying to save the priest from the gibbet. Sir Christopher Hatton, the queen's 'dancing Chancellor', is
treated with surprising gentleness. His 'beauty of person
and grace of action' are mentioned, and it is stated that
he was a moderate man, opposed to the proclamation and
all cruel measures. There is a dark hint about suspicion
of poison when the Chancellor died. The author let
himself go when he came to the subject of the overseas
seminaries. There were in them 'more gentlemen
than in all the [Protestant] clergy in England twice told'.
The English universities, which must have gone down
since the writer was at Balliol, were described as being
in a most parlous state—with no porters to keep dis-

cipline at the gates, and to this is attributed 'the filling
up and pestering all colleges with harlots to be baits
for the young men'. The taverns and the fencing and
dancing schools were crowded, but studies were neg-
lected and the places of fellows and scholars were sold
publicly. We should note, in order to judge Father
Persons' 'treason' fairly, that Philopater declared the
Pope's deposing power to be an article of faith. If that
was his sincere belief, his political efforts in Rome and
Madrid were consistent with it.

The boys' school at Eu, in Normandy, could not be
carried on after the assassination of the Duke of Guise.
Father Persons, who had the knack of loosening the
Spanish purse-strings whenever English Catholics were
in distress, obtained an annual grant from King Philip and
in 1593 established an English college at St. Omer, a
small town in what is now the French department of
Pas de Calais. For the generation that can recall World
War I St. Omer will be remembered as English army
H.Q. in the first part of the war. The English college
(using the word in the British sense to include a boys'
boarding school) carried on the education of the sons of
English Catholics, for the church and for a layman's
life, until the ex-Jesuits had to flee with their students
from the anticlerical fury of the French Revolutionists.
The Welds of Lulworth gave the *emigrés* the old Shire-
burn estate of Stonyhurst, in Lancashire. Alumni of that
great public school may, therefore, regard the Elizabethan Jesuit as their Founder.

Two years after Philopater's brochure appeared,

Father Persons went to press again, this time under the pseudonym of N. Dolman. The famous *Conference about the next Succession* was much more of a bombshell than the *Responsio*. Its actual authorship has been credited to a lay exile, Richard Rowlands, better known under his alias of Verstegan, the antiquary and student of Anglo-Saxon. Father Persons, however, certainly rewrote some parts of the book and revised the whole text, which is of interest to us as an attack on the divine right of kings. The book's championing the claim to the English crown of the Infanta of Spain naturally caused an uproar among Elizabeth's subjects. Most regrettably, from the Catholic point of view, it brought to boiling point the hostility between two sections of the clergy and their lay partisans. The supporters of the pro-Spanish party were aligned with Persons; their opponents, mostly secular priests, stood by their fidelity to the Tudor crown.

The quarrel grew worse as time went on. There were unedifying squabbles between cliques of priests sharing the same hardships in Wisbech jail. Then came the dispute over the archpriest appointed in lieu of a bishop for the persecuted church, and, finally, the formation of a minority group of Appellants who tried to score a victory by playing into the hands of the government.

The indignation in England found expression in Parliament. Legislation was rushed through to make it treason to own a copy of Mr. Dolman's book. Catholics, and not alone English ones, were dismayed, and there is ground for thinking that the Pope himself was none too well pleased.

Father Persons, who was optimistic about such ventures long after other people had given them up, seems to have been taken aback by the hornets' nest he had stirred up amongst his fellow-Catholics as well as the Protestants. He had been too long absent from England, living in the threadbare medievalism of Philip's court and, as we have seen, deluded into accepting a relic of a bygone Christendom as an article of faith. That he had indeed been shocked into some understanding of the contemporary mind in England we deduce from his hiding a manuscript of a book that was all ready for publication. This was *A Memorial of the Reformation of England, containing certain Notes and Advertisements, which same might be proposed in the first Parliament and National Council of our Country, after God in His Mercy shall restore it to the Catholic Faith. . . . Gathered and set down by R.P., 1596.* The book, which did not appear until an enterprising London publisher, Gee, brought it out nearly a hundred years later, is a strange medley of aspirations for a theocracy that might, with elders and ministers substituted for priests and bishops, have been worked out by a committee of divines in seventeenth-century New England. The bishops, for instance, were to have power to veto or confirm elections to the House of Commons. More offensive to the mind of later ages was the proposal to introduce some form of religious inquisition into an England regained for the Papacy. Elizabeth's Protestant subjects, of course, would have bridled at the suggestion, but only because it came from the Catholic side of the fence. It is unhistorical to credit them with eighteenth-century Whig ideas of religious toleration. The author himself had not quite made up his mind 'what forms of Inquisition to bring in, whether that of Spain (whose rigour is misliked by some) or that which is used in divers parts of Italy (whose coldness is reprehended by more).'

Another side of Robert Persons' many-faceted character comes out in the *Memorial*. I refer to his tenderness towards the poor and lowly, the distressed and the exploited among his countrymen. It was a trait he shared with his Founder, St. Ignatius Loyola, who also on occasion could be hard and stern. In an age that to us, despite all we have known of cruelty in Germany and Russia, seems intolerably callous, Persons displays in his book a social conscience worthy of a present-day Catholic Action in a western country. There were to be in every township of his reformed England poor men's savings banks and well-run hospitals. Moreover, anticipating legislation that was still nearly four centuries away, he wanted laws to protect married women's property and their dowries. No, there was no doubt Father Robert definitely held that he was his brother's keeper. Moreover, being a Christian believer, he saw other men as his brothers, not, as with our modern intellectual Leftists, mere units in a Socialist or Marxist ideology.

Cardinal Allen died in the fall of 1594, disillusioned about winning England back to the Faith by means of foreign navies, weary of politics, envious of the young men who had gone to England from Douay and Rheims and won the glory of martyrdom. One may be sure that

Persons, to whom friendship meant much, felt the less deeply. The year after Allen's death Father Persons received the news of the martyrdom of a younger con- temporary and fellow-Jesuit whose character and whose death must have recalled the companion of fourteen years earlier. Blessed Robert Southwell, martyr and poet, was executed at Tyburn in February, 1595. Like Campion, he died protesting that he had never done, desired, nor thought any harm to his queen, and that he was proud to be a priest of the Catholic and Roman Church and a Jesuit. He had endured several years of imprisonment, and repeated tortures under the sadistic brute Topcliffe. Amongst other things, his torturers tried, in vain, to get him to say what he knew of Father Persons' activities.

Did Persons' thoughts at this time begin to take the same direction as his friend Allen's before the end? It is difficult to say, for he was recalled to Rome and given the responsibility which he carried until his death, the rectorship of the English College. This was no admini- strative bed of roses. Elizabethan youths, even in ecclesiastical seminaries, were a full-blooded and high- spirited lot, and the comparable type in our times would be the young Catholic *maquisards* of the Resistance braving the terrors of arrest by the Gestapo.

There had been a spot of trouble in the early days of the college—between Englishmen and Welshmen—of which Persons gave an amusing account in a letter to Dr. Allen, a letter which shows that the Jesuit, unlike too many religious people, had a sense of humour. Remem- bering that in temperament he was wholly English, we must admire his tolerance when, after restoring harmony between Celt and Anglo-Saxon, he writes to Allen, another hundred-per-cent Englishman, '. . . I would the difference between Welsh and English had not been so often named, or so much urged here among strangers, seeing that of both nations there be very good and virtuous people both at home and abroad, who by this open contention may be driven into division. But who can stay young men, or old men either, once incensed on both sides by national contentions?'

More serious trouble arose towards the end of Persons' stay in Spain. In the spring of 1587 he was hurrying Romewards, so far as the term 'hurry' is applicable to sixteenth-century conditions. He had been called back by his father-general. Once more the population of the English College and its partisans, lay and clerical, outside, were divided into two squabbling factions. This time it was worse than the racial clash eighteen years earlier. The supporters of the Jesuits who governed the college were at war with the anti-Jesuit party among the secular clergy. It was a reflection and a preview of the bitter Appellant controversy. The students of the English College were destined for the ranks of the secular clergy.

One might expect that Father Persons, notoriously 'Hispaniolated' and a helper of would-be invaders of England, would have been met with catcalls and jeers when he returned to the college. He may have been; history does not tell us. We do know that in a short time he had restored order. His diplomacy must have come into play, for he apparently charmed away all pro- and anti-Jesuit friction. For the rest of his life, another thirteen years, he reigned in the *Venerabile*, beloved and respected. Undoubtedly, like the priest in the Irish song, he had a way with him. Whatever his faults, they were not those of a cold-hearted man. In those troublesome, fractious young men he saw the zeal, idealism, and courage, moral and physical, which were, generally speaking, the characteristics of the mission priests sent out from Douay, Rheims, Rome, and, after 1580, from Jesuit houses on the continent. There were potential Maynes, Campions, and Southwells among the studnets whom the old saint of the Oratory (the Chiesa Nuova), who had died a couple of years earlier, had gone on addressing as '*Flores martyrum*'.

About this time fresh trouble boiled up among the Catholics in England. For years the Jesuits, along with the secular priests, had urged on Rome the need for bishops in England. We find this plea in some of the earliest letters sent secretly out of England by Father Persons in 1580–1. After the failure of the elderly Dr. Goldwell, expatriate bishop of St. Asaph, to complete the journey to England in 1580, the Pope had appointed no bishops to replace those who had died or were in prison. The new Anglican bishops had taken the territorial titles. Catholic ecclesiastical life became a hole-and-corner business of disguised priests, secular and regular, moving from one country house to another or lurking perilously in inns or rented rooms in the towns. Even an army of heroes and *maquisards* will become a mob without commanders and discipline. Rome at length took action. However, no new bishops were consecrated for England. Clement VIII thought the time 'inopportune'. Perhaps he feared for the dignity and prestige of the episcopal office. The example of the Catacombs had been forgotten, and that of the Iron Curtain was still in the future.

Rome compromised. There should be an archpriest, more than a simple priest, less than a bishop. One George Blackwell, a secular priest working in London, was appointed. Ostensibly he had a great deal of authority, but was given secret orders to consult the Jesuits in all major decisions and to act in collaboration with them. Secrets do not seem to have been well kept in Elizabethan England. The virtual subordination of all the English Mission priests to Jesuit control led to hard feelings between the Society and the secular clergy. Echoes of it could be caught in later generations. It took several years and some scandalous deals with the government by a disaffected minority, for the quarrel to run its course. Finally the archpriest's dependence on Jesuit approval was swept away, but the unfortunate Blackwell burned his fingers over James I's oath of allegiance and died in disfavour with Rome. Father Persons has been much blamed, in his own time and since, for his part in the turmoil about the archpriest. We are told he engineered the orders for the Society's control of the archpriest's actions and fought hard and unscrupulously to prevent the appointment of bishops for the English Mission. We do not know the whole truth about this.

More documents must be brought out from archives before we can judge the case fairly.

Elizabeth was becoming an old woman, as age was reckoned in her time. She was full of vitality and could outdance much younger men and women, but she was nearing her childless threescore years and ten. Who was to succeed her? The question was troubling the minds of English statesmen. Disputed successions, with resultant civil war, are old, far-off things in our history books. To Elizabeth's Privy Councillors they were still a fearful possibility. The Tudors, as the line neared extinction, were still parvenus. James VI of Scotland was the logical choice, but neither his own person nor his race was loved in England. Scotsmen were foreigners and had often been troublesome. Persons, in the pious seclusion of the English College, watched events at home. He himself was watched, not without a touch of apprehension. There was still a pro-Spanish party in the Court. Lord Burghley had died in 1598, but his mantle had fallen on his second son Robert, the clever little hunchback, as adept as his father at throwing the stone so as the hand be not seen. He was well ahead of rivals in making friends with James of Scotland, but he was shrewd enough to hedge against possible contingencies by being very friendly for a time towards the Spaniards and their English sympathizers or, more correctly, their pensioners. It is even possible that he, or more probably some go-between, kept in touch with the redoubtable Jesuit—just in case. However, the Stuart claim was accepted peacefully, with Robert Cecil cheering more loudly than any. Father Persons took the news of James Stuart's accession tranquilly and supported the Pope's admonition to the Catholics of England to accept their new sovereign loyally and to refrain from conspiracy. Catholics hoped for much from the Stuart king, who had shown himself glad to have Catholic support. Father Persons, as well as his countrymen at home, had yet to hear of James' 'Na, na, I'll nae need the Papists now,' when he was safely on the throne, and before the criminal folly of the Gunpowder Plot had given colour to the suspicion Protestant Englishmen have felt for Catholics right down to our own times.

The years which Father Persons spent as rector of the English College will be pictured as peaceful by those who know something of the calm routine of an ecclesiastical community. The duties and responsibilities of his rectorship could not have sufficed to burn up all this dynamic priest's energy. The organization and running of the English Mission was mainly his affair. He was the chief, almost the sole object of attack in the Appellant controversy. He was brought into the business of James I's oath of allegiance and its condemnation by Rome. Even Douay College, to which the Rheims faculty and students had been able to return in 1593, was indirectly under Father Persons' control, for its new rector, Dr. Worthington, was bound by a secret vow of obedience to him. As if all this were not enough, he kept up a spirited controversy with various Protestants at home, including England's great lawyer, Sir Edward Coke.

The end came in typically Jesuit fashion and as Robert

Persons, no doubt, would have wished it, that is to say, quietly, undramatically, and in the midst of work, with just time and opportunity for the Church's deathbed pieties and for a last recalling of what was, perhaps, the most heartfelt of the dying priest's memories. His old enemy, the Roman malaria, had troubled him through the spring of 1610. The college professors and students could see that their sixty-five-year-old rector was failing in health. There was no let-up in his activity, and he kept the severe Lenten fast of those more austere times as strictly as ever. By mid-Lent, however, he was in a bad way. The Pope, says More, the official historian of the English Jesuits, sent his blessing and all indulgences and favours which are accustomed to be given on the approach of death.

On Holy Saturday the dying man was still at work. From his bed he dictated letters in Latin and English to his fellow-countrymen in the Society, using as his rubric the text, 'Love ye one another.' One of his last letters is inscribed in his characteristic fashion, 'Given at Rome from my bed in the English College on this the vigil of the Lord's Resurrection in the year 1610. Yours wholly and ever.' At this time, also, he dictated a paper for the father-general on the future running of the English Mission.

The dying Jesuit seems a different person from the political priest at the Escorial, the aggressive and at times bitter controversialist, the Hispaniolated Englishman urging a foreign monarch to invade Queen Elizabeth's kingdom. In this sick room in the college lay the English students' shrewd and kindly rector, the solicitous Padre Roberto of the Italian lay brothers and servants, the big-hearted Somerset man who would always beg from a foreign nobleman or squeeze out of the community finances an alms for any exiled Englishman in distress.

At the very end Father Persons made a sign and whispered a request to someone, lay brother infirmarian, student, or his *socius* (priest assistant). From among the scanty personal belongings which a Jesuit can call his own, more or less, there was brought him his most cherished possession, the rope with which Edmund Campion had been hanged at Tyburn on the stormy morning of December 1, twenty-nine years earlier. Father Persons kissed the rope and had it put round his own neck as the ministering priest read the prayers for the dying, which begin, '*Proficiscere* , *anima Christiana* . . .' ('Go forth, Christian soul . . .').

Father Persons was buried, as he had asked, beside the body of his friend, Cardinal Allen, in the church of the English College. Some day, one hopes, a full and frank biography will do justice to Robert Persons. The evil, if it be such, of his career has lived too long in his country-men's memories; it is time the good was disinterred.

III

JOHN DEE
THE QUEEN'S ASTROLOGER

A TRIP by the Underground railway out from central London to Kew Gardens to see an astrologer and crystal-gazer in the riverside suburb of Mortlake nearby, calls up a picture of the rows of brick villas that within a few decades have swallowed orchards, water meadows, market gardens, and a good deal of old-world atmosphere. In one of the shabbier and drearier streets there will be a commonplace little house where the seer plies his, or more probably her, trade. Both the astrology and the clairvoyance are, as such, within the law, but they must observe the statutory limitation—no pretence at telling the future. The future, however, is just what a credulous and romance-hungry proletariat wants to hear and will pay its half-crown or its ten bob for. Every so often, therefore, a seer foretells a future, read from a horoscope or crystal ball, to a plainclothes man whose identity the stars or the spirits did not reveal. Then there is a minor case before a stipendiary magistrate, a fine, and another visit to the pawnbroker.

It is all rather pathetic and a bit sordid. Not so to the

Elizabethans. They went down to Mortlake in style—
the queen herself, her Secretary of State, admirals,
knights, men of letters, distinguished foreign visitors—
by river, in gay barges or tilt boats, with flags flying and
bands playing, to consult the great John Dee. Doctor
Dee everybody called him, although no one was quite
sure when or where he got his doctorate, and none of our
painstaking researchers have made quite sure of anything
beyond his M.A.

To the Elizabethan mob, a violent, brutal, superstitious
mob, with all the modern Cockney's irreverence, but
little of his tolerance and good nature, Dr. Dee was an
evil man, in partnership with fiends. His soul was
mortgaged to an eternity of roaring hot fire, the medieval
hell whose horrors had been augmented when the
Reformers blotted out the merciful concept of Purgatory.
The educated minority, Queen Elizabeth, Cecil, Walsingham, Ralegh, Sidney, Dyer, and the like, knew Dee
for a learned man, a scientist, a mathematician, and
bibliophile. Even to some of his distinguished patrons,
however, his astrology and his clairvoyance, the latter
practised at second hand, came uppermost. The queen's
astrologer they called him, on the strength of a horoscope
cast for the young Princess Elizabeth in the perilous
years under her half-sister, Queen Mary.

The popular title, handing down to posterity an image
of blended superstition and quackery, is unfair both to the
queen and the Doctor. He was more than an astrologer,
even in the worthier Tudor use of the word. Elizabeth,
one of the most erudite of queens, but too delightfully

N

feminine for a bluestocking, played with such things, but it is improbable that she took them very seriously. She valued Dee for more than supposed preternatural dealings. She respected his learning, listened to his views on England's navy and maritime affairs, and obviously liked the man for his genial, kindly nature. Perhaps she smiled to herself a little at the foibles of a genius—the naïve vanity, the impracticality in money matters, and his failure to keep his offspring from bumps and bruises, and the danger of drowning in the Thames that flowed below the back garden.

It is a pity that more people did not share Elizabeth's perception of John Dee's intellectual greatness. He was much more dupe than charlatan where the spirits and the visions in the crystal ball were concerned. Still, both failings are minor blots on a record of solid achievement in the English Renaissance. If, then, we find amusement in Dr. Dee's spirits, his 'controls' in modern spiritual- istic jargon, his phoney mediums, and their paraphernalia of crystals and 'mystic' tables, well and good—too many of history's great men serve only for boredom—but let us give him the credit for abilities that impressed the best minds in England's most brilliant era.

Milton, Wordsworth, and, at greater length, Dr. Freud, have told us that the child is father to the man. John Dee's early life adds confirmation. He was a studious little boy, with the neat, systematic sort of mind that takes readily to Latin. He had been born in 1527 in London of a father whom one antiquary describes as a vintner, another as a gentleman 'sewer', or server, to

Henry VIII. The family claimed Welsh origin, and John in later years drew up a genealogy showing his descent from a ninth-century Welsh king, but that probably was a bit of his harmless vanity.

At the age of nine or ten years the boy, who had been at a day school in London, was packed off to a boarding school at Chelmsford, run by a Mr. Peter Wilegh, who enjoyed some reputation as a headmaster. The life at an Essex boarding school in the sixteenth century was rather grim for a book-loving child of ten. John Dee's soul does not seem to have been indelibly scarred by it, for he tells us little in his autobiography except that he left school 'metely well furnished in understanding of the Latin tongue'.

He was somewhat over fifteen years old when he entered St. John's College, Cambridge, in the winter of 1542. There is not much to record about his under-graduate years except his passion for study and the amount of time he gave to it. A modern student would certainly consider him an unmitigated swot. I quote his own testimony. 'In the years 1543, 1544, 1545 I was so vehemently bent to studie, that for those years I did inviolably keep this order: only to sleep four houres every night: to allow to meate and drink (and some refreshing after) two houres every day; and of the other eighteen houres all (except the time of going to and being at divine service) was spent in my studies and learning.'

We are not surprised to hear that as soon as he had his B.A. (1545) he was made a foundation fellow of his college. A further stroke of luck came his way about a year later. Henry VIII established Trinity College, and the young B.A. of St. John's was made one of the original fellows of the new foundation. Also, he was appointed to a readership in Greek. The enthusiasms of the Renaissance had reached England from the continent, and classical Greek was all the rage at the universities.

In these early months at Trinity College the under-reader in Greek was credited, quite unjustly, with magical and, as his contemporaries saw them, sinister powers. His reputation as a wizard then began, and he spent the rest of his life disclaiming it. It all started with a job of stage production for amateur theatricals. Some of the students in his Greek classes were going to do Aristophanes' Εἰρήνη (*Peace*) as a Christmas play. The comedy is an Hellenic anticipation, one might say, of Henry Ford's Peace Ship in the First World War. The hero of the play, Trygaeus, vinedresser and rustic pacifist, decides to call on Zeus and the other deities to see about stopping a war that had been going on for ten years. For the trip to heaven, where wars, if not marriages, were made in classical times, Trygaeus had brought up and trained a gigantic dung beetle, a *Scarabaeus* Dr. Dee more elegantly calls it. The task of getting the monstrous beetle, 'with a man and his basket of victuals on her back', up in the air to Jove's palace was a problem in stage carpentry. John Dee tackled it successfully, but there was 'great wondring, and many vain reports spread about, of the means how that was effected'.

In the early summer after the too-successful production

of Aristophanes' play Dee made a trip to the Low Countries, and came back with various astronomical gadgets and a pair of globes made by Gerard Mercator. This was the beginning of a friendship between the young Englishman and the Flemish cartographer fifteen years his senior. Dee became a Master of Arts in the following year and made another trip to the continent. The friendship with Mercator was renewed, and became a close and affectionate one which lasted until the great mapmaker's death nearly half a century later.

The new M.A. had gone abroad with letters of recommendation from his university, testifying to his industry and good conduct. They served to get him admitted to Louvain University for post-graduate work. As though it were merely a side-line to more arduous studies, Dee tells us he 'looked into the method of civil law'. It is even possible he took a doctorate in it, which would justify the 'Dr.' he was known by later on. His 'studies philosophicall and mathematicall', as he calls them, apparently attracted a good deal of notice and even brought distinguished visitors to Louvain. One of them, Sir William Pickering, afterwards an ambassador, employed Dee to coach him in mathematics and astronomy.

At Louvain began a lifelong interest in alchemy, stimulated, it may be, by the fact that in the Flemish town a dozen years earlier had died the German savant, an alchemist among other things, Henry Cornelius Agrippa von Nettesheim. We know that Dr. Dee read Agrippa's writings, and that the treatise on the excellence of women was one of the treasures of his library.

From Louvain, in the summer of 1550, he went to
Paris. Here he gave lectures, open to the public, in the
College of Rheims, on Euclid's geometry. Something
about the lecturer or his subject, a novelty for the general
public in those days, made a hit with the Parisians. They
swarmed into the lecture room and filled it to over-
flowing, with eager auditors peering in through the
windows. The sensation was like that in our own times
when Bergson expounded his philosophy at the Collège
de France. Dee was urged to stay in Paris, but even a
regius professorship with a good salary attached could
not keep him abroad. It was ever the same. Tempting
offers were made, wealth dangled before his eyes, but
always he went back to England, to family worries,
inadequate means, and an uncertain future. However,
he kept up his contacts with the intellectual world of
Renaissance Europe by correspondence with learned men
at a dozen universities.

He was back in England in 1551, and towards the end
of the year his prospects were encouraging. He found a
friend and patron in Sir John Cheke, tutor to the young
King Edward VI, Jane Seymour's sickly child, whose
birth had killed his mother. Cheke introduced Dee to
William Cecil, who as Secretary had begun to hold the
dominant position in English politics which was his for
nearly half a century, through three reigns, the ruthless
scrambles of the Edwardian Protectors, and several
changes of religion. It was a useful introduction. The
great Lord Burghley found time to do Dr. Dee several
good turns later on, although the scientist, who was a

touchy man where his reputation was concerned, seems at times to have felt he was not duly appreciated. However, he made a promising start under Edward VI with the grant of a rectory in Worcestershire—at Upton-on-Severn. A monetary pension had been assigned him, and the Worcestershire living was in lieu of the hundred crowns annuity originally given. It was a poor deal in the end, like most of Dee's financial arrangements.

Dee never resided in his parish and never took orders, Catholic or Protestant. One presumes that, like William Cecil and other careerists, great and small, he made the appropriate gestures for his country's official changes from Protestant to Catholic and back again.

About the time of Queen Mary's accession he was in touch with the new queen's half-sister, Princess Elizabeth, possibly casting a horoscope for her. The service, whatever it was, was an innocent one, but the timing was bad. The young princess was imprisoned, and for a time she was in grave peril. An informer, George Ferrys, thought it worth his while to get John Dee's name put on the list for the threatened purge. The young scientist had, said the informer, killed one of the Ferrys' children and blinded another by magic. Further, to give Dee's evil activities a more public interest, the informer hinted that the magician was working against the queen's life. This, of course, was a more serious charge. For a time things looked very bad for John Dee.

He was seized, his lodgings searched and sealed, and he had to submit to various interrogations by one of the Secretaries of State, the Lord Chief Justice, members of the Privy Council, and, finally, the Star Chamber, a body with wide powers feared even by citizens with a clear conscience.

Dr. Dee was cleared of all suspicion of treason, which suggests that Star Chamber was more of a genuine court of justice and less of the Fascist (or Communist) tribunal the Whig historians have made it out to be. However, the scientist's troubles were not yet over. The idea of guilt by association is not a product of our modern campaign against the Nazi and Communist forms of fascism. It flourished in the sixteenth century. Dr. Dee had been seen in bad company, which is what Protestants were under Queen Mary and her Spanish consort. The Doctor was handed over to Bonner, the Bishop of London, who has been so much blamed, and over-blamed, in connection with the Marian burnings for heresy.

While he was in custody Dee associated with another prisoner suspected of heresy, but when his turn came he convinced the bishop of his orthodoxy so thoroughly that he was retained by Bonner to help in the examination of other suspects. It is on occasions of this kind that the reader feels John Dee must have been a bit of a charlatan. However, let martyrs and heroes throw the first stone. The Smithfield fires, even to a sixteenth-century spectator, were a grim reminder of the perils of heterodoxy.

Dee evidently felt his credit was good after the Bishop of London had given him an honourable discharge, for a little later we find him presenting to Queen Mary 'A Supplication for the recovery and preservation of ancient writers and monuments.' It was a petition for the estab-

lishment of a National Library, set up and run by the
state. Two centuries later England got around to doing
what Dee had suggested. We may hope that the col-
lections in the British Museum are a compensation to his
spirit for our tardiness in following his advice.

With the accession of Queen Elizabeth began a time of
greater tranquillity for those Englishmen who scurried
about, figuratively speaking, to find out whether their
spiritual home should be Rome, Geneva, or Canterbury.
They soon found out that a moderate and Erastian Canterbury was the correct thing. Only the logical extremists,
Catholics at one end, Puritans at the other, stuck to their
convictions and were persecuted accordingly.

Dr. Dee had made a good start by his approaches to
Princess Elizabeth when her star was not in the ascendant,
approaches which suggest that he did not altogether
lack moral courage. He enjoyed the good will of Lord
Robert Dudley, the future Earl of Leicester, who now
introduced him into the presence of the queen. Elizabeth took an immediate liking to him. Doubtless his
good looks had something to do with it. The Oxford
portrait, which shows him later in life, suggests well-bred
features, good bone formation, and calmness and dignity
of expression. Aubrey, who collected oddments of
gossip and old people's memories half a century after
Dee's death, tells us he was tall and handsome, with a
good skin and complexion. His personality was *simpatico*.
Aubrey tells us he was a great peacemaker. One suspects
that he had good hands, perhaps with graceful, tapering
fingers. They were a passport to the queen's approval.

Queen Elizabeth showed her favour at this interview by a fine promise in terms of the English currency. 'Where my brother hath given him a crown (5 shillings)' she said, 'I will give him a noble (about 10 shillings).' As with too many of the queen's gestures where money was in question, the recipient ended up with a good deal less than he had been promised.

In these early days of the new reign Dee may well have thought he was on the way to riches and high position. He was promptly commissioned, probably through Robert Dudley, to choose by means of astrology a suitable day for the coronation. To Elizabethan ears there was nothing fantastic, quaint, or superstitious about this, although later on we see Shakespeare giving utterance to a growing scepticism about astrology.

> 'The fault, dear Brutus, is not in our stars,
> But in ourselves, that we are underlings.'

Dee picked out January 14, 1559 (new style) as the auspicious date.

Immediately after this achievement as augur to the queen he received a promise of preferment. He was to be made 'Master' of the hospital or almshouses of St. Katharine-by-the-Tower, a charitable foundation going back to the Middle Ages, with its buildings and gardens on a site now covered with docks and warehouses just below Tower Bridge. The mastership was virtually a sinecure. Such duties as there were could be taken over by a deputy for a small sum. The position carried with it a moderate but secure income, a certain prestige, and a pleasant dwelling on what was then the eastern fringe of London. John Dee's prospects looked encouraging, but even Tudor monarchs could not be wholly arbitrary about patronage. One Wilson, a Doctor of Letters, had got ahead of the astrologer. 'Dr. Willson politickly prevented me,' says Dee.

About this time a mild panic was caused by an ominous discovery in Lincoln's Inn Fields—a doll or wax figure of Elizabeth pierced to the heart with pins. Malevolent persons—they would be Communists nowadays; then it was probably claimed that they were Catholics—were seeking to destroy the queen by sympathetic magic. Dr. Dee was hastily called in. He reassured the members of the Privy Council who took the matter seriously, and was then sent along to Richmond to carry his reassurances to the queen in person.

Presumably he hoped that his buttressing of morale at high levels would be rewarded by something to take the place of the lost mastership of St. Katharine's. He was quite specific in his requests to friends at Court. He needed a substantial benefice to live on, but he would accept no spiritual responsibilities. 'A *cura animarum annexa* did terrifie me to deal with them,' he told the queen on a later occasion. There is matter for speculation about his psychology here, although it is unlikely we can reach a firm conclusion. In medieval society, and to a less extent after the break with Rome, ordination was often and quite casually accepted as merely a useful prerequisite for a good job, much like a university degree in our modern world. Why, then, Dee's terror of such a thing? Was there enough of his Marian Catholicism lurking in his subsconscious for him to retain a horror, not merely of eating and drinking the Lord's Body unworthily, but still more of calling It down to the altar by the priestly words of consecration?

In the winter of 1562 he crossed the North Sea to Antwerp. He had for the time wearied of royal promises that came to nothing. He hoped to arrange for the publication in Germany and the Low Countries of some of his writings. Towards the end of the winter he wrote to William Cecil asking whether he should come home or spend more time abroad in research. Also, he slipped in a fresh hint about his need for preferment.

In the same letter Dee titillated the imagination of Cecil, who was a connoisseur of books, with news of a bibliographical treasure. This was the manuscript of what we may describe as the pioneer of all shorthand manuals, the *Steganographia* of Trithemius, a German ecclesiastic.

Dee stayed abroad for some time longer, evidently at the suggestion of Cecil, who gave good reports of his industry and success in research. Part of the sojourn overseas was spent in visits to Venice and to Hungary. To the Emperor Maximilian II he presented a copy of his book *Monas Hieroglyphica*.

In 1564 he was home again. That summer he was called to Greenwich to instruct the queen in occultism. Again his hopes of preferment rose. He was to get the deanery of Gloucester, said Her Majesty, and by December everything seemed to be going smoothly, but once more he was out of luck. An Oxford don had been beforehand with him and was given the benefice.

Friends at Court then tried to get him the provostship of Eton College. This was to be an appointment in reversion, that is, one that becomes effective on the death or retirement of the present holder. The Provost neither died nor retired, unfortunately for Dee. It was not until 1566 that he received a tiny bit of encouragement. Then Matthew Parker, Elizabeth's Archbishop of Canterbury, a kind, scholarly prelate and a book-lover, confirmed the former grant of the living of Upton, together with Long Leadenham, in Worcestershire. Further, the archbishop authorized him to hold and enjoy any other benefices that might be bestowed on him. Actually, the Upton living was all he ever got from the Church, and it certainly was not much of a plum as preferment went in those days. We are told that it never amounted to more more than about fifty pounds a year, and out of that sum a curate had to be paid to do the work. Dee stuck to his resolve not to take holy orders, and he never lived in his parish. He would have done better to keep the original pension he had exchanged for the benefice.

Another friend at Court, the Earl of Pembroke, kept Dee in the queen's memory by presenting her, on the author's behalf, with a learned treatise, the *Propaedeumata Aphoristica*. This, we are told, Elizabeth graciously accepted. The earl received a copy for himself and in return gave the author twenty pounds.

The earl's efforts did some good. A few weeks later Dr. Dee could be seen in private conference with the queen in the garden at Westminster. She was very gracious to him, and he apparently promised to reveal some great secret to her. It was probably something to do with alchemy, and if it meant transmuting base metals into gold to enrich the royal treasury, we may be sure the queen was deeply interested. We shall do her an injustice, however, if we see her friendliness to the Doctor motivated only by his possibilities of gold-making. On several recorded occasions she went out of her way to do personal kindnesses to him, and she had enough respect for his mental powers to become his pupil.

About this time he settled at Mortlake with his mother. The riverside village was a convenient spot for the contact between scientist and royal pupil. Within easy reach were all of Queen Elizabeth's favourite haunts outside London—Nonesuch Palace, Hampton Court, Sion House, Greenwich, Richmond. The last four lay on London's great east-west thoroughfare of those days, the River Thames.

With Renaissance enthusiasm and versatility Dee, like Francis Bacon, took the whole of learning for his province. In the earlier years he kept his deepest affection for mathematics. Of arithmetic he writes with an ardour that sounds strange to those of us who have memories of schoolday encounters with that subject. 'It lifts the heart above the heavens by invisible lines,' says Dr. Dee, 'and by its immortal beams melteth the reflection of light incomprehensible and so procureth joy and perfection unspeakable'.

In 1570 was published, with a learned preface by Dr. Dee, the first translation into English, from a fifteenth-century Latin version, of Euclid's 'Elements'. The translator was a man with the same passion for mathematics as Dr. Dee, but gifted with a business sense which the queen's astrologer lacked. Henry Billingsley gave promise of becoming a great mathematician, but his family had other ideas for his future. They apprenticed him to the haberdashery business. He made a fortune and became Lord Mayor of London. Success in the bustling world of Elizabethan trade did not kill his interest in things of the mind. He endowed scholarships at Cambridge and became a member of the Society of Antiquaries which the book-loving Archbishop Parker had founded.

Dr. Dee dated his preface to Billingsley's *Euclid* from his home in Mortlake. Probably he wrote it in the library in which he was building up his collection of books and objects of scientific and antiquarian interest. The age of intense specialization had not yet arrived. The Mortlake library was rich in classical authors, Persian and Arabic manuscripts, and the works of two English pioneers of inductive science, Roger Bacon and Bishop Grosseteste. A big wooden chest was filled with seals bearing coats of arms. This formed a reference library of heraldry.

From time to time a Thames waterman would land his passenger at Dr. Dee's river steps, a member of the College of Heralds or a clerk of the Tower records come to do research work in Dr. Dee's library.

All manner of scientific objects were scattered about

the Doctor's library. There were a large quadrant, a ten-foot *radius astronomicus* or early form of telescope swinging in a frame, a large piece of lodestone, and, later in Dee's career, his 'gazing table' to hold the crystal or the polished mirror in which his seers or 'skryers' would behold materialized beings from the spirit world.

Sometimes the visitor would be the Doctor's friend John Stow, who made the trip up the river when he could take time off from his tailoring business in the City. Mr. Stow, like Billingsley, combined a business career with intellectual hobbies. He was a respected member of the Merchant Taylors' Company, as well as the greatest English antiquary of his time.

Sometimes the queen herself visited Dr. Dee in his Mortlake home. She was jolted over the rutted country road from Richmond to Mortlake in a coach or litter, or, in fine weather, came riding her horse. Courtiers and armed guard waited outside, their horses pawing the ground, while queen and savant conferred in the book-lined room within the house. The tall, slender man of learning in his simple black gown who gazes thoughtfully from the canvas in the Ashmolean Museum, and the queen, red-haired, sparkling with jewellery, lively, satirical, loud-voiced, were strangely contrasted. Dee was a gentle, kindly scholar, rather ingenuous in practical things, and rather easily fooled by a plausible rogue. The queen, who could be something of a virago when she was annoyed and who had a habit of deflating minds swollen with their own importance, was invariably kind and mild with her astrologer. In fact, one might almost describe her attitude as maternal, though there was only about six years' difference in their ages, Dee being the senior. He himself bears witness to her kindness, and gives himself a little pat on the back at the same time. 'In her princely countenance I never perceived frown towards me, but at all times favourable and gracious, to the joy and comfort of my true, faithful and loyal heart.'

After one of his early trips abroad Dee was gravely ill with an infection he had picked up. The queen was quite perturbed about it, sent two of her own physicians to attend him and dispatched Lady Sidney to him with 'kind, gracious, and pithy messages', and 'divers rareties' from the royal table to tempt the sick man's appetite. Unfortunately these kindly gestures in time of sickness were not followed up by more substantial favours when he was well again. The various promises of preferment had a distressing way of fading out just as Dee felt he was reaching financial security and the peace of mind he needed.

Several years after he had waited in vain for the royal bounty to advance beyond gracious messages and some palace dainties in time of illness he wrote to Lord Burghley complaining of the lack of encouragment for years of laborious study. With the frank and naïve estimate of his own qualities which shows up amusingly from time to time he tells Cecil of his years of toil in pursuit of learning, assuring the statesman that 'this land never bred any man, whose account therein can evidently be proved greater than mine'.

o

The letter to Burghley, which runs to four and a half folio pages, passes from complaints to a business proposition. The writer can locate a valuable vein of gold or silver, apparently by means of a divining rod. He will offer all the precious metal to the Crown in return for a monopoly on all treasure trove in the realm. As an inducement to push the case at Court, Lord Burghley was offered a fifty-fifty partnership with Dr. Dee.

Nothing came of the offer. Dee, who must have been of a sanguine temperament, struggling on and hoping for some stroke of luck to the end of his poverty-stricken old age, went on buying books and scientific instruments. Also, he took to himself a young wife. He showed he had something of the serpent's cunning as well as academic dovelike innocence. He asked the queen's permission to marry, and sought, or pretended to seek her advice. The queen disliked all marriages of her male admirers, and although Dr. Dee was only on the periphery of the charmed circle he thought it desirable not to show himself too independent of Elizabeth's good will. He did well. He received 'a very gracious letter of credit for my marriage'. His satisfaction was increased by messages of congratulation from two of the top favourites at Court, the Earl of Leicester and Sir Christopher Hatton, the latter a future Lord Chancellor who owed his high office, said his enemies, to the pleasure Elizabeth took in his dancing.

John Dee was an affectionate man by nature and a born paterfamilias, but his happiness in his first marriage was shortlived. The young Mrs. Dee died in the early part of

March, 1575 (new style). On the tenth of the month, the day of the burial, the queen all unwittingly turned up at the riverside house to talk with her pet scientist and browse in his library. She found the poor man dazed and depressed by the irruption of tragedy into his life of study and domesticity. The kindliness that in Queen Elizabeth lay below the brilliant Renaissance surface responded to the simple, human grief of her friend. Dee, for all his intellectual power, was a simple man; his unselfconscious vanity is proof enough.

The courtiers, the officers, the fashionable young men, were left to cool their heels in the village streets or admire the daffodils braving the winds of March with beauty. The queen drew Dr. Dee aside. She would not enter the house. Everything there would remind him of his loss and renew the pain in his mind. She made him fetch out his latest piece of scientific apparatus, his famous convex lens, which she had heard about, and explain it to her and show her how it worked.

We are not disparaging Dee's qualities of heart if we surmise that in giving this extempore lesson in optics to his royal pupil he could forget for a time the sorrow and the loneliness that had overwhelmed him. Moreover, it is delightful to think of those exquisites of the English Court, fashionably tailored, arrogant probably, like most 'new' men, as they waited in the Mortlake streets or on the village green, curbing their restless horses and cursing the English climate.

Dee was soon at work again after his first wife's death. In the number and diversity of his interests and activities he has a kinship with such men as Roger Bacon, Da Vinci, and Michelangelo. In the year following Mrs. Dee's burial he made a study of the English fishing industry and drew up a scheme for its organization worthy of the ablest of our contemporary planners. At the time of this venture herring abounded off the east coast of England, but only the Dutch went after them in a big way. The shrewd Hollanders paid for all their imports *and* financed the anti-Spanish effort with the profits from their fisheries. The concept of territorial waters was a vague one in those days, so hundreds of Dutch fishing vessels were at work within hailing distance of the Suffolk and Norfolk shores. This was not a cause for any kind of sanctions or even a conference between the two governments, but it seemed to Dee and to Robert Hitchcock, who actually broached the scheme to his fellow-Parliamentarians, to call for some initiative on the part of England.

Dr. Dee's plan provided for a fleet of four hundred 'large' ships. A large ship was one of some seventy tons burden. Each would have a captain, twelve trained seamen, and, for what we should called unskilled labour, twelve 'lusty beggars'. These last were an integral part of the scheme, and they represent an Elizabethan forerunner of Works Progress Administration and similar government agencies. Elizabethan statesmen feared widespread unemployment as keenly as any modern administrator. There was less of humanity than policy in the sentiment. Some three and a half centuries were to pass before social security would come to Britain. In time of general distress—expensive war, a prolonged winter, crop failures—the unemployed, swarming in slums and purlieus of the towns and wandering in hordes over the countryside, were a menace to law and order, to private property, and to the public health. A big fishing fleet, partly manned by sturdy vagabonds, with casualties constantly being replaced, would go a long way towards solving unemployment problems.

The sturdy beggars who survived scurvy, drowning, frostbite, and all the horrors the North Sea can produce on occasion, would be turned into able seamen who would be useful when the day of reckoning with Spain should arrive. The invasion effort of the Spanish Armada was a dozen years away, but clear-headed Englishmen like Mr. Secretary Walsingham and young Mr. Ralegh of Devonshire could see what was coming.

There was, of course, the consideration of the herring as an article of food. In the ages before artificial refrigeration was possible, the herring was a valuable item in the Englishman's diet. The fish salted down well; 'pickle herring' was a topic for wise-cracking in the sixteenth century. Also, it could be dried or smoked to make palatable food. This was important in the winters, when fresh food might be hard to get. Dee overlooked no details. The average take of fish was calculated and allotted to various sections of the country. London, already so much bigger than any other city in the kingdom, got the largest allocation.

Mr. Hitchcock had his fellow Members of Parliament in to dinner and laid Dr. Dee's scheme before them.

They thoroughly approved of it, but decided it was too expensive to undertake. The queen's government, administered by the queen herself, was a thrifty one. She would not embark on spending her own money in the light-hearted way that modern governments spend other people's. Dee's work was not wholly fruitless. The scheme awakened interest and encouraged maritime enterprise, and we may credit it with some part in the increase in both fishing and cargo tonnage in the years before the Armada.

About the time of his first wife's death Dr. Dee began to keep his diary. It brings its writer to life with a vividness like that of Montaigne's *Essays* or Pepys' *Diary*. Important schemes for national defence, for naval reform, visits of distinguished people, the queen, Mr. Secretary Walsingham, the Earl of Leicester, Sidney, Edward Dyer, alternate with such trifles as a note on the weather, the cure of a cold or some small ailment, and details of household and gardening chores.

A visit of 'the Earl of Leicester, Mr. Philip Sidney and Mr. Dyer' dazzles us with the picture it conjures up— the royal favourite, rather solid and middle-aged by now, but still good-looking and magnificently dressed and mounted, and with him the two brilliant young men, courtiers and poets. We read a few more entries and learn that one of the succeeding days was notable for 'a great wynde' from the south-west, and that the weather was 'close and clowdy'. A minor mishap is then recorded. 'My fall upon my right knucklebone about nine o'clock. Wythe oyle of Hypericon in 24 hours eased above all hope. God be thanked for such his goodness to his creatures.' The discomfort of the bruised knuckle was forgotten next day in the excitement of a visit from the famous Dutch map-maker Ortelius.

An amusing detail of craftsmanship before the era of trade unions and specialization appears under the date of May 20, 1577. 'I hyred the barber of Chyswick, Walter Hooper, to keep my hedges and knots in as good order as he seed them then, and that to be done with twice cutting in the year, at the least, and he to have yearly five shillings and meat and drink.'

Occasionally the Doctor lets himself go in an outburst of emotion, generally of indignation. Ever since the too-successful bit of stage mechanics in the college production of Aristophanes there had been whispers of black magic. That was no laughing matter in an age that took witch-craft seriously. All his life long Dee had to defend him-self against suspicions which, if followed up, might lead to torture and execution. One Vincent Murphy tried to stir up trouble by calling Dee 'the arch-conjuror of the whole kingdom'. This calls forth an exclamation of anger, probably mingled with fear, in the diary. 'Oh, a damnable sklander, utterly untrue in the whole and in every worde and part thereof, as before the King of Kings will appear at the dreadful day.'

At other times the diarist's mind is wholly on plans for his country's welfare and security. He has, for example, a sound scheme for a Royal Naval Reserve, a 'Petty Navy Royall' as he calls it. There was to be a force of 'sixty tall ships or more in which thousands of soldiers (i.e. "sea soldiers" or sailors) could be trained', so that 'in time of need we shall not be forced to use all fresh-water Soldyers.' The cost of training these 'hardy sea-soldiers' was to be met by a small tax levied on every subject of 'the British Empire'. Dee, so far as I can gather, was the first Englishman to use this phrase.

On another day the writer expressed his indignation at what we call the export of strategic materials. English forests were being destroyed, while ordnance, gunpowder, and saltpetre were going overseas to potential enemies. 'Good God!' exclaims the diary, 'who knowth not what proviso is made and kept in other Common Weales against armour carrying out of their Limits?' There must have been grounds for the Doctor's anger when so patriotic an Englishman as Sir Walter Ralegh could contemplate selling to Spain an armed vessel which he owned. Substitute Elizabeth II's reign for her namesake's, and the U.S.S.R. for Spain, and it will be easy to enter into Dr. Dee's feelings.

A mere listing of some of Dee's activities in these years of his early middle life gives us a good idea of the versatility and energy of the man. In 1577, for example, a new comet swam into the astronomers' ken and there was widespread excitement and a good deal of alarm, by no means confined to the credulous mob. Whether the queen, who seems to have had a streak of superstition along with intellect, wit, and erudition, was seriously perturbed, we do not know. Anyhow, she sent for Dr. Dee. At Windsor he calmed everyone's fears, but the

queen was so fascinated by his exposition that she kept
him in the Castle expounding astronomy to her.

The following year he was called into conference with
one of the royal physicians. The queen was suffering
agonies from toothache and rheumatism. No doubt the
two afflictions were causally connected, for Elizabeth's
teeth were notably bad even for that age of much sugar-
eating, neglect of the teeth, and only the most primitive
of barber-shop dentistry. It was decided Dr. Dee should
go to Germany to seek advice and prescriptions from that
country's specialists.

Possibly the Doctor was given a hush-hush political
mission at the same time. There were rumours to that
effect. As Mr. Secretary Walsingham, the English
Machiavelli, had a good deal to do with the journey,
it was thought the government might be killing two
birds with one stone. That would be in keeping with
Walsingham's methods, as well as with Lord Burghley's
technique of throwing the stone so as the hand be not
seen.

In the fall of 1580 the queen put Dee on to a project
of research dealing with the 'British Empire' he speaks
of in the diary. She wanted to know how good her claims
were to various territories in the New World. They
were being rapidly opened up to European colonization,
and England was lagging behind. As these lands were
on the western continent we may regard Dee, along with
Sir Walter Ralegh, as one of the pioneers, at least in
desire and intention, of an English-speaking civilization
in America. America is Atlantis in Dr. Dee's writings

and maps, and in the latter is bounded on the north by an area marked 'Infinite yse'.

The maps and data were duly got together and sent to the queen at Richmond. The cautious Burghley took a poor view of them and the claims they were meant to back up—until he found the queen thought very well of them. A few days later Elizabeth visited Dee at Mortlake and graciously told him that her Lord Treasurer Burghley highly approved of the work that had been done for her.

Somewhat over two years before the incident of the colonial claims Dee had made his second marriage. It would perhaps be more accurate to say the queen made it for him. She seems always to have taken this personal interest in her astrologer's life. Perhaps there was something pathetic about him, living alone with his aged mother, who was now only two years from her end. With books and scientific paraphernalia he was competent and happy, but in domestic matters he may have been a good deal of the absent-minded genius. He had now passed his fiftieth year, an age for slippers and the fireside in Tudor times. However, the queen made up her mind marriage was his vocation. She must have been right, for he had eleven children by this marriage.

The wedding took place on February 5, 1578 (new style). The bride, Jane Fromond, was twenty-two. This is the 'paynfull Jane' of the diary. She came of a good family living at Cheam, in Surrey, and had been a lady-in-waiting to Lady Howard, wife of the Lord-Admiral who was to command England's navy when Philip II's

Armada was defeated. Besides being well-born, the new Mrs. Dee apparently was good-looking and affectionate, but she had a quick temper and perhaps she was a bit inclined to henpeck her elderly husband. Used to the ducal magnificence of the Howards she was probably more than a little house-proud. If the Doctor was as absent-minded and untidy about the house as many scientific geniuses, he doubtless got his share of curtain lectures. Mrs. Dee had her own worries. There was seldom enough money for all the expenses of the rapidly increasing family; there was trouble with the servants. The children were constantly tumbling down the water stairs and risking death by drowning in the Thames. Greatest trial of all—about three years after the marriage the Doctor's sinister partner in occultism came on the scene.

In July, 1579, Jane gave birth to her first child. It was a boy, named Arthur, who was destined to follow a career not unlike his father's. Late in the fall of the following year the Doctor's mother died. The queen, duly informed of the bereavement this time, paid Dee a visit of condolence. The Cecil family showed their sympathy in a practical way by sending the Doctor a haunch of venison.

Now began the devotion to occult practices and what we should call spiritualism. This, amid the multifarious interests of Dee's life, was the ruling passion for many years to come. It survived poverty, ill-health, disappointments of all kinds, the chicanery of assistants and partners. Occasionally we suspect Dee of being something of a charlatan himself, but on the whole he seems to have been the dupe rather than the deceiver.

The reason for holding that John Dee was, in the main, sincere and straightforward is that he never claimed so-called psychic powers for himself. Neither did he exploit the supposedly other-world visitations to refill his grievously empty coffers. Perhaps he embroidered the truth a little, but who shall cast the first stone in our acquisitive and publicity-loving society? When he describes one of his friendly spirits, embodied in visible form, as stepping from the gazing crystal on his table and tripping playfully about the library, at least he believed the spirit *was* visible in the crystal ball. Perhaps he truly believed the rest of the story—on the say-so of his assistant. Thereby came all his woes.

We know of a magic crystal, which sounds like the crystal ball used, at least in comic drawings, by gipsy fortune-tellers. The ball, of smoky quartz, had allegedly been given Dee by an angel. There was also a magic mirror. This was a disc of cannel coal, which had been given a high polish. The right person, gazing intently into either of these two media, could see spirits who had taken on human semblance.

Dee seems to have found out quite soon that he himself was not the right person to do this. He was not 'psychic', as modern dabblers in that sort of thing would say. Indeed, he was not: he was a scientist and a rationalist except where his curious streak of credulity about the spirit visitors came into play. An entry in his diary early in these occult adventures says, 'I had sight in

Chrystalls, and I saw.' He does not make it clear whether he meant that he saw with his own eyes. Anyhow, he began to look for a seer or 'skryer'. This was in the spring of 1581.

Sporadic happenings of a ghostly kind had begun in the Mortlake house. There were noises, mysterious rappings, strange dreams which came to the Doctor at night, and unexplained fires, which seem to have done no damage, in the 'maydens' chamber', that is, the servants' quarters. Then Dee found his first medium or skryer, a certain Barnabas Saul, who was given the spare room over the hall. There he was visited at night by 'a spiritual creature'. That, however, was the end of Mr. Saul's part in these peerings beyond the veil. He got into some kind of trouble with the law and although he was acquitted he had lost his mediumistic powers when he came back. Dr. Dee tells us in his diary that Saul now 'confessed he neyther herd nor saw any spirituall creature any more'. The room over the hall was vacant for a time.

When the daffodils were once more braving the March winds in the Thames valley the right man came along; so the Doctor thought. Mr. Clerkson, an acquaintance of Dr. Dee, dropped in for a visit with a companion he introduced as Mr. Talbot. This Mr. Talbot was a personable man, well educated, well dressed, with a fad for wearing a close-fitting black cap pulled down well over his ears. The great point about him was that he was interested in the same things as Dr. Dee—alchemy, the search for the philosopher's stone, intercourse with the spirits beyond the veil. Above all, he claimed to be on familiar terms with these spirits. Dee was enchanted. He wanted to see more of Mr. Talbot, so the visitor came again, without Mr. Clerkson's sponsoring. He was Dee's junior by a quarter of a century, which made him about young Mrs. Dee's age. Also, he had an interest in women who were still a long way from becoming spirits beyond the veil. A more worldly-minded man than the studious, good-hearted scientist would have smelled a rat. Not so Dr. Dee. He ordered the spare room to be furbished and made ready for a new skryer.

The séances began at once. The first one was held on March 10. Dr. Dee describes it in some detail in a new diary, *Liber Mysteriorum* (Book of Mysteries), he started for recording these events.

'. . . thereupon I brought forth to him [Talbot] my stone in the frame, which was given me of a friend, and I said unto him that I was credibly informed that to it, after a sort, were answerable *Aliqui angeli boni*. And also that I was once willed by a skryer to call for the good Angel Annael to appear in that stone to my own sight. And therefore I desired him to call him and, if he would, Anachor and Anilos likewise, accounted good angels, for I was not prepared thereto. He settled himself to the Action, and on his knees at my desk, setting the stone before him, fell to prayer and entreaty, &c. In the mean space, I in my Oratory did pray and make motion to God and his good creatures for the furthering of this Action. And in a quarter of an hour, or less, he had sight of one in the stone.'

The above bears testimony to the Doctor's good faith, as well as to a childlike trust in the stranger who had been brought into the Mortlake household. Mr. Talbot, finding his achievements as a medium so readily accepted, quickly set himself more ambitious tasks in celestial tuft-hunting. Soon Uriel appeared in the magic crystal and, on March 14, the Archangel Michael. This exalted visitor not only appeared in physical form to the skryer; he handed him a ring with a seal for Dr. Dee. The latter was overcome with joy and was all eagerness to go on with the work, but Mr. Talbot had been instructed by St. Michael to go to Lancaster and fetch back some books which formed part of a medium's professional library. He was back in the Doctor's house the next month, and then the two of them got down to work in earnest.

The frame, 'given me of a friend', in which the stone rested, was now replaced by a specially made piece of furniture which Dr. Dee calls 'the table of practice'. Like most practisers of magic, black or white, the Doctor took symbolism very seriously. 'Mystic' colours, hieratic writing, cabalistic formulae, sacred texts, especially in Hebrew or Greek, were all supposed to be very helpful towards establishing rapport with the spirit world and were much used by 'conjurors' in their contacts with extra-terrestrial beings. The table top on which the crystal or the stone rested bore a mystical diagram and a Hebrew text meaning, 'Thou art great forever, O Lord.' Each leg of this 'gazing table' rested on a wax seal, also magically inscribed, and the whole contraption stood on a square of red silk. Dr. Dee notes that the

spirits had 'no respect of collours'. However, he not
only insisted on the red silk, but also provided a green
chair for the seer, who no longer had to spend all the
time on his knees.

To our minds there is an element of the grotesque in
the picture of one of these séances. It is as though some
great and respected scientist, Einstein let us say, or Dr.
Millikan, were caught in solemn collaboration with one
of the gipsy crystal-gazers in a *New Yorker* cartoon. The
Elizabethans, except for a rare sceptic like Kit Marlowe,
saw nothing incongruous in a research team consisting of
England's leading scientist and a shady fortune-teller from
the western shires (Mr. Talbot was a Worcester man).

When all was in readiness—the curtained library, the
lighted candles, the table with its legs on the discs of wax
placed on the square of red silk—the skryer, always in
the tight-fitting black cap, seated himself in the green
chair and concentrated sight and mind on the crystal
or the piece of polished cannel coal, whichever was in
use at the time. Dr. Dee sat at a desk nearby ready to
take notes of all that happened. Lacking psychic faculties
himself, he was wholly dependent on the skryer. In
the early years of their partnership, at any rate, he had
unquestioning faith in Mr. Talbot.

The medium, gazing into the crystal or the stone, saw
a golden curtain which, like that at a theatre in a later
age, was drawn aside for the spirits to make their
entrances and their exits. The spirits usually stayed
inside the crystal, but occasionally stepped down and
moved about the room. A more than usually skittish

one would even jump from the table and skip about the library.

The seer, dictating what he saw and heard for the Doctor's notebook, described everything in a realistic, reportorial fashion. For instance, one of the visitors, Bobogel, appears in the record dressed in a black velvet cloak and close round hose of velvet upperstocks overlaid with golden lace. Dr. Dee, of a more metaphysical turn of mind, put his own interpretation on his amanuensis' descriptions. 'I do think,' said Dee to the spirits, 'you have no organs or instruments apt for voice, but are mere spiritual and nothing corporal, but have the power and property from God to insinuate your message or meaning to ear or eye (so that) man's imagination shall be that they hear and see you sensibly.'

All through the spring, summer, and fall of 1582 the dealings with the spirits continued. A special room had now been set aside, the 'little, farthermost chamber'. It had been a spare bedroom, but the bed was 'taken down' to give more space. Dee was wholly enchanted with his skryer, to whom he was paying a salary of fifty pounds a year, but the intuitions of the quick-tempered 'paynfull Jane' were sounder than the opinions of genius. Mrs. Dee distrusted the seer and, apparently, was repelled by something evil she sensed in him, of which her husband was quite unconscious.

An entry in the diary in the early summer of 1582 suggests a stormy scene with the young wife. The record has been partially obliterated. Perhaps the Doctor felt he had put too much on paper, even in a private diary,

P

but enough is left to tell the story. 'Jane in a marvellous
rage at eight of the clock at night, and all that night, and
next day till eight of the clock, melancholic and ch . . .
(perhaps "chided me") terribly for . . .' Mr. Clerkson,
who had in the first place brought the two men together,
seems to have been called in as peacemaker. 'By Mr.
Clerkson his help was . . .' and there the record
tantalizingly comes to an end.

Mr. Talbot had been told by the spirits to marry, and
in this same spring he wed Joan Cooper of Chipping
Norton. He was very hesitant about taking this step,
despite the orders received and he soon confided to his
patron and partner that he could not stand the sight of the
girl. In view of later developments, we are left wonder-
ing if the marriage was forced on an unwilling bridegroom to save the bride's reputation.

Some time in November of the same year the skryer
confessed that his name was not Talbot; he was Edward
Kelley. What else he revealed to Dee we do not know,
probably not very much, almost certainly not the reason
for the black skull cap. Edward Kelley was a rogue, but
a plausible and educated rogue. He had been trained in
pharmacy and chemistry, and it is probable he was at
Oxford for a time, but under the alias of Talbot by which
Dee knew him for nearly a year. Something went wrong
at Oxford and he left the university in a hurry. Then he
turned up in London as a shyster lawyer or a scrivener.
About 1580 he left London as hurriedly as he had left
Oxford.

We next hear of him in the north of England. History

has recorded the reason for the black skull cap. Up north there had been a serious collision with the law— forging title deeds for a crooked real estate deal, says one authority; making counterfeit money, says another. Whichever the charge, he was found guilty and sentenced to have his ears cropped by the executioner. Presumably the mutilation would have been hard to explain away, even to the credulous Dr. Dee; hence the skull cap worn low down over the ears.

Perhaps the apparent candour of shedding an alias was a cunning move to make Dee feel he now knew the worst about his partner. Further, it may be that the name Talbot, seemingly used as early as undergraduate days, was a more dangerous clue to past misdeeds than the fellow's true name. There is a record in the Doctor's diary of a row at the supper table between the skryer and another, more repellent, scoundrel, Charles Sledd. The latter was a renegade Catholic who had once been a seminarist and now earned money for his keep and his nights in the stews on Bankside, the red light district of Tudor London, by informing against his fellow-Papists. He was at one time on Walsingham's payroll.

Sledd was a violent, quarrelsome fellow and probably started the dispute. Very likely he knew something of Kelley's, or Talbot's past, and it is possible he tried blackmail. According to the diary, the squabble arose 'because Charles Sledd had done him an injury in speech at my table'. Dr. Dee would not, at that time, have listened to anything against his grave, earnest and clairvoyant skryer.

The search for the perfect medium and the essays in preternatural contacts were varied for a time by a project for a new calendar. In 1582 Pope Gregory XIII had published a Bull for the reform of the old and inaccurate Julian calendar. Catholic Europe had promptly accepted the reform. Dee made calculations which would have cut off ten days instead of eleven specified in the Bull. Sensibly, however, he was in favour of uniformity rather than pedantic accuracy. He did not allow for the strength of anti-Roman prejudice in the queen's Church. Grindal, Archbishop of Canterbury, Aylmer, Bishop of London, and others of the Anglican hierarchy, made it clear they would have no truck with anything from the Seven Hills. The government dropped the scheme, and it took England the best part of two centuries to come into line with western civilization on this matter of accurate mathematics.

The zeal for national prosperity which had moved Dr. Dee to work out a scheme for the better organization of the fisheries fired him with enthusiasm for the discovery of a North-west Passage. A short cut to China and all the wealth of the Orient by a sub-Arctic route would have by-passed the Atlantic crossing jealously guarded by Spain, as well as the long journey round the Cape of Good Hope used by the Portuguese.

Most Englishmen at the time saw the object of overseas discovery as large and quick returns in a spectacular investment. Gold, silver, precious stones, spices, and the bodies of black men for slave labour, were the commodities most desired. If trade and piracy were sometimes rather hard to distinguish, no one worried very much. The queen, Lord Treasurer Burghley, and the courteous Machiavellian Principal Secretary Walsingham would give soft answers to angry ambassadors. At Court there was a sudden blaze of new jewellery and precious stones when an admiral, backed by shrewd merchants and gentlemen-adventurers, had successfully hijacked the galleons of Spain. Only Burghley seemed disturbed by the fact that Spain was nominally a friendly power, whose king was once consort of Elizabeth's half-sister.

A few of the queen's subjects thought of colonization and of a genuine British Empire. Dr. Dee was one of them. So was Mr. Secretary Walsingham, likewise Sir Walter Ralegh and his half-brothers the Gilberts. Ralegh was the greatest of these colonial pioneers. Acquisitive as he was in his early days, an 'upstart knave' in the eyes of the old aristocrats, he yet spent a fortune for his colony on the shores of what is now North Carolina. We justly regard him as the precursor of all western-looking Englishmen who founded an Anglo-Saxon civilization in North America.

Early in 1583 Dee records that 'Mr. Secretarie Walsingham came to my house, where by good luck he found Mr. Adrian Gilbert, and so talk was begonne of North West Straights discovery.' Ralegh seems to have cherished a particular liking for John Dee. We find several records of special kindnesses to the Doctor, as well as reminders given to the queen when she and her 'Water' were riding by on their way to Richmond or Nonesuch Palace. Beneath the go-getter, the courtier, and the man of fashion, was the philosopher, the speculative theologian, and the scientist, who found a congenial mind in the needy scientist among his books, manuscripts, instruments, and too numerous children in the Mortlake house.

The Gregorian Calender reform, and its rejection by the Anglican bishops, was for Dee a minor affair beside his commerce with the spirit world. Even the implications of a North-west Passage and dreams of a British Empire were secondary to the revelations made through the psychic Edward Kelley, alias Talbot. The first heavenly visitants, archangels and angels, gave way to a new 'control', one II, who seems more akin to Shakespeare's fairies. Dee describes him as 'a merrie creature, apparelled like a Vice in a play'. 'He skipped here and there,' says the diary.

For a short time Dee suffered a set-back in his spiritualistic research. Kelley had moral scruples. In view of what we know of his character, and its mingling of brilliance and charlatanism, the scruples are hard to understand. What if the heavenly visitors were really evil spirits, asked the skryer. Perhaps there had been more trouble with 'paynfull Jane', for Kelley never made a good impression on the second Mrs. Dee. Anyhow, there was another rumpus of some kind, and this time Adrian Gilbert was called in as peacemaker.

When outward calm had been restored, the séances were resumed. The seer had a vision of 'a beautiful woman having her head cut off by a tall, black man'. This was afterwards interpreted as a prophecy of the execution of Mary, Queen of Scots. Then Kelley saw 'the seas covered with many ships', and Uriel, again appearing at Mortlake, warned against foreign aggressors. This, of course, was recalled when the Spanish Armada sailed.

Some years before these prophecies could be checked by events in the outer world, the Dee household was excited by the prospect of a visit from a distinguished foreigner. Albert or Adelbert Laski, the Palatine of Siradz, a Bohemian nobleman, visited England in 1583, chiefly, one suspects, in the hope of a hand-out from Queen Elizabeth. He was learned, handsome, richly dressed, and he had graceful manners. These were qualities to recommend him to the queen's favour, but not sufficiently so to inspire gifts from the royal exchequer. Then Laski heard of Dr. Dee's interest in what we may call Elizabethan atomic research, the transmutation of metals. Gold for a bankrupt palatinate! The visitor expressed a wish to see Dr. Dee. Perhaps the queen suggested it, as a means of evading requests without discourtesy. Laski was a supporter of the elected King of Poland, Stephen Batory, which may account for Dee's references to him as the 'Polonian lord'.

The English scientist and the foreign nobleman supped together, and got along well with each other. Then Dr. Dee let himself in for issuing a formal dinner invitation. It was a blunder. Those were the days of easy and lavish hospitality. A man of Laski's rank would turn up with a whole army of servants and hangers-on. Dee, kindly and courteous, was worried about the resources of his household, and was solicitous for his good name as an English host. He lived most of the time in a state of financial insecurity, and there were moments when things looked desperate. This was one of them. Fortunately the queen, who was staying at Sion House, heard of his plight, and she came across handsomely. She sent along Mr. Lloyd, a secretary to her 'dear Robin', the the Earl of Leicester, with a gift of forty gold marks (about $100.00) for the Doctor's entertainment account. With the money came 'Mr. Rawlegh his letter unto me of her Majestie's good disposition with me.' Dee was very happy. He set his painful Jane and her servants to work getting ready for the visitor, but, more important still, the spirits had to be consulted. Kelley was on his mettle.

This resort to spiritualism for diplomatic guidance led to one of the strangest of the Doctor's contacts with the other world. We do not know whether to marvel more at Kelley's chicanery or his employer's gullibility. The séance that was held in connection with Laski's visit brought forward a new 'control'. This was Madimi, the first female spirit to appear in Dee's house by way of Kelley and the crystal. The angels of medieval theology were, of course, sexless, the pure essences of scholasticism. In fact, any hint of sex in a spirit was of itself cause for suspicion. Spirits could assume male and female forms, the *incubi* and *succubi* of diabolism, but if so they were up to no good. Dee, well read in the subject, knew that Trithemius had authoritatively stated that no good spirits ever took the shape of a woman.

Madimi seems to have banished Dee's suspicions. She made her first appearance on May 28, 'like a pretty girl of seven or nine years'. She wore a gown of 'changeable green and red, with a train'. Kelley had a sharp eye for girls. He observed that Madimi's hair was 'rowled up before and hanging very long behind'. He even noticed the sequins on the gown of shot silk.

This winsome creature made herself quite at home. She stepped out of the crystal into the little room set aside for these meetings. In spite of the smart hair-do and the silk gown, she was definitely an intellectual, for she quickly studied and mastered Greek, Arabic and Syriac, to help the Doctor in his researches. Her polyglot attainments annoyed Kelley at times, especially on one occasion when her fluent Greek was too much for him and she then dropped into Arabic. The skryer burst out angrily, 'Unless you speak some language which I understand, I will express no more of this Gibberish.' At another time Kelley took a rest from his medium's chores and went fishing, a neglect of duty which brought him a reprimand from another of the spirits called Gabrah.

Kelley had other and more terrestrial troubles about this time. The law was after him, or so he thought, for previous misdeeds, including coining. Moreover, his marriage was going badly, and when his wife found out that he was a 'cozener', she left him for a time and went home to her mother. Madimi, however, began to appear again and restored the skryer's spirits somewhat. Dee, who thought his failure to get a good, fat sinecure was due to hostility at Court, made enquiries of Madimi through

Kelley. 'How is the mind of Mr. Secretary (Walsingham) towards me?' he asked. Madimi had no consolation to offer. The people at Court, she answered comprehensively, hated him. This was less than fair to the queen, Mr. Secretary Walsingham, Ralegh, and even the cautious Lord Burghley, who had all shown good will to Dee in one way or another.

Perhaps Kelley had good reason to fear the law in England and was anxious to promote a scheme which Dee and Laski were discussing. It called for a foreign voyage meant to fill Laski's empty coffers and enrich the scientist. Dee's finances were badly in the red, and his only assets were a beggarly stipend and the queen's unfulfilled promises. Gold was to be manufactured on the continent by a process which Kelley claimed to have ready. Various foreign rulers were to be brought into the scheme, with Laski as the intermediary.

This venture began with a 'secret' departure from Mortlake on an afternoon in the latter part of September, 1583. Three o'clock of a Saturday afternoon seems a strange time for secrecy, especially as the party comprised Laski, Dr. Dee and Edward Kelley, the Dee and Kelley wives and children—the Doctor had three by this time— Laski's attendants, Dee's servants, and two horses. Besides their personal things and household goods, they took with them a quantity of drugs and chemicals which were the raw materials for the 'projection' of gold. These materials may have been the reason for secrecy. The goods had been bought on credit, and there was no money to meet the bills. There is also a suggestion that fear of Burghley and Walsingham had something to do with it. These high officials might, as we should put it nowadays, refuse exit visas to travellers carrying so much potential wealth out of England. The dodge of freezing the currency was not left to our age to discover.

The moment the house was empty, the mob had a good time. The Elizabethan *canaille* loved a bit of violence— a public hanging and disembowelling of a traitor, the burning alive of a woman for husband-poisoning, ear-lopping for forgery or making counterfeit money. A lynching would not have come amiss, but since the wicked magicians were beyond their reach, the poorer villagers of Mortlake, reinforced probably by sightseers from town, stormed the house. They wrecked the library and laboratory, smashing furniture and apparatus, including a valuable quadrant, carried away a great magnet that Dee had paid a high price for, burned precious books and manuscripts, and, one supposes, did some looting on the side. Such was the superstitious hatred of the Elizabethan mob for what they thought was witchcraft.

After the rigours of crossing the narrow seas at a time of year when they are likely to be tempestuous, the party rested in Holland for a time. Financial worries and the discomforts of the sea voyage appear to have bred a slight friction between Dee and his skryer. Anyhow, the Doctor, indefatigable in keeping his diary posted, suspected Kelley of snooping among his private papers. A new volume of the diary, especially for this overseas trip, was started, the *Liber Peregrinationis*, and although the

writer used his native English he wrote it in Greek
characters. This checkmated Kelley, who had already
been rather short with Madimi when that blithe spirit
addressed him in Greek.

Madimi, as 'a little wench in white', appeared at a
séance held one Sunday after the travellers had got over
their seasickness and their frayed nerves. She had, so she
told Dee by way of Kelley, just been back to Mortlake.
She was able to give reassurances of the queen's favour,
but warned of Burghley's hostility.

A more exalted visitor was the Archangel Gabriel, who
appeared briefly to supply a code of conduct to guide the
travellers when meeting foreigners of high rank. Incon-
gruously, this visitation was soon followed by the re-
appearance of the playful Il, in a 'white satin jerkin,
ragged below the girdle'. The curtain visible within the
crystal went up and Il tripped forward, gazing in apparent surprise at Dee and his medium. 'Room for a
player!' exclaimed this debonair spirit, 'Jesus! who
would have thought I should have met you here?'

For the next few years the fantastic cavalcade wandered
back and forth across Central Europe, Holland to Poland,
Poland to Bohemia, then to Germany, back to Bohemia,
and, finally, the year after the defeat of the Spanish
Armada, back to England. Sometimes the party enjoyed the semi-barbaric luxury of castles and palaces as
the guests of great land-owning noblemen; at other times
they were hard up for mere subsistence and the means of
transport.

The interviews with royalty, in spite of Gabriel's help,

were a failure. Laski had become sceptical of Kelley's experiments, but he evidently thought that a profitable thing might be made of them. Accordingly he introduced his friend to the Emperor Rudolph at Prague. Kelley unfortunately overplayed his part and the emperor would not even invite the visitors to another interview. Then they tried Poland, after a bit of trouble from the Papal Nuncio in Prague, and King Stephen condescended to sit in on a spell of crystal-gazing and to listen to an exposition of atomic research on the philosopher's stone. It was a simple matter. The 'marriage of the red man, copper, and the white woman, mercury,' correctly managed, was bound to produce gold. Again Kelley was too glib, Dee too credulous, and the royal patron they had hoped to find dismissed them ignominiously.

At this time the party was in low water financially. Madimi had sent them to Limburg, but they had no luck there. Dee's wife, Jane, who usually kept aloof from the dealings with spirits and distrusted Kelley, now proposed that an appeal should be made to the angels for monetary help. If this was done, there is no record of any result.

To money troubles was added emotional tension. Jane Dee was loyal, affectionate, and dutiful, despite her quick temper. Joan Kelley, reconciled to the skryer, was lively and docile, and everyone with the possible exception of her husband, liked her. However, Jane was suspicious of Kelley, the latter's wife was hurt by his coldness, and even the patient and credulous Dee became at times exasperated with his seer.

Dee made a few attempts to replace Kelley by another medium. For a short time an Italian named Pucci joined the household, and Dee had hopes of his powers. He was a man of ability, but he turned out to be a brazen charlatan, and Dee sent him packing. The next experiment was with little Arthur Dee, a rather delicate, sensitive child, not yet eight years old. As we might expect, this venture ended in failure and might have been a tragedy. Faced with the paraphernalia of spiritualism, and perhaps the glowering face of Kelley below the black cap, the wretched little boy fell to the floor in a 'swound' and was ill for some time afterwards. Several years later, when he had to face boarding school life, he still showed the effects of his experience.

Dee made up his quarrel with Kelley, and the latter promptly got *en rapport* with the female spirit Madimi again. She had grown up by this time, and we gather that she was a very alluring young woman. In the glamour of her maturity and in her subsequent behaviour we recognize the hand, or, perhaps one should say, the cloven hoof, of Edward Kelley. When we read the story we are astounded at the credulity shown by a man of Dee's intellectual powers and moral integrity.

Early in the spring of 1587 Madimi, who, despite a suggestion of archness, was formerly a polyglot linguist and rather a bluestocking, now appeared in a very different character. Under the eager gaze of Kelley she took off all her clothes and standing unabashed in her nudity before the seer she gave her latest directive from the spirit world. Her friends, John Dee and Edward Kelley, were to engage in a voluntary Communism that had no limits. Specifically, they were to have their wives in common. At first this was too much even for the gullible Doctor. He was a moral man and a faithful husband, married to a loyal and high-spirited wife of good breeding. Madimi's shameless conduct and her latest instructions deeply shocked him. We may imagine the effect on the gentle, unassertive Joan Kelley and on Jane Dee, whose intuitive dislike and distrust of the seer were now justified.

It seems incredible that no one denounced Kelley for the charlatan and lecher he was. Although shocked and chagrined, Dee still believed in the fellow's good faith. What Jane and Joan thought about it is not recorded. Joan Kelley, probably, was too meek to protest. Jane may have been overawed by her husband's learning and intellect. Perhaps, also, she shared the credulity of the age enough to think Madimi more than a figment of Kelley's sexy imagination. Anyhow, there were further conferences with the spirits. Madimi insisted on her original orders and even demanded their formal acceptance in writing. We are not told if she remained a nudist all through the negotiations.

On April 26 a pact was drawn up, and on Sunday, May 3, it was signed by the two husbands and their wives as the high contracting parties. They pledged themselves to perpetual and irrevocable friendship and absolute community of goods and of their own persons, 'as God, by sundry means, willed us to do'. Dee, still troubled in mind in spite of his credulity, insisted on a codicil which protested that 'this last mystical admonishment be not imputed to them for rashness, presumption, or wanton lust'.

This repulsive scheme of Edward Kelley had its inevitable effect on a man of Dee's wholesome character, and two well-bred and normal young wives. Everyone got on everyone else's nerves. There was constant friction in the joint household, sometimes leading only to petty squabbles, but often finding an outlet in violent quarrels. By the end of 1588 all could see that a break-up of the 'indissoluble and inviolable' design for living was in sight. Kelley, moreover, was beginning to chafe at his partnership. Possibly he felt a certain contempt for a man he had so easily gulled despite his learning and intellect, nor can we believe that Jane Dee was readily amenable to the practical details of Madimi's household and sexual communism.

Above all, Kelley was now eager to launch out on his own. He was not without education, and he must have been very plausible. However, he was definitely a rogue, a confidence trickster, with his spiritualistic nudists and his projection of gold, whereas Dee was an honest man. So long as Dee could be hoodwinked, well and good. On the other hand, if the Doctor's intellectual honesty should lead to a show-down and a public denunciation, Kelley's prestige and consequently his ability to live on his wits would be destroyed.

Just before the final rupture Dee heard of the defeat of the Spanish Armada. For a time he put aside his quarrels with Kelley, the emotional distress of his wife, and the interviews with the spirits. Madimi had made her last

appearance early in the preceding summer. One is surprised that she had the nerve to revisit the household she
had so disrupted. Dee, however, never became wholly
disillusioned about her. At the moment he forgot he was
an expatriate and an occultist, and brimmed over with
patriotic fervour. He sat down and wrote a congratula-
tory letter to his queen. Reading it, we feel that he
could not much longer tolerate his exile from England,
spirits or no spirits.

Kelley, meanwhile, was making himself thoroughly
objectionable. He demanded as his own various papers
and materials that had been the working equipment of
the two researchers. Dee's diary was safeguarded against
his snooping by its Greek characters, so the fellow took
his revenge by destroying such of the Doctor's papers as
he could lay his hands on. Then he stole a couple of
crystal-gazing or 'shew' glasses, one of which was later
found under Mrs. Dee's pillow.

In February, 1589, the parting took place. Some kind
of reconciliation had been patched up. Dee, good-
natured and a lover of peace, kept in touch with Kelley
by letters for some years, and his diary records his ex-
partner's death in 1595. Kelley's life in the half-dozen
years after the break-up was full of vicissitudes and ended
in sordid tragedy. The barefaced fraud of the gold production led to imprisonment, an attempt at escape by a
leap from a window, two broken legs, and death shortly
afterwards. Dee, in recording Kelley's end, makes no
comment.

Queen Elizabeth had invited Dee to return to England.

Q

The royal condescension coincided with his own nostalgia. He wrote to the queen (November, 1588) of his intention to fall in with the royal wish, and then began his preparations for the end of his sojourn abroad.

His worldly fortunes had looked up somewhat during a stay in southern Bohemia, thanks to the generosity of Count Rosenberg, a firm believer in the spirits who visited Dee and his skryer. Other noblemen were friendly, also, and Rudolph II had got over the disgust and disbelief with which he had once snubbed Dee and Kelley.

The journey northwards was something of a triumphal procession. There was an armed guard, because of the danger from robbers and highwaymen. There were coaches for the Doctor, his wife, children, and servants, and several waggons for their baggage. At length the whole caravan reached Bremen without any serious mishap. On November 19, 1589, they sailed for England on the *Vanguard*.

The ship tied up at Gravesend on December 2, and the Dees gazed through the mist at the country they had not seen for six years. A great deal had happened since their departure. The queen was an old lady by Elizabethan standards, her Lord Treasurer Burghley nearly seventy. Walsingham, still in harness but suffering frequent and intense pain, was near his end. However, he had lived long enough to see the Queen of Scots meet, with great dignity and fortitude, the death he had planned for her. Leicester, the queen's 'dear Robin', was dead. In London, a young fellow from Warwickshire, one William Shakespeare, was beginning to be spoken of as an actor who did quite well in some minor parts in one of the new theatrical companies. Mr. Lyly and the ornate prose of his *Euphues* were the talk of those who considered themselves connoisseurs of literature.

A couple of weeks after his arrival Dee had an interview with the queen at Richmond. He still hoped for preferment, and put his needs before the elderly queen. Then he moved into his Mortlake house, which his father-in-law Fromond had been keeping an eye on. It was a depressing experience to see the damage that had been wrought by the mob six years earlier. Most of the money Dee had been given by Count Rosenberg had been spent in transporting the family and their goods from Bohemia to England.

Very soon the unhappy scientist's accounts were in the red again, and he had to be helped by one or two friends. Adrian Gilbert, one of Ralegh's half-brothers, generously came to the rescue of the geographer with whom he had worked on schemes for finding the Northwest Passage.

Money difficulties were increased by periodical additions to the family. One of these took place early in the year after the return to England. Jane gave birth to a daughter, who was christened early in March, with Lady Walsingham as one of the godparents. The baby girl was given the name of Madimi, so clearly the father bore no rancour against that shameless young female from the spirit world.

The presence of Ursula, Lady Walsingham, at the child's christening suggests, too, that Dee had got over his suspicions that Walsingham was unfriendly. In 1590, when the Principal Secretary, worn out by illness, over-work, and financial worries, passed away, the diary records the fact under date of April 16. 'Good Sir Francis Walsingham died at night *hora undecima*.'

If Dee had hoped to find peace and financial security by coming back to England, he was disappointed. Money troubles pestered him for the rest of his life. Jane was a faithful and affectionate wife, but at times she must have been difficult to live with. Then there were various domestic troubles. A servant went mad and committed suicide. The children were constantly hurting them-selves. Their favourite way of doing this was to fall down the river steps at the foot of the garden, a mishap which further worried their parents because of the danger of drowning.

Little Arthur, who had reacted so disastrously to mediumship, was particularly ingenious at finding trouble. His father's diary records the misadventure in which the child hurt himself with a brick weighing two and a half pounds, by 'wanton throwing of a brick-bat upright, and not avoiding the fall of it again'.

In 1592 the Doctor sent the boy off to boarding school. The choice was Westminster School, where Dee's friend William Camden was the second master, that is, the assistant head. Camden succeeded to the head-mastership the next year, and so was able to keep a quasi-paternal eye on the thirteen-year-old Arthur, who was destined to follow his father as alchemist and student of the occult sciences. Dr. Dee gave more attention to his eldest son's traits of character and special needs than was common with parents of that era. We find him carrying on a detailed correspondence with Arthur's headmaster about such matters as food, drink, and washing. 'The boy liketh abundance of meat well: but very bashfully he said that their proportion of drink is somewhat too little.' Arthur, wrote his father, was 'of an exceeding great and haughty mind naturally, ready to revenge rashly'. The headmaster, however, 'may alter this natural courage to true fortitude and not to frail, rash fancies'.

After the birth of his third daughter, Frances, in 1592, Dee was in a very bad way financially. In desperation he appealed to various friends for loans and raised money by pawning the family plate and jewellery. Added to these troubles was his apprehension about the spread of rumours concerning his dealings with the occult. The heyday of the witchcraft phobia was near at hand, so a reputation for black magic could not be laughed off. Dee made a personal appeal to the queen for an inquiry that would clear his name and he wrote his *Compendious Rehearsall* as an apologia for the commission she appointed.

One useful result this investigation had for posterity. We have the catalogue of his library which formed part of the evidence to show that he was a serious student and investigator. Many of the titles have little or no interest for the modern reader, and are only items in the category vaguely named *curiosa* in antiquarian booksellers' lists. The title of one of Dee's bibliographical treasures, however, has a very modern flavour. The book is by Agrippa, alchemist to Margaret of the Netherlands, and its title is *De Nobilitate et praecellentia feminei sexus* (On the nobility and excellence of the female sex). Nearly a century later it was translated into English and published under the title of *Female pre-eminence; or, the Dignity and Excellence of that Sex above the Male*. With, one supposes unconscious irony the translator dedicated the volume to Queen Catherine of Braganza, Charles II's long-suffering spouse.

The outcome of the inquiry was satisfactory, but it did not put any money into Dee's pocket. He tried another appeal to the queen. The mastership of the hospital or hostel of St. Cross at Winchester was about to fall vacant because its holder was to be made a bishop. It was just the kind of thing Dee needed, practically a sinecure, with the chaplain's work performed by a curate at a small stipend. There would be a dwelling house and other amenities, and the holder of the position would be accepted in the society of the old cathedral city. The queen was gracious. Dee should have the post, with a pension squeezed out of the diocese of Oxford meanwhile. There was even a generous hand-out to Mrs. Dee through her old patroness, the Lady Howard.

Alas! nothing came of all these fine prospects. Poor Dee at length sought another interview with the queen. Again she was gracious to her old friend and astrologer as she talked with him in the privy garden at Greenwich (May, 1594). Dee begged her to expedite the Winchester appointment. Gently she explained that there were difficulties.

Another place-seeker had muscled in. Even a Tudor queen, it seems, could be entangled in the red tape of her own administration. Then Dr. Dee tried for other posts —in vain, until the Archbishop of Canterbury, Whitgift, came to the rescue. Of all the Anglican ecclesiastics in her time, Elizabeth had most respect and liking for this energetic and competent prelate, whom she spoke of playfully as her 'little black husband'. When, therefore, the archbishop put in a word for Dr. Dee, the situation was saved. The wardenship of Manchester College was going begging, and, as the prelate pointed out, the disposal of it was in the queen's gift.

The necessary papers were prepared. It took a long time. Even in the embryonic civil service of those times the accumulation of documents was formidable. By the end of May, 1595, all the legal formalities were complete and Dee received his patent under the Great Seal.

In the following February he set out for Manchester with his wife and children, arrived in the middle of the month, and about a week later was solemnly installed as head of the college. It would be pleasant to record that after all his vicissitudes, travels, hardships, worries, and disappointments, John Dee, aged nearly seventy, settled down to the Indian summer of an Elizabethan scientist, with an adequate income, a tranquil donnish routine, and a reputation safe from evil tongues. Unhappily this was not the case.

Being warden of Manchester College was no bed of

roses. Despite the fanfare of his appointment and in-
auguration the new head soon found himself mixed up in
various disturbing squabbles, opposed and thwarted by
his subordinates, and, financially, worse off than ever.
The college had a chequered past and at the time of Dee's
installation as warden it was in the doldrums.

As a medieval, and, therefore, Catholic institution,
Manchester College had been suppressed under Edward
VI, revived under his Catholic half-sister Mary, and now
had been drawn into the movement to impose Protestantism on the conservative Catholic north. We do not
know how much of a convinced Protestant Dee was. He
was not of the Anglican left wing favoured by Walsingham, and he was by nature a tolerant man, so he would
not have been very acceptable to the 'hot' Protestants on
his staff. Perhaps, too, some of the friction was due to
his own highhandedness. He had waited long for preferment, brooding meanwhile on the neglect of talent and
erudition, while go-getting and sycophancy won other
men position and wealth. Anyhow, there were undigni-
fied quarrels between warden and fellows of the college,
while academic progress was lost sight of in a fog of
personal animosities.

Then there were disagreements over witchcraft. Dee,
this time, was on the side of a civilized scepticism against
the witch-hunters. Called upon to exorcize some women
allegedly possessed by evil spirits, he refused. Let them
resort to certain worthy ministers of religion, he replied,
who were fitted by their training and their profession to
deal with such things. We must bear in mind that Dee

had remained a layman and when he went to Manchester he paid curates to look after the spiritual welfare of the college. Evidently he disappointed people by refusing a sensational series of exorcisms. Probably some of the local gentry had hoped for the kind of macabre entertainment Aldous Huxley has chronicled in *The Devils of Loudun*. Dr. Dee's decision was a sound one. The old queen had not many years to live, and when her Scots cousin, James, came to the throne of England, it was best to have as little connection with magic as possible.

In the turbulence of the Reformation years and the general scramble for wealth from monastic sources the finances of Manchester College had got into a confused state. The stipend of the warden, not a princely one at any time, was a fluctuating quantity when Dee was appointed. It depended partly on the income from certain parcels of land, but the warden's title to these monies was distressingly vague. While he sued, petitioned, and counter-petitioned, the money was going regularly into someone else's pocket. Again he had recourse to the pawnbrokers, and more of the family plate had to be pledged.

After a couple of unhappy years we find Dee back in London or at his Mortlake house on a kind of self-appointed Sabbatical leave. This may have been for reasons of health. His robust constitution was beginning to give way under the strain of years of vicissitude and intense mental labour. The diary, too, suggests a touch of hypochondria. There are frequent notes on insomnia, bizarre dreams, and records of the diarist's pulse. When a man not only takes his own pulse often, but also records it meticulously, we may suspect him of overmuch worry about his health.

It is possible that in absenting himself from his post the Doctor had, at least as a secondary motive, the desire to lay before the Privy Council a statement of all that was wrong with the institution up north. He described Manchester College as almost 'no college', with its finances in confusion, its faculty squabbling among themselves and at loggerheads with their warden. The students, one supposes, did little or no academic work unless they chose, and could give most of their time and attention to their mentors' quarrels or the tippling and wenching which, Father Persons tells us, were rife in English universities at the time.

After the opening of the new century Dr. Dee allowed even his diary to lapse. He had kept it faithfully for many years, but now his enthusiasms were growing weaker and the struggle with failing health and monetary worries used up most of the old man's energy. He had made a half-hearted attempt to find another skryer to replace Edward Kelley, but was unsuccessful and let the matter drop. There were a few more entries in the *Book of Mysteries* and then that record of occult experimentation came to an end.

Back in the north he struggled on at his uncongenial job, but we know little of these last years at Manchester except his increasing poverty. When the plate was all sold or all pawned, with no money at hand to redeem it, he started selling choice items from his library. Only a true bibliophile can know the straits he must have been in and the agony of mind he must have suffered.

In the small hours of a March night in 1603 Queen Elizabeth died. With her passing Dee lost a good friend. She had been, it is true, but an indifferent patroness, but she appreciated the scientist's zeal for knowledge, she liked him personally, and she was too intelligent and too well-informed to listen to the calumnies against him. With the royal pedant James VI of Scotland and I of England, who fancied himself as an authority on witch-craft and a smeller-out of subversive black art, things were different.

Dr. Dee was uneasy about his standing with this 'most learned fool in Christendom', and petitioned the new king for a further inquiry into the slanders in circulation. Gladly, he said, would he accept the capital sentence were he judged guilty of black magic, so clear was his con-science of all guilt. James I, who for all his faults seems not to have been a harshly intolerant person, had the matter looked into, and refused the petition. As nothing untoward happened to Dr. Dee, the presump-tion is that James considered the slanders baseless.

In the winter of 1604 the Doctor, now in very poor health, once more went back to Mortlake. Those were the days when a return to one's native air was the last desperate prescription of a baffled physician. The old energy and enthusiasm flared up for a few years more. There were fresh attempts to find a successful medium. Séances with a couple of skryers, one of them an old

practitioner of continental days, led to a few incon-
clusive 'actions' with the spirits.

One of the periodical epidemics of bubonic plague
reached out from the foul slums of London in 1605 and
claimed victims in the Middlesex and Surrey hamlets.
There was illness in the Mortlake house, but the energetic, hot-tempered, but devoted Jane Dee nursed the
sick, kept up the family's spirits, and cherished her
ailing, elderly husband. No one in the household suc-
cumbed except Jane Dee herself. She caught the infection
and passed away quickly, leaving the distraught widower
to be cared for by his daughter Kate.

The nagging poverty and the loneliness of his last
years drove Dee once more to seek the aid and advice
of his spirit guides. A skryer named Bartholomew
Hickman claimed to make contact with the Archangel
Raphael. It may have been on a hint from the archangel
that Dee began to dream of a foreign trip to make the
money he needed so badly. He had his eye on Germany
as a country whose princelings might once again help
him out. It was too late. The flame of that ardent
Elizabethan nature was burning very low through 1608
and before December was over it had flickered out.

In accordance with an immemorial practice the old
scholar's corpse was buried in the chancel of his parish
church. A stone was inscribed and set in place to com-
memorate him, but something happened to it and it
disappeared. Half a century later the antiquarian Aubrey
visited Mortlake. He was seeking for scraps of history
and tradition about the occultist and scholar who had

been the queen's astrologer nearly a century before the Civil War had swept away king and kingship for nearly a dozen years. There were only old wives' tales, of doubtful authenticity, to be picked up. Mr. Aubrey returned to town with scanty notes of his contact with the ghosts of an age that was already becoming fabulous in English eyes.

IV

MARY FRITH, THE ROARING GIRL

THE 'Roaring Boys' were the bane of peaceful Londoners in the sixteenth and seventeenth centuries. They were, we are told, 'riotous blades, who abounded in London and took pleasure in annoying the quieter inhabitants'. In the eighteenth century they were replaced by the Mohocks, well-heeled and well-born young hoodlums whose exploits, always lawless, frequently indecent, often cruel, made the ill-lighted streets of the city a place of terror. Fielding, novelist and magistrate, showed his courage, both physical and moral, in a judicial war on these aristocratic young criminals. Whether they were much worse than the 'Roaring Boys' who preceded them, it is hard to tell. Certainly they were no better.

The women of England, in their successive generations, have invariably brought forth at least one or two of their sex to challenge male supremacy—and monopoly—in nearly all the activities of our western civilization. We take that sort of thing for granted nowadays. No doubt a few reactionaries in men's bars and the locker rooms of

country clubs still get together over their whisky and
soda and decry the invasion of business, the professions,
the arts by what used to be called the weaker sex.
Probably the critics carry very little of their criticism
beyond the hide-outs where they give tongue to it; they
dare not. On most of the battlefields the war between
the sexes has already been won—by the women. It was
not always so. The pioneers who began the movement
were lone fighters.

They had need of strength and endurance, of mind
always, often of body also. Curiously, it is in the tougher
professions that they first made themselves felt. The
Amazons, female commando troops, figure in literature
long before the bluestockings, like Hypatia, and the
lawyers, like Portia. Boadicea, warrior and Resistance
leader, was a national, almost a mythical figure in Britain
many centuries before any woman engaged in the gentler
professions of law, medicine, authorship, and the arts.
We shall not be surprised, therefore, to find that the
roaring boys were not left in possession of a monopoly
of their chosen form of life.

Roaring girls, though never so numerous as roaring
boys, appear as a distinctive part of English life quite
early in the Tudor period. The term 'roaring girl',
however, has been given a wider connotation than
'roaring boy'. Some of the ladies included in the category were by no means counterparts to the male hoodlums and criminals. Some of them were included in the
genus simply because they were conspicuously active in
things hitherto regarded as a male preserve, like warfare.

Others earned inclusion, it would seem, by the mere fact they sometimes wore male clothing.

Their prototype, who had been honoured in an old ballad, is Mary Ambree, who served as a soldier under Henry VIII. She appears as an English Joan of Arc, courageous—'foremost in battle was Mary Ambree'— soldierly, and fiercely chaste.

> 'But this virtuous mayden despised them all,
> "I'll ne'er sell my honour for purple or pall;
> A mayden of England, sir, never will be
> The whore of a monarch," quoth Mary Ambree.'

Our Mary Frith was, perhaps, not quite so much an idealist as the Mary of ballad fame. At the same time, she seems to have led an equally blameless life so far as her personal chastity was concerned. One writer, careless of the truth, and followed sheeplike by several others, includes 'prostitute' among the epithets he applies to Mistress Frith. The evidence is against him.

Unfortunately the records of this interesting female's character and exploits are all too scanty. She intrigues the historical imagination. Anyone who has read Middleton and Dekker's *The Roaring Girl* will wish to know more about the lady. Obviously she impressed herself on her contemporaries. The impression was very favourable in one case, anyhow, for her biographer says that, 'He that looks not on Mal Cutpurse with Admiration is not fit to carry Guts to a Beare.'

Several poets and dramatists have commemorated her. An anonymous *Life and Death of Mrs. Mary Frith* has the

merit of being virtually contemporary. It was published
in 1662—and she had died in the summer of 1659. Possibly the book was already being written while she was
alive, or, anyhow, the author may have been collecting
his material from her own lips, for there are numerous
quotations in the first person singular, and much that
could scarcely have come from outside sources. The
Mrs. of the title is, of course only the 'Mistress' of the
period, applicable to an unmarried woman.

The book contains a portrait which, with some
painted panels recently discovered in an old house in
Huntingdonshire, enables us to picture Mary Frith as she
was in her lifetime, both as a well-dressed woman of her
period and in her favourite male attire. Her biographer
appears to have been unmoved by her looks, which he
regarded as unimpressive beside her achievements, for
the following verse accompanies the portrait:

> 'See here the Presidesse o'th pilf'ring Trade,
> Mercurye's second, Venus's onely Mayd,
> Doublet and breeches, in a Un'form dresse,
> The Female Hummurist, a Kickshaw messe;
> Here's no attraction that your fancy greets,
> But if her Features please not, read her Feats.'

It would be pleasing to trace an association between
our Moll Cutpurse and Shakespeare in the allusion by Sir
Toby Belch to 'Mistress Moll's picture', but it is unlikely Shakespeare was thinking of her, for *Twelfth Night*
was written before she had made a reputation for herself.

Mary Frith was a Londoner and, like many Londoners,

R

happiest when she was within the confines of her native city, a tiny, compact metropolis compared to the sprawling 'Greater London' that now contain nearly a quarter of the population of Great Britain. There was no criminal element in the family background. The Friths were of the respectable tradesmen class, the urban equivalent of the solid yeomen who would in time become the middle class that was so influential in English life right up to our own day.

Mary's father was a shoemaker, with a house and shop combined, in the Barbican, at the upper end of Aldersgate Street. There she was born in 1589, says her earliest biographer. Malone, the Shakespearian editor, says 1584, which tallies with the record of her death in her seventy-fifth year.

All tradesmen except the most exalted merchant princes lived 'over the shop' in those times, so it may be that the child's life was as normal and happy as that of anyone else born in that section of society. Anyhow, we have no evidence for a psychiatric explanation of the female gangster's career in a frustrated or warped childhood. Moreover, in an age when illiteracy carried no stigma in the class of craftsmen and small tradesmen, Mary received an education that certainly included the fundamentals and even some of the accomplishments. Her later skill as a swordsman, for example, suggests that she had early lessons in fencing. If that was so, her parents were undoubtedly on the way up. We must bear in mind that Elizabeth's reign was very much an age of profiteers and climbers. The old aristocrats were still rich and powerful, but they were getting thrust aside by the 'new' men, the Cecils, Raleghs, Hattons and the like. It is not unreasonable, then, to imagine that Frith *père* had dreams of some position in English society a bit above that of a respectable small business man in the Barbican. It should be noted that he was a 'shoemaker', not just a 'cobbler'.

Perhaps some talk of her parents or the success stories which a bright child like Mary would have picked up from the gossips around her may have stirred the spirit of adventure in her. More probably, however, the traits of character which account for some of her later habits and actions were already decisive. Definitely she was a tomboy, 'a very tomrig or rumpscuttle', says the seventeenth-century biography. In our age we should have seen her in slacks and a lumber jacket, running around with the boys, not because she was sexually attracted to them, but because in those days it was only in male company that she could find the sort of active mischief she enjoyed. Young females were kept at the jobs thought suitable to them—in kitchen, dairy, and still-room, at the embroidery frame or sitting demurely beside the sewing-basket. Young Mary Frith cared for none of these things.

Very early in life she showed her fondness for dressing in men's clothes. It was not merely the phase of blue jeans and bobby sox. She started at an age when most little girls like to wear their pretty party frocks and hair ribbon, and she kept it up until her death. 'From the first entrance into a competency of age,' says the biographer, 'and to her dying day she would not leave it off, till the infirmity and weakness of nature had brought her abed to her last travail, changed it for a wastcoat, and her pettycoats for a winding sheet.'

Modern parents would not worry too much about a childish predilection for boy's attire, so long as suitable womanly qualities were otherwise evident. Not so in former ages. We do not need to go back to St. Jeanne d'Arc and the charges against her—the cavalry soldier's armour only slightly less reprehensible in ecclesiastical eyes than the alleged witchcraft. We know how our grandparents regarded George Sand, execrating her almost as much for strutting about in male attire as for the picturesque liaisons that followed her separation from her husband. Although we are lamentably short of data on the domestic situation in the shoemaker's household in the Barbican, we may be sure that Mr. and Mrs. Frith took a poor view of Mary's tomboy spirits and her dressing up in hose and doublet. Men's fashions, at the time Mary started her nonsense, must have struck her parents as particularly immodest and unsuitable for a young girl. The later male mode of the Protectorate and Commonwealth, when she was middle-aged, would have seemed less objectionable. English Puritanism, we must remember, had a large following by the time Mary was born, and its adherents were chiefly in the class of tradespeople and craftsmen to which the Friths belonged.

She 'delighted and sported only in boys' play and pastime, not minding or companying with the girls', we are told, so at least we may conclude she was a healthy adolescent, morally and physically. In modern times she might have gone into business, taught equitation, collected wild animals for zoos, been a stewardess on a plane, or held a pilot's licence, and have become and remained a useful and respected English citizen.

Unfortunately there were very few opportunities for a career girl in Tudor and Stuart times, especially if she lacked the advantages of aristocratic birth. By the time Mary Frith had grown into 'a lusty and sturdy wench' the shoemaker and his wife felt that something had to be done about her. The obvious career, of course, was marriage, and one presumes that her father could have provided a dowry adequate for a girl of her social class. Despite the rather unchivalrous verse accompanying her portrait in the 1662 edition of her biography, she seems to have had her share of good looks. If the painted panels in the country house are to be trusted, she was by no means averse from being the well-dressed woman on occasion. The artist shows her in the fashionable attire of James I's reign—in a man's plumed hat, indeed, but with grey-green ruff and gloves, cream skirt and bodice, picked out in red. Beneath her portrait is a couplet which reads:

'Not soe quicke sighted is ye eagle for her prey
As I new fashions spie to make me gay.'

However, Mary was the androgynous type, slim, youthful, athletic, inclined to be flat-chested. Perhaps she would have aroused male admiration at a college athletic meeting in our own time, but the smooth, oval face is definitely boyish, certainly quite as masculine, let us say, as Pontormo's *Halberdier*. Her eye, blue, I imagine, although it is impossible to be sure now, was a cold one, except when warmed by the emotions of friendship and patriotism. I do not think an Elizabethan or Jacobean counterpart of a 'wolf' would readily have made a pass at her, or, having tried it once, ever have made a second essay.

The Friths, father and mother, did the best they knew. Had their troublesome offspring been a boy, they would have apprenticed him to his father's trade. They put Mary out to domestic service, perhaps in the household of some well-to-do customer of the Barbican shoe shop. That might or might not be a career with a future to it. There was, of course, the chance of meeting the 'right' man, a steward, bailiff, or other household official, even a young parson, now that clerical celibacy was no more. If something like that failed to come her way, then a career might be made of domestic service. There were, doubtless, very respectable and well-paid jobs in the big households of the wealthy 'new' men of Renaissance England. Young Mary left the Barbican for her first job accompanied by the hopes and wishes of her worried parents.

Unfortunately for parental hopes and her own chance of finding a niche in the middle-class society of her time, Mary had two pet aversions that unfitted her for the life chosen for her by her elders. She hated household work of any kind, and she loathed the task of looking after children. As hers was the era before any of the work in a house, large or small, was mechanized in any way, she obviously was not going to be happy as an apprenticed domestic help, whatever administrative status in the future might free her of the actual physical labour. The dislike of baby-sitting and other departments of child care was an even greater handicap in a period before female emancipation, birth control, and high taxation put any check on the size of families. Those hordes of children seated meekly at table in old prints or kneeling in serried rows on sepulchral monuments in churches and cathedrals were not Mary Frith's idea of a congenial environment. Animals—yes; she was an animal lover and kept interesting and unusual pets all her life; children—definitely, no. The company of the other servant wenches bored her. She could not abide their 'magpie chat'.

One suspects that the attempt to make her conform to a recognized pattern of petty bourgeois life failed chiefly on account of her temperamental make-up. It was not due to laziness or lack of will power. She just didn't fit into the conventional design for living for one of her sex and class—marriage to a plodding young tradesman or crafts-man, the chores of a house where everything had to be done by manual labour, the care, on a small income, of a rapidly growing family—with luck, not more than one a year.

'No man could affirm that she had a Sweet-heart, or any such fond thing to dally with her,' says the *Life and Death of Mrs. Mary Frith*. Perhaps she was sexually cold, and resented the fact she had been born a woman. Her obstinacy about male clothing in the face of convention and even legal penalties suggests that as a key to her psychology. Certainly, it was no case of perverted instincts with her. Women bored her, more so perhaps than they would have done had she been able to meet on a footing of equality some of the women with brains and character who were her contemporaries—Queen Elizabeth herself, for example, Frances Walsingham, Lady Fairfax. But her associates were necessarily women with the untrained minds and limited interests of her own class, the fellow domestics in the household where she held her short-lived job. Their empty-headed gossip and their giggling were highly distasteful.

Presumably there was a flare-up in the shoemaker's family circle. Whether Mary donned her male clothing and stalked out of the house, careless of the family's shame and the raised eyebrows of the neighbours, or whether Papa Frith told her never to darken his Barbican door again, we do not know. It seems certain, however, that she entered the underworld of London and quickly made a place for herself in it. How she got her start we do not know. Probably it was by strength of will and a natural talent for leadership. We may be sure she did not adopt the standard practice of becoming mistress and pupil of a male practitioner in crime. In view of the nickname she early acquired—Moll Cutpurse—we may reasonably surmise that she started her profession as a pickpocket. Strictly, it was a matter of cutting rather than picking a purse. The sausage-like purse of the time, woven of silk or other material, could be cut in half and freed from its owner's belt or other fastenings. This was the technique of the 'nip' or cut-purse. The pickpocket properly so-called, a 'foist' in Elizabethan slang, despised the use of the knife and relied entirely on sleight of hand, like his modern descendants.

Mary Frith did not waste time acquiring, by painful practice and at great risk, the skill of the experienced foist. Her ambition was to be head of an organization, a lady gangster, not a mere pickpocket risking, at every operation, a broken head from a cudgel, a sword through the body, or a horrible death by strangulation at Tyburn. She must have been a just and even a kindly boss, for there is no record of misfortunes from false brethren, dis-gruntled henchmen, or stool-pigeons. The icy chastity and the male attire gave her the authority of a man in the same position. The fact that the leader, despite the semi-military costume, the tobacco-smoking, and the swords-manship, was actually a woman added piquancy to service with her. Her inaccessibility kept out the sexual jealousies which play havoc with the spirit of co-opera-tion, whether in crime or politics. 'An Hermaphrodite in manners as well as in Habit, she was not moved nor solicited by any man,' says her chronicler.

Apart from the great exploit of her later years, wherein the motive was patriotism rather than profit, the only open collision with the law on record had nothing to do with a crime against property. The trouble came from ecclesiastical quarters—the shocked abhorrence of the clergy for Mary's mannish style of dress. Until recent years in the Anglo-Saxon world, and still amongst the Latins, the sight of a woman in trousers suggests to the clerical mind a suspicious tendency at least, if not actual depravity. To the Anglican clerics in the London of Elizabeth, James I, and Charles I, and their Presbyterian and Independent usurpers under the Protectorate, a woman whose legs were covered by hose or breeches instead of a skirt was a monster. They seem to have regarded her as the Pharisees did the woman taken in adultery. Fortunately for Mary Frith, English canon law did not allow the sort of penalties which the more fiercely Puritanical of the clergy would have liked to see inflicted.

By 1611, when the trouble arose, Mary was pretty well established in her chosen profession. By contrast with the perils and nervous strain of a modern criminal career, crime in the ill-lighted, unpoliced, and very bribable London of the late sixteenth and early seventeenth centuries was easy, of a leisurely tempo, and often highly remunerative. Mary should have dressed with more regard for convention; that was all that was needed. Voluminous skirts for everyday wear, for parties a farthingale as long as it remained in fashion, decorous feminine headwear—and all would have been well until her impudent attack on a Party bigwig later in life. She could not, however, resist her childhood's urge, now a confirmed habit, to swagger about town in a man's clothes.

It was the Church of England, not the State, that brought her to book. The scandal of the male attire was too much for the official guardians of morality. Prostitutes and kept women were bad enough in ecclesiastical eyes, but the lax standards of much upper-class society and the unedifying example of James I's court discouraged the clergy in their fight for better sexual morals. Occasional diatribes from the pulpit were about the limit of their efforts, and even so they had to be discreet. King James I lacked the high standards and the integrity of life of his son and successor Charles I, and he would have resented attacks on his favourites. The enormity of a woman in trousers, however, was too much even for Erastian consciences. Moreover, Mary Frith was only a shoemaker's daughter. She had no friends with Palace influence. Accordingly she was cited to appear before the Court of Arches on a charge of lewd and indecent behaviour. The Court of Arches, a judicial body with disciplinary powers in the established Church, plays an inconspicuous part in present-day English life. The ordinary layman seldom hears of it, and has very little occasion to worry about its authority. It may punish an Anglican cleric who gives scandal by drunkenness or sexual misbehaviour, although it seems unable to touch him if he undermines the basic doctrines of Christinaity or espouses Russian communism. Mary Frith was almost certainly of unimpeachable Anglican orthodoxy, but she wore trousers, and that to the divines and lawyers of the Court of Arches was an abomination.

She was tried and found guilty. Ecclesiastical courts imposed milder punishments than the secular courts in those days of whipping, branding, strangulation, and disembowelling. Mary was sentenced to do public penance at Paul's Cross. This might be very humiliating, and to a shy or self-conscious penitent must have been exceedingly embarrassing, but it was not physically cruel. The guilty person had to appear in a white garment—a long robe or a sheet—and listen to a sermon delivered by a selected preacher. An armed guard was at hand to assure safety from mob violence or lynching if the offender were unpopular and to prevent rescue if the penitent enjoyed the favour of the London rabble.

Mary Frith was popular. The Cockneys turned out in force to see her. Their minds were pleasantly titillated by the shameless behaviour that had brought her to Paul's Cross, and the deep grief and copious tears of her penance. The edifying picture of Mary's contrition is marred by the probability that she went to Paul's Cross primed with alcohol to get her through the ordeal as comfortably as possible. She was 'maudlin drunk' says the biographer, which she might well be, as she had drunk three quarts of sack before going to the place of penance.

The preacher, a Reverend Mr. Radcliffe of Brasenose College, Oxford, was a pulpit spell-binder. He was 'the daintiest preacher or ghostly father that ever I saw', says Mary's biographer, but adds critically, 'a likelier man to have led the revels in some Inn of Court than to be where he was'. Neither his oratory nor his personal character made much impression. 'He did extreme badly, and so wearied the audience, that the best part went away, and the rest tarried rather to hear Moll Cutpurse than him.'

The extant portraits, the anonymous biography, and the remarks of contemporary writers enable us to con-

jure up a reasonably likely picture of Mary Frith in early
womanhood—'the maddest, fantasticalest girle', as the
dramatist Middleton calls her—as she impressed herself
on her fellow Londoners and, less favourably, on the
clergy. Butler, whose *Hudibras* was published within a
few years of her death, speaks of:

> 'A bold Virago, stout and tall,
> As Joan of France, or English Mall.'

The costume which has been recorded by artists of her
own time has nothing shameless or improper about it
according to present-day standards. Mary would, we
may be sure, have been immeasurably shocked by our
sweater girls and bathing beauties. The plumed hat, a
copintank or sugar-loaf hat, was a common headgear
in early Stuart times, and with slight variations could be
worn with male or female costume. The doublet or
tunic, a more or less soldierly garment, was not designed
for the provocative display of female charms, as was the
extreme décolletage we see in portraits of high-born
ladies of the period.

The nether garment which was the acme of Mary's
depravity by clerical standards appears as a very modest
and decorous affair to our eyes. It was a pair of rather
ample breeches of the cut known as Dutch slop, not
unlike the plus fours in vogue some years ago. The cloak
or mantle worn for warmth or protection against rain can
have given offence only because it was of a type that went
with male rather than female costume.

The pictures of Mary Frith, whether in man's clothes

or woman's, draw attention to a habit which in her time was considered almost as unsuitable to her sex as the Dutch slop—smoking, or as the seventeenth century called it, drinking tobacco. She is shown with a clay tobacco pipe in her right hand. The panel-painting of her in woman's dress shows a half-filled drinking glass in the left hand. She was as fond of her glass as her pipe, although we are not told of any excess, except on the occasion of the penance imposed by the Court of Arches. Mary took up tobacco smoking partly as a matter of bravado and so that she could boast of being the first woman addict in England. 'Tobacco was grown to be the great Mode,' she is quoted as saying, 'and a set of Swaggerers there were denominated Puffers and high Huffers. I was mightily taken with this vanity, because of its affected singularity, and as no Woman before me ever smoaked any.' We are not told if this boast went unchallenged. There is a record of Sidney's sister *buying* tobacco, but we do not know who smoked it; probably Sir Philip and his friends.

The practice Mary Frith started as a piece of ostentation she kept up for enjoyment and because, like Sir Walter Ralegh and other early smokers, she believed it beneficial to health. It gets the credit for her survival to a comparatively ripe old age, in spite of the dropsy she suffered from in later years. The Huntingdonshire painting of Mary in her smart female costume depicts the tobacco pipe, while below it a rhymed couplet makes play on the words *nonsense* and *incense*, the latter a slang term for tobacco smoke in the early seventeenth century.

Another of Mary's traits commemorated by the painters of her portrait is love of animals. The age was very callous in its attitude to animals. Englishmen found pleasure in bull and bear baiting, while cockfighting was called the royal diversion. James I and his son and grandson were all devotees of 'cocking'. The royal cockpit which Henry VII had built for himself gave its name to a section of the palace at Whitehall. Mary Frith's unusual pets—a monkey, a tame eagle, and, according to one record, a lion—suggest an affection for animals more comprehensive than the traditional English devotion to dogs and horses. She had a dog as well as her more unusual pets, but in this case business as well as affection seems to be involved. The dog was specially trained to help her in her work. This tickled the popular fancy. We find a reference in a play that was acted in 1632 to a dog named after her. This, however, was a dog used for bull-and-bear baiting, sports she would undoubtedly have disapproved of because of the horrible injuries inflicted on the dogs used for the baiting.

By the time she was a middle-aged woman Mary appears to have been generally accepted as the queen of London's underworld. She was solidly established as a city householder, with a property in Fleet Street, near the Conduit. The house served as both residence and place of business, like her father's home in the Barbican. The business premises comprised a kind of informal tavern or public house and a pawnshop or lost property bureau. The house was the headquarters of the criminal gang she controlled—burglars, pickpockets (both 'nips' and 'foists'), and specialists in hooking movable goods out of ground-floor windows. Possibly some highwaymen dealt with her as a discreet 'fence', or receiver of stolen goods. Two distinguished members of the highway fraternity were personal friends of hers.

Her henchmen and assistants were all kept very much under control. 'Your Governesse was famous;' says the biographer, 'your Government under her Discipline no less reputable for its due regulation.'

As her business grew and prospered, it took on an aura of near-respectability. Solid citizens thought less about the criminal underlings who might have filched their goods and more about the competent, reliable business woman, also a friendly and jovial person so long as no liberties were attempted, who could be trusted to recover them—for a consideration. In a play that was put on the stage in 1632 the dramatist has one of the characters say, 'My watch is gone out of my pocket too o'th'right side. I'le go to honest Moll about it presently.' Mary herself describes this business with a touch of pride in its commercial integrity.

'In my house,' she said, when giving what we should call a press interview to her future biographer, 'I set up a kind of brokery for Jewels, rings or watches which might have been stolen or pinched. . . . I might have called it the Insurance Office, for the losers were sure upon Compensation to Recover their goods.'

Outside business hours she was a good companion, always ready for a drink, a pipe of tobacco, and a song, with a large circle of men who accepted her as one of themselves. She left a record of some of her special friends, such as 'my fellow humorist Banks the Vintner in Cheapside, who taught his horse to dance and shood him with silver.' Then there was Mulsack, the chimney sweeper, who was one of her special circle. She knew most of the 'keepers' of the London jails, and was especially friendly with Ralph Briscoe, the Clerk of Newgate. Presumably a ready access to the prison population in those days of easy-going administration and widespread bribery was a help to business. Mary, however, had her altruistic side. On Sundays she regularly visited the Ludgate and Newgate jails to carry charity—food and alms—to poor prisoners. This may have been a shrewd casting of her bread on the waters. Those of the poor prisoners who were not 'going west', the jargon of the period for a trip to Tyburn gallows, and who survived typhus, cholera, bubonic plague and so forth, became her devoted henchmen when they came out. However, all the evidence suggests a woman of great good nature, with a ready hand-out for those in distress.

The two high spots of Mary Frith's career are connected with her ardent royalism. In 1639, when she was well established in London, middle-aged, prosperous, highly respected in criminal circles, King Charles I returned to his capital after leading a military expedition against a Scottish rebellion. There was great excitement in London, and much patriotic fervour was displayed. Mary's account of her part in it shows a journalistic flair that would have served her well in a later age.

'I was also resolved to show my Loyal and Dutiful

s

Respects to the King in as ample a manner as I could.
. . . I undertook to supply Fleet-street Conduit adjacent
to my House with Wine to flow continually for that
Triumphal Day, which I performed with no less Expence
than Credit and Delight, and the Satisfaction of all
Comers and Spectators . . . and as the King passed by me,
I put out my Hand and caught Him by His, and grasped
it very hard, saying *Welcome Home*, CHARLES! His
Majesty smiled, and I believe took me for some Mad,
Bold Beatrice or other, while the people shouted and
made a noyse in part at my confidence and presumption,
and in part for joy of the King's Return. The rest of that
day I spent in jollity and carousing and concluded the
Night with fireworks and Drink.'

Then she adds, with a touch of complacency, that she
was 'the Talk of the Town, and made people look upon
me at another rate than formerly. . . . I was no more Mal
Cutpurse, but Mrs. Mary Frith.' The wine in the conduit cost her twenty pounds, a generous sum when we
translate it into contemporary spending power.

The second great ebullition of her royalist patriotism
took place early in the Civil War, that is, some time
after 1642, so she must have been getting towards her
sixties when it happened. It took the form of an attack
on Lord Fairfax, the Parliamentarian general, on Hounslow Heath. Robbery entered into the affair, but was
probably an afterthought. It is unlikely she expected
Fairfax to be carrying much money on him at the time,
although she took two hundred Jacobuses off him.
From some of the wealthy merchants and Puritan war

profiteers who were to be found in the London area and East Anglia she might have taken heavier spoils with less risk. Lord Fairfax, however, stood for everything she abhorred, the Puritan attitude to her easy-going ideas of personal property, the Puritan distrust of good fellow-ship and conviviality, above all, the treachery, as she regarded it, of a nobleman and a soldier bearing arms against his anointed king at the behest of a group of Puritan lawyers in Westminster.

The set-to on Hounslow Heath was quite an affair as hold-ups went in the seventeenth century. Mary Frith, mounted and armed, attacked in person. We do not know if any of her assistants, except possibly the well-trained dog, accompanied her. Lord Fairfax was shot in the arm, and two of his servants had their horses killed under them. Then Mary put spurs to her horse and made her escape, taking the general's two hundred Jacobuses with her, but with a posse of Parliamentarian staff officers in hot pursuit. She galloped down the road that runs from London to the west, but at Turnham Green her horse collapsed. Probably his rider was putting on weight in later middle age. Anyhow, she and the Jacobuses were too much for the poor beast.

The Parliamentarian officers caught her, put her under arrest, and hurried her off to Newgate. She had com-mitted what in those days and for long after was a capital offence, but it is unlikely she was other than very com-fortable in jail, for the officials at Newgate were friends of hers. Anyhow, she had not long to wait behind bars. The Fairfaxes were a magnanimous family. The general was quite willing to come to terms. Probably, too, he admired the sheer impudence of the lady gangster. He compromised for two thousand pounds. It was a large sum in those days, but then Mary was a well-heeled capitalist. One presumes that Fairfax' officers retrieved his two hundred Jacobuses for him.

After this adventure Mary appears to have settled down to a tranquil life of well-run crime, assorted pets, pleasant evenings of song, drink, and tobacco with her numerous men friends, and, we may be pretty sure, a good deal of a helping hand for the royalist underground. There is an intriguing irony in the life of this woman, with her male attire, her menagerie of strange pets, and her stolen property bureau run with the efficiency of a well-audited business, in the dreary Puritan London of the Protectorate—the theatres and concert halls closed, the churches stripped bare of their ornaments and handed over to dour Calvinists, the weekly day of rest a nightmare of Sabbatarian gloom. But there were rich pickings for people with initiative and no scruples. There were phony contracts for army supply, bootleg song and dance, bootleg royalist books, even bootleg Anglican worship. Moreover, commercialized vice flourished as never before. The city was packed with soldiers whose activities were officially limited to military drill under a system of harsh discipline and brutal punishments, and, on Sundays and at periodical 'lectures', attendance at long-winded predestinarian discourses. It is no wonder that brothels sprang up all over the city and its suburbs and did a roaring trade.

We have no conclusive evidence that the sexagenarian Mary Frith, so chaste and immune from calumny in her own life, muscled in on this golden harvest of sin. However, it is indisputable that she has been dubbed 'procuress', and that an old manuscript devoted to her 'Madde Prancks' purports to record her walks about Bankside in man's attire. Bankside, across the river, had been for many generations the recognized red light district of London. Although the law of supply and demand, operating in Cromwell's London, had caused the Bankside industry to spread beyond its original limits, those Southwark slums were still the headquarters of metropolitan vice. Mary's frequent presence there, and in the safe disguise of male clothing, is suspicious—if the report is truthful. Perhaps, however, it is as calumnious as the inclusion of 'prostitute' among the epithets once applied to her.

In view of the lady's ardent devotion to the English crown and to its Stuart wearers, it is sad to know that she died just too soon for the Restoration. A little longer and she might have welcomed the restored King Charles II, grasping him by the hand and crying, 'Welcome home, Charles!' as she had done for his father twenty-two years before. However, she lived long enough to outlive the powerful Oliver Cromwell, accursed regicide and usurper in her eyes, by nearly a year. Moreover, she had seen his son Richard, Tumbledown Dick as she and her royalist friends called him, lay down the burden his father had bequeathed him, while events shaped themselves for the glorious Restoration she had awaited for more than seventeen years.

By anticipation, at least, she took part in the re-joicing. In her will she arranged for another twenty pounds' worth of wine in the Fleet Street conduit to celebrate Charles II's return.

She was in her seventy-fifth year, a ripe old age in those days. During the last uneasy months of the Pro-tectorate she had been suffering from dropsy, although she claimed to have kept it at bay by her free use of tobacco. Now, as the summer of 1659 drew towards its end (July 26), she knew that her 'merry pranks', her swaggering about town as a gallant and a swordsman, her prosperous 'brokery', her convivial evenings with the vintner and the chimney sweeper, were over. The Elizabethan sun was setting when she started her career. After Elizabeth I's death she had lived through two Stuart reigns and a Puritan dictatorship. Now the end was at hand.

One hopes that some good-hearted royalist parson was able to visit the dying woman in her Fleet Street house and help her prepare to face a Judge more to be feared, but also more understanding, than anyone in the Court of Arches. The Caroline clergy of the Church of England were, by and large, an earnest, devout, and kindly body of men. Were there some saintly pastor of the type of George Herbert at hand when Mary lay dying, it is a safe guess that the wandering sheep would have been gathered in.

In death she was Mary Frith, daughter of a respectable tradesman and London citizen. The 'maddest, fantastica-lest girle' had exchanged her 'merry pranks' for the stillness of death, and her scandalous male attire for a winding sheet. The church of her baptism, which was just beginning to raise its head after a generation of outlawry and usurpation, took her to its bosom again. She was buried with Anglican rites on August 10 in the Church of St. Bridget (St. Bride), near her Fleet Street home. The old church was destroyed in the Great Fire of London in 1666, and it was more than a dozen years later before a new one, designed by Sir Christopher Wren, took its place.

V

SIR JOHN HARINGTON,
THE MERRY POET

THE queen's godson had a happy disposition. Formidable as Queen Elizabeth I was on occasion—many occasions—she always kept a warm spot in her heart for the young courtier, nearly thirty years her junior, whom she befriended from his babyhood to the end of her own life. It was, I think, the survival of a strain of naïveté in his character that endeared him to his royal godmother. He was scholarly and well-read, a true child of the Renaissance in that, but so was Elizabeth herself; that did not impress her. He was a go-getter, but the queen was surrounded by such. Go-getting was an accepted practice at the courts of the Tudors, and the queen could resist its insinuations well enough when she chose. Harington was something of a poet, a versifier, anyhow, but she had better poets among her followers. She even granted a small pension to one of them, Edmund Spenser, over the protests of the budget-cutting Lord Treasurer Burghley. No, when all is said and done, it must have been that youthful insouciance that won Gloriana, that and her gratitude for the courageous loyalty of the Haringtons in her own early years of peril.

Harington's likeness, preserved for us in the miniature by John Hoskins, confirms this impression of his character. There is a touch of foppery in the picture—curly hair brushed off the forehead in something like the 'quiff' of later times, an ear-ring of four large stones set in brilliants worn in the left ear, more jewels in the necklace worn like a lord mayor's chain, a ruff of fine lace delicately worked, a doublet richly embroidered. We miss the severity and restrained good taste of Walsingham's clothes, but the foppery was not greater than that of Ralegh. The face, moreover, is very different from the Principal Secretary's stern, swarthy countenance or Sir Walter's thoughtful, aloof and rather disdainful features. Harington's, in fact, is scarcely an Elizabethan face at all. It is good-natured, easy-going, with a kind of wide-eyed innocence betrayed only by the lower lip, which is just sensual enough to hint at an Horatian acceptance of life's minor pleasures. The mere shadow of a moustache on the upper lip and the little point of beard on the chin suggest that the wearer was just another courtier and dandy. That is not so; he had an excellent record as a cavalry officer in Ireland during the Earl of Essex' campaign.

The Haringtons were a family on the losing side in the last scene of the thirty-year dynastic struggle we call the Wars of the Roses. They were loyal to the White Rose, the Yorkists. Sir James Harington the younger fell at Bosworth with King Richard III in 1485.

The dead knight's estates were confiscated, and his family had to get along as best it could under the tight-fisted Tudor King Henry VII. Sir James' grandson made a successful come-back. He combined wit and administrative ability, qualities that found favour with Henry VIII, and he was given a post whose functions bore some resemblance to those of the modern Office of Works. Doubtless there were some more or less legitimate perquisites. Tudor courtiers went into the civil service with one eye at least on the chances of quick enrichment.

This John Harington lived near London, in what was then the pleasant village of Stepney, and supervised the accounts of various royal buildings and camps. At one time he was in an embarrassing position because of a sum of money that found its way into his own coffers instead of those of the royal exchequer. His clerk, one John Bradford, later a Protestant martyr in the Marian burnings, comes into the story, but the assessment of guilt is impossible at this date. Bradford's eulogists represent him as the sea-green incorruptible forcing his crooked employer to make restitution. Other writers picture Harington as the magnanimous chief shielding a light-fingered but penitent accountant and making up the deficit out of his own pocket.

Nothing untoward happened to either master or clerk. The king very likely never heard of the affair, or was too busy with theology, love, marriage, and the royal navy. Anyhow, he continued the royal favour by graciously allowing Harington's marriage to Etheldreda Dyngley (or Dobson), a girl born of one of the king's unacknowledged love affairs. She had been well brought up by John Malte, tailor to his Majesty. The king ordered the polite fiction that Etheldreda owed her existence to the tailor's moral lapse, but did not fail to endow his love-child with a handsome dowry carved out of various monastic lands in Somersetshire. The newly married couple started their life on the best of these properties, Kelston, near Bath, but Etheldreda died early, leaving John Harington a childless widower.

We know practically nothing of the Harington fortunes during the unsettled years of Edward VI's reign. John became friendly with the Princess Elizabeth, and frequently visited her at Hatfield, braving Queen Mary's suspicions and disfavour by doing so. He exercised his talent for poetry by producing a sonnet, *The Prayse of six gentlewomen attending on the Ladie Elizabeth her Grace at Hatfield House*. These six ladies, we are told, were all conspiciuously beautiful, but after a time Harington fixed his attention on one of them, Isabella Markham, whom 'he first thoughte fayre as she stode at the Princesse's window in goodlye attyre, and talkede to dyvers in the courte yarde.'

Another sonnet was composed, headed this time *John Harington to sweete Isabella Markham*, and a betrothal soon followed. Elizabeth must have been less jealous of her courtiers' marriages than she became later, for the young widower and the glamorous lady-in-waiting were married with her approval some time before 1554.

This was the year of greatest peril for Princess Elizabeth. She was imprisoned in the Tower, and for a time her death seemed more likely than not. The Haringtons were imprisoned also, for no other reason than their friendship with Elizabeth. John Harington passed the time by translating Cicero's *De Amicitia* and by composing a letter of protest to Bishop Gardiner. That masterful prelate did not deign to answer it, and Harington then wrote a satirical poem about the bishop, which saw the light when the danger had passed with Mary Tudor's death.

Queen Elizabeth I did not forget the fidelity of her former maid-of-honour and her husband. When their son John was born at Kelston in 1561 she willingly became godmother, and a quasi-maternal relation existed between queen and godson for another forty-two years. The family divided its time between Kelston and the house at Stepney, so it is probable that baby John Harington saw his royal godmother at intervals before the day came for his departure to boarding school.

I have spoken of his happy disposition. We have heard so much in our time of young lives blighted by English boarding school life that it is refreshing to hear of happy schooldays in an age when English Public School life was truly something to endure. Young Harington was a happy Etonian. Thomas Gray, it may be mentioned, was another such, and he was far more of a sensitive plant than any Elizabethan—in an age, too, when English boarding schools had become even tougher than in Elizabeth's time.

William Wickham, an Anglican divine who became Bishop of Winchester, was a vice-provost of Eton when the clever young lad from the country house near Bath came as a new boy to the College. The vice-provost was kind to young Harington, who includes a grateful reference to him in the miscellaneous jottings that make up the *Nugae Antiquae*, collected and published by a Harington descendant two centuries later.

'In the schoolmaster's absence,' says Sir John, 'he (Wickham) would teach the school himself, and direct the boys for their exercises, of which myself was one, of whom he shared as fatherly care as if he had been a second tutor to me. He was reported there a very mild and good-natured man, and esteemed a very good preacher.'

The queen, meanwhile, was keeping an eye on her godson and, no mean classical scholar herself, watched his progress in the studies Eton made the backbone of its curriculum. Possibly he started his Italian at school, for Italian was often the Renaissance Englishman's second language. When John was fourteen his godmother sent him a copy of her 1575 speech to Parliament, accompanied by the charming exhortation, 'Ponder my poore words tyll they enter thyne understanding; so shalt thou hereafter perchance fynde some goode frutes hereof when thy Godmother is oute of remembrance, and I do thys, because thy father was ready to serve and love us in trouble and thrall.'

From Eton young Harington went to Cambridge in 1578, starting his university career as an undergraduate of Christ's College. Here, as in school, good luck and his own disposition combined to assure him the happy life. He was as fortunate in his college tutor as he had been in his teacher at Eton. Dr. John Still, afterwards Bishop of Bath and Wells, having ensured the respect due to authority from an exuberant youth, then became father, philosopher and friend to him.

The young student managed to get into some of the usual undergraduate scrapes, despite Dr. Still's friendly care, to say nothing of a letter of advice from that Polonius among English statesmen, William Cecil, Lord Burghley. John ran into debt, was pestered by dunning tradesmen, tailors, coiffeurs, and jewellers, one suspects, and had recourse to an older family friend to act as go-between with Harington *père*. It is unlikely the father was very stern about it. He himself was something of a wit and Epicurean, and, if John Bradford's friends were accurate, not over-scrupulous in a small matter of a gentleman's creditors.

'When I came to sue to be bachelor, first he (Dr. Still) examined me strictly and after answered me kindly,' says Harington, making it clear that the degree with which he left Cambridge was genuinely earned and not just handed out as a favour to her Majesty's godson.

Young Harington followed up his graduation from the university by a sojourn in London as a law student of Lincoln's Inn. We need not take this too seriously. It did not imply any intention of making a career of law or even completing the ordinary courses of instruction in it. The Inns of Court, then and in later times, were pleasant places for a well-heeled young bachelor's residence, with less irksome restrictions than school or university. Ralegh spent some time as a nominal law student in

London, and, so far as one can judge, did little except
sow wild oats before settling down to more serious occu-
pations. In a later age Oliver Cromwell did the same,
and laid up matter for a lifetime of bitter repentance, and
fear of his stern, Calvinistic Jehovah. Harington probably gave rather more time to study than either of these
men, although he tells us that he 'studied Lyttleton but
to the title of discontinuance'.

The trouble was that John was already making a reputation as a wit, a master of epigram, and a good companion,
and he felt bound to live up to it. With his seductively
ingenuous features, rich, curly hair, genial manner, and
tolerant good nature, combined with a sparkling wit, he
made a ready appeal to men and women both. I suspect
that he had neither the whole-hogging sensuality which
probably preceded Cromwell the Huntingdon gentleman-
farmer's conversion, or Ralegh the Devonshire squire's
passionate intensity. His relations with pretty girls were
chiefly flirtatious and playful, a fact which his royal
godmother, who could be very stern about sexual
laxity, saw with her usual perceptiveness.

Tired of Lyttleton's legal treatises and, perhaps, a
little worried by finding how quickly his accounts were
in the red when he tried to keep up with the sons of the
London 'new' men, John Harington left town and settled
down to matrimony and the life of a country squire in
Somerset. He married Mary, daughter of Sir George
Rogers of Cannington. Whether she was as beautiful as
the court ladies and London belles whom he had ogled
and made up epigrams and pretty verses for, we are not

told. Elizabethan love affairs were often devastatingly passionate, but marriages tended to be prudent and well planned. Harington's conformed to the usual pattern, but from his references to his 'dearest Mall' and his affection for his children, his pet dog, and even the cattle on his estate, it is clear the marriage was a happy one.

As against the mythical hatefulness of mothers-in-law, a fiction of the Victorian music hall, it is pleasant to record the friendship between the young, debonair son-in-law and the elderly, jovial, and salty mother of the bride. From the mists of Elizabethan family history we can pick out the spirited lineaments of Lady Rogers, a composite of the good-natured vulgarity of Jane Austen's Mrs. Jennings and the Rabelaisian heartiness of Chaucer's Wife of Bath, but with an education that made her superior to both. The young husband, it is true, looked forward to solid benefits under his mother-in-law's last will and testament, but, apart from that, he obviously enjoyed her companionship and her ready ear for his wisecracks and amusing anecdotes, many of them indecorous by later standards. Whether young Mrs. Harington disapproved, we are not told. Probably not; she would have been brought up to respect her mother's judgment, and in fact, the Elizabethan woman, like her medieval sister, could combine the strictest integrity of life with a striking degree of plain speaking.

There is a chameleon-like quality about John Harington as he passes back and forth between the fashionable world of London and the Court and his well-ordered life at the family seat of Kelston, near Bath. In town he was wit, courtier, epigrammatist, man of fashion. In Somerset he was the solid country gentleman, busy with building, landscaping, agriculture, dividing his evenings between quiet domesticity and studious hours with the classics and the poets of Italy. He appears as a kindly employer, with the easy-going relationship between master and man which can flourish in a well-ordered, hierarchical society not based exclusively on wealth. Servants were not ashamed of their status, and good employers looked to more than the money nexus between themselves and what, ancient Roman fashion, they called their 'families'.

Harington cracked doggerel rhymes with his gentleman's gentleman, when the latter had the wit for it, but sloppy and inefficient service was not put up with at Kelston. Thanks to the squire's voluminous jottings we can read the complete schedule of penalties for minor lapses. Probably it was first compiled by his father, but he kept it in force when he ran the estate. Absence from household prayers, morning or evening, 'without lawful excuse', was punished by a fine of twopence. Bad language was checked by a penny fine 'upon pain of every oath'. A bed left unmade after 8 a.m. also involved a fine of one penny. The traditional excuse of, 'It slipped out of me 'and' was not accepted; the price of a broken glass was to be stopped out of wages. If dinner, a formal affair in Tudor times, was late because of mismanagement in the kitchen, the cook forfeited sixpence. Personal neatness and cleanliness were assured by a penny fine imposed on any servant who failed to change his shirt on

T

Sunday or was remiss in replacing lost buttons on his doublet. Finally, that there should be no reflection on the master's motives, the money, when deducted from the wages each quarterly pay day, went into a kind of Elizabethan community chest, to be 'bestowed on the poor, or other godly use'.

In spite of the charms of his dearest Mall, his children, and his pets, and the Somersetshire countryside, Harington had periodical attacks of nostalgia for London, his godmother's brilliant Court, her diamond-hard courtiers and her beauteous ladies-in-waiting. Also, he liked the opportunity to show off his fine clothes and scintillating wit to others than his faithful, affectionate wife, taken up with her babies and her household. Even Lady Rogers, with her hearty coarseness and her appreciation of her son-in-law's lewd epigrams and stories, palled as an audience. Then the squire ordered out his horses, his personal 'man', and a few armed attendants, and rode to town. His geniality and wit were becoming legendary along the road from Bath to London. We hear of a dinner en route at an ordinary. The serving maid gave him more than the usual share of attention and prompt service. Intrigued, and perhaps tickled, at getting priority over other customers, Harington asked her for an explanation. 'I understand you are a very witty man,' the girl said, 'and if I should displease you in anything, I fear you would make an epigram of me.'

Unfortunately these expeditions ran into a distressingly large sum of money. There was a harmless, but expensive, streak of the show-off in Harington, and, good-natured and warm-hearted, he probably tipped extravagantly in an age when a gentleman's household staff was reckoned not by ones and twos or dozens but scores and hundreds. Anyhow, even the long-suffering creditors of an Elizabethan gentleman had to be paid eventually—or perhaps the exuberant squire had got into the hands of Lombard Street 'goldsmiths'. These financiers charged a stiff rate of interest on long-term loans in those halcyon days of financial free enterprise.

The consequence was an unfortunate lawsuit and something had to go, so Harington sold one of his landed properties, the estate of Nyland. In later years, riding over its fields with his 'man', he is supposed to have improvised the couplet,

> 'John! John! this Nyland
> Alas! was once my land.'

The faithful 'man', with equally ready wit and the permitted freedom of an old servant, replied,

> 'If you had had more wit, sir,
> It might have been yours yet, sir!'

The anecdote, whether true or not, is at least in character. Things would have had to be in a much worse way for Harington to be greatly upset. Anyhow, his interests and affections were centred on the Kelston house, which had been designed by the Italian architect Barozzi of Vignola. Harington spent a great deal of money on it, especially when, in the course of her western progress, the queen stayed at Kelston as his guest. One of these royal visits was a mixed blessing. The presence of the queen was a great honour, but it often strained the householder's finances badly or left him burdened with debts and mortgages for years afterwards. Harington, we know, was thus afflicted, but we cannot justly blame his god-mother, although she would have resented any miserliness in doing honour to the crown. On this occasion, however, her host exceeded all reasonable limits in altering and beautifying his place for her sojourn.

Among the improvements he introduced was the construction of a fountain and a pool, or 'swimming place', as he called it. Swimming was at the time becoming a fashionable athletic exercise among well-to-do Englishmen. They chose lakes or river holes or built pools in spots where privacy would be assured, for the sport was a male monopoly and the swimmers were naked.

Shortly before the royal visit the incident occurred that puts Harington among the Elizabethan translators. He was always something of the *enfant terrible* in his periodical visits to London and took a schoolboyish delight in shocking anyone who would rise to his bait. Dabbling in Italian literature, as became a Renaissance Englishman, he came across Ariosto's story of Giocondo, one of the less edifying passages in the *Orlando Furioso*. He translated the section of Book 28 in which the story occurs, and circulated it in manuscript at the Court. Elizabeth took him to task for, as she said, corrupting her maids of honour. The queen was no prude and it is unlikely she could have been shocked by anything in

Ariosto, but she was strict about the bevy of aristocratic young virgins who attended her. Perhaps, too, a
touch of jealousy came into it; she was fifty-eight years
old.

Harington, whose affection for his godmother was
tempered with fear of the royal temper, was called into
the Presence and reprimanded. Moreover, he was to
receive punishment. He awaited his sentence; perhaps
the vision of a dark, chilly room in the Tower floated
through his mind. Then her Majesty announced the
penalty, rustication. He was to leave London and go
back to Somerset—until he had translated the whole of
Ariosto's poem.

Doubtless he was relieved to get off so lightly. Queen
Elizabeth, who had her own vein of mischief, would have
enjoyed giving her ebullient godson a temporary scare.
He went back to the country and tackled the long Italian
poem at once. His brother Francis gave him some help
with it, at least to the extent of fifty stanzas in the
thirty-second Book. The whole thing, with explanatory
footnotes and a prefatory 'Apologie of Poetrie', was
finished in time for the queen's visit. It was dedicated
to her, and she graciously accepted it when she arrived.

The reading public was allowed to share the royal
privilege later in the year, for Feilde, a London book-
seller and publisher, brought out a folio edition. It was
so successful that a second edition came out in 1607 and
yet another in 1634, more than twenty years after the
translator's death. Those who are good enough Italian
scholars to compare original and translation tell us that

Harington's version is patchy, sometimes admirable and exact, sometimes 'careless and coarse'. It was, after all, a 'rush job'. The translator wanted to mollify his godmother and resume those junketings in town, with meetings of the London wits in taverns and ordinaries, and flirtatious interludes among the court beauties.

Also, he hoped that attendance at Court might lead to some fat sinecure or, perhaps, one of the royal monopolies like those on which Ralegh grew rich. He was disappointed. Nothing came his way, and he writes of court sycophancy with a fervour that protests too much. '. . . Be it remembered that he who castethe up this reckoning of a courtlie mission, will settle his summe like a foole at the ende, for not beinge a knave at the beginninge. Oh, that I coud boaste with chaunter David, *In te speravi, Domine*!'

He readily consoled himself with the rural and domestic joys of his home near Bath, where undoubtedly his deeper affections were rooted. However, although he does a bit more moralizing, he likes to think that he is not wholly cut off from contact with the Court. 'I came home to Kelstone, and founde my Mall, my children, and my cattle, all well fedde, well taughte, and well belovede. 'Tis not so at cowrte; ill breeding with ill feelinge, and no love but that of the lustie god of gallantrie, Asmodeus. I am to send goode store of news from the countrie, for hir Highnesse' entertainment. . . . Hir Highnesse loveth merrie tales.'

In the winter of 1591 Harington was appointed High Sheriff of Somerset in succession to his friend Sir Hugh

Portman, and he settled down to whatever duties that office imposed on him, and to further work on his estate. Also, he took an interest in the restoration of the Abbey Church in Bath. One of his jottings at the time depicts his condition with a touch of humour. 'I am very busy, yet very idle; very merry, yet very sad; well in my body, but sick in my purse, merry to think my house well nigh done, and sad to say 'tis not well nigh paid for.'

The following year he was mixed up in a legal squabble of which most of the details have been lost. It concerned one Thomas Wells, an apprentice to the printing and engraving trade. Harington was accused of trying to lure him away from the master to whom he was bound by his apprentice's contract or indenture. Why, if there was any truth in the charge, Harington should have done this, we do not know. The only plausible suggestion is that he wished to set up a private printing press. We know that he was interested in the technique of engraving. In any case, despite his dignity as High Sheriff of his county, he was rebuked by the Council for 'so uncharitable an action, not fitting a gentleman of his quality'. He had to send the erring apprentice back to his master in London, under pain of making 'personal appearance without delay to answer his default'.

When this disturbing incident was over, Harington settled down to writing again. He enjoyed writing. There were none of the agonies of gestation and delivery some of our contemporaries describe in their self-revelations. Harington wrote easily and fluently, and after nearly four centuries we still savour the enthu-

siasm, the exuberance, and the ingenuous delight in anything mildly shocking or a bit scatological. I find it hard
to sympathize with the righteous anger of a Victorian
writer who castigates Harington's *Ajax* as 'an indescribable cloacinian satire'.

Those who know nothing else about John Harington
have heard at least that he is credited with a great
English invention—the W.C. or flush toilet. It is this
discovery, and a good deal of playful satire centring on
it, that is the subject of his book, *A New Discourse of a
Stale subject, called the Metamorphosis of Ajax*. Dealing with
the same subject, in the same frivolous mood, were the
subsequent booklets, two published under pseudonyms,
the third anonymously, entitled respectively, *Ulysses upon
Ajax*, *An Anatomie of the Metamorphosed Ajax*, and *An
Apologie*, 1, *Or rather a Retractation*, 2, *Or rather a Recanta-
tion*, 3, *Or rather a Recapitulation . . .*' and so on to Number
12, '*Or rather none of them.*'

The first of these, the *Metamorphosis of Ajax*, is the
chef d'oeuvre of the series. The *Ajax* of the title is a pun
on the good old English noun 'jakes', a privy or earth
closet. Harington, who seems to have been fastidious,
with ideas of personal cleanliness ahead of his generation,
might well have been disgusted by the primitive sani-
tary arrangements of Elizabethan households. He decided
the time had come for a change, and offered his *Metamorphosis*, so in the *Ajax* we have the full specifications of
the ancestor of all water closets or flush toilets. There
is even a clearly executed diagram, reproduced in a rare
nineteenth-century edition, showing the design and

method of operation of the new contrivance. Lest there should be any doubt as to the purifying element, the draughtsman has drawn several little fish swimming about in the overhead tank.

In the studious seclusion of his library at Kelston the author dismissed any qualms about the propriety of his subject, for, he said, 'pens may blot, but they cannot blush', and then, in reference to the naughty story from Ariosto that shocked the ladies-in-waiting, 'If you can but tell a homelie tale of this in prose as cleanlie, as you haue told in verse a baudie tale or two in *Orlando* mannerlie, it maie passe among the sowrest censurers verie currantlie.' He dedicated the work to his uncle, Thomas Markham of Ollerton, 'a right Englishman, a faithful, plain, true, stout gentleman, and a man of honesty and virtue'.

The book is largely filled with the writer's pseudo-classical satire upon his subject, but in the later pages, along with the informative diagram, he gives practical details of engineering and cost-accounting. The price list of parts, even when we make allowance for the value of English money in the late sixteenth century, compares very favourably with modern plumbers' bills. The cistern, of stone or brick, cost eight shillings and six-pence, the pipe from it, 'with a stopple to the washer', three shillings and sixpence, a waste pipe one shilling, and 'the stem of the great stopple, with a key to it', one shilling and sixpence. The 'stool pot, of stone', was eight shillings and sixpence, while the most expen-sive item of all, 'the great brass sluice, to which is three inches current to send it down a gallop into the jax' cost only ten shillings. The seat, we are told, was made 'with a peak devant for elbow room'. The total cost, concludes the inventor's amanuensis, was 'thirty-three shillings: yet a mason of my master's was offered thirty pounds for the like'.

John Harington, who seems always to have been ingenuously surprised when his indiscretions got him into trouble, found that he had once more incurred his royal godmother's displeasure. One cannot believe that she was greatly put out by his 'cloacinian satire', and she showed her appreciation of the new gadget by having one installed in Richmond Palace. It seems, however, that one of the author's remarks in the course of his book was taken as a sly allusion to the Earl of Leicester, who had died several years earlier. Probably he was the only man Elizabeth had ever been truly in love with, and the sorrow of his death was still fresh.

Harington took alarm. There was talk of an indictment and further action by the Council. He hastened to bury himself away in Somerset and there he stayed until a letter from his cousin, Robert Markham of Cottam, gave him some reassurance of royal favour, but also warned him about his verbal indiscretions.

'Your book is almost forgiven,' writes Cousin Robert, 'but not for its want of wit and satyre. Though her Highness signified displeasure in outward sort, yet did she like the marrow of your booke. The Queene is minded to take you to her favour, but she swearethe that she believes you will make epigrams on her and her courte; she hath been hearde to saye—"That merry poet my godson must not come to Greenwich tille he hathe growne sober, and leaveth the ladies' sports and frolics." Yet you stand well in her highnesse' love, and I heere you are to go to Ireland with the Lieutenant Essex. If so, mark my counsel in the matter: I doubt not of your valour nor your labour, but that damnable uncovered honestie will marr your fortunes.'

When he was already middle-aged by Elizabethan standards—he was about thirty-seven—Harington saw active service as a cavalry commander. He also won a knighthood, which at one time looked like a doubtful blessing. The important thing for us who wish to see this Elizabethan as he indeed was, is that he proved himself a true man of the Renaissance in his hardihood, his physical courage, and the readiness to exchange his dallyings at Court, his scholarly hobbies, his interests as a country gentleman, for the dangers and discomforts of sixteenth-century campaigning. The newly dubbed Sir John, ennobled for valour and endurance, was a genuine, if an amateur, soldier. His military record as captain of a troop of horse in the Irish campaign is the needed counterpoise for the queen's godson, the dandified trifler in London, the dabbler in Italian classics, the country squire, and even that benefactor of our modern world, the inventor of the English water closet.

Harington's service under Robert Devereux, Earl of Essex, in the Irish expedition of 1598 may have been largely a matter of chance. Harington's cousins, the Markhams, were followers of the earl, and perhaps their influence led Harington to seek and obtain a commission in Essex' forces. Like most of his generation, he was an opportunist, but, perhaps, a less unscrupulous one than most of the 'new' men at Elizabeth's Court. Anyhow, he hitched his waggon to the Essex meteor rather than the steady, inexorable Cecil star. Young Robert Cecil, the brilliant hunchback, had quietly taken over his father's power and authority after William Cecil's death. The feud went on between the 'new' men who clustered round the Cecils and the old nobility—and the populace—who regarded the dashing, handsome, thirty-year-old earl as their leader. The moves on the Cecil side were more tortuous, the technique more subtle than when Lord Burghley held the reins.

After Essex' Cadiz expedition ten years earlier, an honourable place in the 1589 expeditionary force against the Irish, who were undergoing one of their periodical conquests by England, appeared to be a very good seat on a popular band waggon. The band waggon, however, was destined to a calamitous flight downhill, even had the earl not hastened the process by his own presumption. Robert Cecil, old Burghley's second son, had been well trained by his father in the art of 'throwing the stone so as the hand be not seen'. He was resolved to complete the task of transferring power from the old nobility to the 'new' men. Essex played into his hands by an intolerable arrogance towards the queen and her instructions and by questionable negotiations with the Irish leaders. He had been sent to Ireland as a *gauleiter*, but had ended up almost as a peace-maker.

The details of that tragic expedition, leading to the execution of the earl in 1601, have little to do with Harington's career, except for one false move, probably an innocent one, made by Essex in the course of the campaign. Like all commanders acting in a viceregal capacity, he held deputed authority to confer knighthoods. It was, however, a power to be used with great discretion and moderation. Even the great Leicester, for whom Elizabeth had an affection far deeper and more passionate than her quasi-maternal, half-sentimental emotion for Essex, had greatly offended her by a too free creation of new knights. Essex now made the same mistake, and one of the officers knighted was John Harington, the queen's own godson.

Riding into the wilds of Connaught with his Markham cousins, Sir John, we may be sure, glowed with satisfaction in his new dignity. Until the invalidism preceding his death he always had a schoolboyish zest in all his projects and activities. It must have been pleasant to dwell on the details of that knighthood conferred by the beloved leader. It offset the discomforts of Irish weather and Irish food, long hours in the saddle, cheerless bivouacs, the nervous strain of guarding against ambush. Nor can we blame him much if he dwelt a bit on the mental picture of the people at home—the faithful servants and the honest rustics in Somerset, with their, 'Ay, Sir John,' and 'No, Sir John,' the London tailors and jewellers who would bow obsequiously as the apprentices doffed their caps and made way for the gentleman whose credit had been extended because of his knighthood and his service for queen and country against the Papistical Irish rebels.

Sir John had a rude awakening in England. The Earl of Essex, angry and uneasy because of the royal displeasure and the machinations of his enemies at Court, had, in defiance of the queen's orders, abandoned his post in Ireland and hurried home to see what he could do in person. His method and his manner led to a crisis with the elderly queen. The Cecil party, rightly or not, was able to make his conduct appear as disobedient, disrespectful, even disloyal. It was unlucky for Harington that he was one of the earl's entourage on the journey to London.

Perhaps Elizabeth was angered that John Harington should have been knighted in Ireland. She, if anyone, should have had the knighting of her own godson. We cannot believe that she suspected him of any part in a treasonable plot, even if she had begun to suspect the earl's motives at this time. Her treatment of Harington suggests only an outburst of nervous irritation. 'What, did the fool bring you too?' she asked, and then exclaimed impatiently, 'Go back to your business!' Even her godson's falling to his knees did not mollify her. She seized him by his girdle and swore one of her favourite oaths. 'By God's Son, I am no queen! This man (Essex) is above me.' Harington needed no urging to leave the Presence. He went as if all the Irish rebels were after him. 'In good sooth, I feared her Majesty more than the rebel Tyrone, and wished I had never received my Lord of Essex' honour of knighthood.' A little later he made an entry in his journal—'Thank heaven, I am safe at home, and if I go into such troubles again, I deserve the gallows for a meddling fool.'

The queen's anger against him did not last very long. He had not himself disobeyed any royal orders, and his acceptance of knighthood from his lawful superior could not be held against him. Elizabeth was not an unjust woman, and, anyhow, she had an affection for her amusing and sometimes naïve godson. We must bear in mind also, her gratitude to his parents who had stood loyally by her and shared her imprisonment in Queen Mary's time. It is very improbable that the new knight was in danger of anything more awesome than the queen's displeasure. although that, as he well knew, could be a very disturbing experience.

A letter he wrote to a friend some time after Essex' return to London speaks of a threat of transfer to naval service. That worried the veteran of Sligo and Connaught, but perhaps his godmother was merely giving him a jolt. His very submissiveness, by contrast with the Earl of Essex' arrogance, may have been a source of irritation. 'I came to Court in the very heat and height of all displeasures,' says the letter to Sir Anthony Standen, 'and after I had been there but an hour I was threatened with the fleet. I answered that, coming so late from the land service, I hoped I should not be prest to serve in her Majesty's fleet. After three days every man wondered to see me at liberty. After four or five days the Queen had talked of me, and twice talked to me, though very briefly. At last she gave me a full and gracious audience in the withdrawing room at Whitehall, where herself being accuser, judge, and witness, I was cleared and graciously dismissed. In December I came hither.'

Back at Kelston, with his dearest Mall and his family and animals, he settled down again to the life of a country gentleman, but there was one worry from which he never wholly freed himself—the disparity between income and expenditure. In that age of lavish display, of fantastically rich male attire, of bribery and jobbery to get or retain favour at Court, being in financial straits was a common enough thing among the men of Harington's set. The trouble was that there were virtually no honest jobs of work to which a gentleman and a courtier could turn to get himself out of the red without loss of prestige. 'Adventuring' or speculating on one of the semi-piratical voyages of Drake or a Hawkins might bring in a handsome percentage of profit or leave the investor deprived of his last shilling. In any case, some capital or a degree of credit was needed. Harington was unable or unwilling to invest in any of the 'adventures' and the loss of the Nyland estate stirred him to making efforts for easy money.

Legacy-hunting seemed to be the road to affluence. His mother-in-law, Lady Rogers of Cannington, was getting old, her health was breaking down, and evidently she had not many years to live. She had always been friendly to her young, gay son-in-law, read his verses and translations, laughed at his slightly off-colour jokes and stories, and gossiped with him in a hearty man-to-man fashion. She appeared to be heaven's answer to the prayers of a hard-up knight. The idea was that she should cut out her son in favour of her daughter, Harington's wife. Her will, alas, was a bitter disappointment.

Family sentiment about the male heir had been stronger than the good-fellowship between mother-in-law and son-in-law. There was nothing for Sir John. This did not deter him from trying to enforce what he regarded as a moral claim. When the old lady was dying, he had already broken open a few chests in her house, taken over her papers, and done his best to establish himself as master. After her death he tried to shut out her son Edward, the legal claimant. This led to more trouble—a Star Chamber case this time. There might have been a sentence of imprisonment, but the merry poet's knack of getting into hot water was balanced by a facility in getting out of it again. Nothing serious happened to him, except the disappointment. Soon he managed to resume his London interludes, with attendance on his aging godmother as a sop to his conscience.

History is the richer for these last visits of Harington to the queen in the opening years of the seventeenth century. He was a keen observer and he transcribed accurately what he had seen and heard. His entries in his journal at this time conjure up for us a poignant likeness of the dying Elizabeth—the gloom and disillusion, the inner loneliness, the remorse over Essex' execution, the doubts and fears, perhaps, assailing that brilliant, sceptical mind. And then there was the sudden touch of petulance, followed by a sad, tolerant smile for the well-meaning godson.

U

The sense of time, past and present, was becoming vague at the end. The queen, harking back to the Essex tragedy, asked Harington if he had ever seen Tyrone, the Irish leader. 'Oh, now it mindeth me that you was one who saw this man elsewhere.' Then the memory of the beheaded favourite was too much for her. A few tears rolled down the haggard cheeks and on to the embroidered bodice. Sir John tried to cheer her up by reading some of his amusing verses. They had acted as a tonic before, but now such things had lost their savour. The queen managed to smile, but her words were full of sadness.

'When thou dost feel creeping time at thy gates, these fooleries will please thee less: I am past my relish for such matters.'

Harington records also the evidence of suspicion and disquiet, bred of memories of treasonable intrigues, deposition schemes, plots for assassination, the Earl of Essex' abortive rising.

'The many evil plots and designs have overcome all her Highness' sweet temper. She walks much in her privy chamber, and stamps with her feet at ill news, and thrusts her rusty sword at times into the arras in great rage. My Lord Buckhurst is much with her, and few else since the city business, but the dangers are over, and yet she always keeps a sword by her table. So disordered is all order that her Highnesse hath worne but one change of raiment for many days, and sweers much at those that cause greefs in such wise, to the no small discomfiture of all about her.'

Before these words were written, perhaps some six

months before the queen's death, her godson had begun to get ready to seek the favours of her successor. We need not write him down callous and ungrateful. English history already carried its warning record of disputed successions and dynastic rivalries, resulting in lawlessness, civil strife, and insecurity. Elizabeth was nearing her seventieth year. She would die, as she had lived—*pace* Cardinal Allen and Mr. Belloc—the Virgin Queen. The succession was not a matter only for heralds and genealogists. It concerned the rich man's security in his possessions, the poor man's freedom to live out his life in his craft or on his few acres. Few Englishmen would willingly see the strong rule of the Tudors followed by anything like the anarchy of Stephen's reign or the thirty years' struggle between the houses of York and Lancaster.

Catholics tended to support the claims made for Arabella Stuart, daughter of the Earl of Lennox. From the continent the redoubtable Father Robert Persons, writing under a pseudonym, supported the claim of the Spanish Infanta. Most Englishmen, and Harington along with them, saw Elizabeth's cousin, James VI of Scotland, as having the best claim. For some years the aging queen had apparently accepted James as her heir, although she refused to name her successor explicitly. It is doubtful if she ever did so, although a feeble gesture of the dying queen was interpreted as a definite 'Yes' to the question of James as heir to the English crown. Opportunistic Englishmen in high places, including Sir Walter Ralegh and possibly Robert Cecil, kept in touch, however, with the pro-Spanish faction. Hedging one's bets had always been accepted in sporting affairs. In Elizabethan times a quisling was wrong only if his forcecast had been in error, but the man who spread his risks prudently—and discreetly—was almost without blame.

Harington, with less opportunism or more loyalty to the known wishes of his queen and godmother, was wholly for James. If self-interest seemed to point in the same direction as loyalty, so much the better. He set to work on a treatise to back up the Stuart king's title. This *Tract on the Succession to the Crown*, completed the year before the queen died, was unsigned, but its authorship has been established. There seems to be little doubt that Harington looked forward to its being read by James and thereby winning goodwill for the author. This did not come to pass, nor did Harington for some years make much headway with the Scottish king. The latter's attention was fixed on younger and more personable men than the middle-aged knight from Somerset.

Towards the end of March, 1603, the old queen died. Whitgift, the Archbishop of Canterbury, attended her on her death bed. Her Councillors stood around her, urgent for a word or other token of her wishes for the succession. When speech had left her and consciousness was flickering, she made the movement into which the bystanders read her assent to James' claim.

Whatever his anxiety to stand in well with the new monarch, Harington, warm-hearted and affectionate, grieved for Elizabeth, the brilliant queen-godmother who had smiled on his babyhood and schooldays and his years at the university, and then the rather tart old lady who frightened and snubbed the tactless author of *Ajax Metamorphosed*, and, later still, terrified the new and perhaps slightly absurd knight who had come home with the Earl of Essex.

Harington had last seen her at Christmas time in 1602, that is, about three months before her death, and he had been touched and shocked by the change in her looks. Writing to dearest Mall, who was down at Kelston with the family and the animals, he says, 'I cannot blot out from my memorie's table the goodnesse of our Soveriegne Ladie to me, even (I will saie) before borne; her affectione to my mother, who waited in privie chamber; her bettering the state of my father's fortunes, her watchings over my youth, her likeinge to my free speech, and admiration of my little learninge and poesy, which I did so much cultivate on her commande, have rootede such love, such dutyfull remembrance of her princelie virtues, that to turne askante from her condition with tearless eyes, woud straine and foule the springe and founte of gratitude. '

A letter to one of his Markham cousins three years later reiterates his sentiments of affection and gratitude, but ends with a sentence that points up the Tudor character of Gloriana—'Againe she coude put forth such alteracions when obedience was lackinge, as lefte no doubtynges whose daughter she was.'

The efforts to get into the good graces of the new king, James VI of Scotland and I of England, and to reap some solid benefit thereby, were pathetic in their futility. The

Succession Tract had lost its usefulness by the time it was finished and never came before the eyes it was written for. The new king was safely on the throne. The Lady Arabella Stuart found few backers—even had she wanted them—and the ingenious treatise on behalf of the Infanta Isabella by Dolman, that is to say, Father Robert Persons, S.J., cut no ice even with the Catholics of England. In fact, when James' accession was a *fait accompli*, the great English Jesuit admonished his Catholic fellow-countrymen to be loyal to their new king. It was a sad thing for the Catholics of England that the Gunpowder Plot conspirators did not follow his advice. Harington's *Tract* found its way into the possession of Archbishop Toby Matthew and lay forgotten in the Chapter Library at York until modern times.

Presents at holiday times—Christmas, Easter, birthdays, and so forth—were a recognized way of seeking royal favour. Queen Elizabeth's coffers and wardrobes bulged with the accumulated gifts of her long reign. There was no reason to think that her Scots cousin would be less willing to accept a token of a loyal subject's devotion. Unfortunately for his own prospects, the Somersetshire knight, a good husband and father, could offer the king neither youthful male beauty nor money to lavish on those who had it. He did the best he could, an elaborate and curiously wrought lantern as a New Year's gift. James, an ungrateful and insensitive man where others' feelings were concerned, gave only a note of thanks in return, despite the flattering symbolism of the new light shining forth over England. We are not told what he thought about the application to himself *vis-à-vis* Harington of the dying thief's words to Christ, 'Lord, remember me when Thou comest into Thy Kingdom.' The crucifixion was included among the ornaments of the lantern so as to bring in the words. James, the wisest fool in Christendom, seems to have had little sense of the absurd where flattery of himself was concerned. Perhaps he liked the blasphemous compliment.

Harington, meanwhile, was importuning his courtier friends to do the wire-pulling that would secure him a personal interview. In the year following James' accession Lord Thomas Howard, who had been doing his best as his friend's advance agent at the Court, wrote to him that the time was ripe. 'You may set forward for Court whenever it suiteth your own conveniency: the King hath enquired after you, and would readily see and converse again with the "merry blade", as he hath oft called you, since you was here.'

The long letter which carried this welcome news also had in it some advice on winning James' favour. The royal pedant liked 'learned discourse', but more important was 'good fashion in clothes'. The writer went into detail for his friend's guidance. 'I would wish you to be well trimmed; get a new jerkin, well bordered, and not too short; the King saith, he liketh a flowing garment; be sure it be not all of one sort, but diversely coloured, and the collar falling somewhat down, and your ruff well stiffened and bushy.'

'You must see Carr before you go to the King,' says Howard. Young Robert Carr, who had been a page in attendance on James when he went to England, was now the royal pet. In a few years he would be knighted and later made Earl of Somerset. Harington's friend was candid about the difficulty of competing with Carr under the circumstances. 'I tell you, good knight, this fellow is straight-limbed, well-favoured, strong-shouldered, and smooth-faced. . . . You are not young, you are not handsome, you are not finely, and yet will you come to Court and think to be well favoured?' Harington's learning, his wit, his mastery of languages and literatures, *may* help him for a while, just because they were novelties in the new Court, but, adds Howard bitterly, 'These are not the things men live by nowadays.'

Another piece of advice about handling the new king leads our thoughts on to Mr. Gladstone. He and James I, so different in most ways, had one thing in common; they must never be contradicted. 'Do not of yourself say, "This is good or bad", but, "If it were your Majesty's good opinion, I myself should think so and so."'

We are not surprised that the letter was entrusted to the writer's own son for safe delivery, 'that no danger may happen from our freedoms'.

Lord Thomas Howard's letter might have deterred a less sanguine man, but Harington had the amiable optimism of a Micawber. He went to Court, dressed in his finery, as we see him in the old miniature, and ready to dazzle the learned fool with his erudition. The King was polite and friendly, and things seemed to be going well until James I got on to his special topic, witchcraft, the seventeenth-century obsession that sent a good many

innocent or deluded people to torture and death.
Harington's irresponsible levity got the better of him.
The king pursued the subject in his didactic manner and
'asketh me, with much gravitie, if I did trulie under-
stande why the Devil did worke more with ancient
women than others.' At this, Sir John confesses, 'I
could not refrain from a scurvy jest.' It is improbable
that King James was shocked by any coarseness or bawdry
in the knight's answer, but he was nettled by anyone's
joking when he, the royal dominie, was holding forth.
The interview petered out, and Harington had nothing
to show for it but tailor's bills and the loss of money
spent on tips to royal flunkeys.

Hope sprang eternal in Sir John's breast. Courtly
hangers-on, badly in need of money but very averse from
unnecessary labour, scanned the news of what we should
call government jobs very much as an out-of-work
citizen pores over the *Situations Vacant* column in the
newspapers. The falling-in of a sinecure or the creation
of a new monopoly brought the knightly spongers or their
letter-carrying messengers swarming to London to see
what could be done about it. Harington watched his
opportunity. In 1605 he thought he saw his chance.
It was in Ireland, a country he knew at first hand.

The Lord Chancellorship of Ireland had fallen vacant.
The income from this high office was what the Harington
finances needed, and the knight had no objection to a
period of residence in Ireland. In fact, he seems to have
developed something of a liking for Ireland while he was
soldiering there. His love of a joke and a certain good-

natured scurrility may have called forth a congenial response from the Irish. Anyhow, he wrote to Robert Cecil proposing himself for the job. It might not have been at all a bad appointment. Harington was tolerant in matters of religion, wholly devoid of the persecuting spirit of his generation, and his ideas on conciliating and governing Ireland were far ahead of the times. Of technical qualifications he probably had none, but such appointments were royal favours, and bore little relation to the public welfare.

Another and very different Irish vacancy occurred at this time—the Archbishopric of Dublin, the Protestant one, of course. With a seriousness that was either incredibly naïve or unblushingly impudent, Harington proposed himself for this dignity also. Not only did he propose himself for this, the highest position in the new Church which England was trying to force upon the Irish, but he compiled a brochure containing data on Irish affairs and setting forth his reasons for combining the temporal and spiritual functions of the two positions of Lord Chancellor and Primate in one person, Sir John Harington's. The salaries of the two lofty dignities would, of course, be paid to him. The pamphlet came to light in Victorian times and was published as *A Short View of the State of Ireland*.

The Elizabethan and Stuart sense of humour, if less subtle than ours, was more violent. Whether its sense of the ridiculous operated on the same lines, it is hard to know precisely. However, the 'merry poet', with his naughty verses from Ariosto circulating among the ladies of the Court, his 'cloacinian satire' on flush toilets, his foppery in dress, and his chronic indebtedness, as Archbishop of Dublin would have been a bit too much even for the era of graft and jobbery that came in with the advent of James I and his feather-brained wife Anne of Denmark. Little Robert Cecil, the hunchback political genius, must have smiled cynically at a proposal that would have genuinely shocked his father, the 'Old Fox', but the Cecils were very discreet about what they put on paper or said in the hearing of others. Robert did not commit himself; he did not even acknowledge Harington's letter.

Sir John still spent a good deal of time at the Court, but its manners and morals under the new ruler disgusted him. He was by no means squeamish about trifles, but even if we allow for some bias due to his disappointment about jobs and salaries, we must sympathize with his revulsion. He contemplated the gluttonous and bibulous king, who had a pathological horror of soap and water, living in a separate establishment from his wife, and slobbering over his handsome but worthless young Robert Carr; the frivolous Anne of Denmark, intent only on feasts, masques, and pageants; and the swarm of ready-made knights and baronets, the latter a new, money-raising device of the king; the scarcely concealed lechery and the quite unconcealed drunkenness in Court circles. It was too much for Sir John. 'In the Queen's days I never did see such lack of good order, discretion and sobriety as I have now done. I wish I was at home.'

In spite of his disgust at a king who had to be helped
to his feet in the middle of a masque, and ladies of the
Court who fell down drunk while trying to perform their
amateur theatricals, Harington hung about London hoping
for some kind of official appointment. His persistence
gained him a vague kind of tutorship to the young Prince
Henry, the elder of James I's sons. The boy, who was
good-looking, athletic, studious, and serious, was as
unlike his parents in character as a child could be. His
father was annoyed with him because, although a skilled
rider, he preferred golf, and swimming in the Thames, to
hunting. The mass of the people idolized him, and when
he was made Prince of Wales a few years later they were
full of hope for the future. The young prince's death of a
fever when he was only eighteen years old they looked
upon as a national calamity.

There must have been a core of serious purpose in
Sir John's character for him to have undertaken the
work and given to it the time and energy he did. The
evidence is in the letters he wrote to the prince, and the
work he composed for his instruction. This latter was an
appendix to a contemporary book about pre-Reformation
English bishops. Prince Henry had a touch of the
Puritan about him. Perhaps this was one of the things
that appealed to something in the plebeian mass of the
English people, something that would in time evolve into
the Nonconformist conscience. Harington, a sound
episcopalian, disapproved of Puritan ideas on episco-
pacy and sought to counteract them in his royal pupil.

The official relation between the middle-aged knight

and the youthful heir to the throne developed into friendship, so far as there can be friendship between a com-
moner and the heir-apparent. That this was so is evident
from Sir John's letters to Prince Henry. Harington wrote
to the boy-prince charming and enthusiastic descriptions
of the marvellous sagacity of the pet dog that in its lifetime had been the pride and joy of the Kelston household.
The tutor to royalty would not have done this unless there
had been some degree of intimacy to set against the
contemporary sensitiveness to caste.

Doubtless every cherished dog or cat is in the eyes of
its owner the best and wisest of its species, but Harington's pet dog, 'my servant Bungy', as he calls him, must
have been a paragon among dogs. Bungy, or Bungay, a
spaniel, had an intelligence that rated him a very high
canine I.Q. He served as his master's letter-carrier,
and could be trusted to carry a pair of wine bottles
safely from place to place. He was even shrewd enough
to hide one of them in the bushes and retrieve it later
when the fastenings gave way, and he faced the problem
of transporting two separate mouthfuls of bottle. On
one occasion he strayed, or, perhaps, was kidnapped, and
his master traced him to the Spanish Embassy. Harington
overruled the ambassador's claim to the animal and proved
his ownership by sending Bungy at a gesture to take a
roast pheasant from His Excellency's dinner-table. Then,
on another sign from his owner, the dog took the pheasant
back and replaced it under its cover.

Harington presented a copy of his *Orlando Furioso* to
Prince Henry, chiefly perhaps for the sake of the title

page, whereon Bungy, with his chain fastened to a column, sits contentedly, gazing at his master's portrait. From the dog's mouth a scroll is drawn, with a quotation from the poem printed on it: *Fin che venga* (Until he comes). The prince is told of a portrait of the dog especially painted for the benefit of Harington's descendants. Unfortunately the whereabouts of this painting, if it still exists, is unknown.

Bungy had not remained immune from the occupational fault of courtiers—he was a bit of a snob. He was, says his owner, 'knowne to the best ladies of England'. We may surmise that Elizabeth herself would have stroked or fondled the spaniel's head. The gesture would have given her a chance to display her long, graceful fingers, of which she was very proud.

The influence of Harington was just what was needed to offset a too serious, almost a priggish streak in Prince Henry's character. It was a revulsion against the spirit of James I's Court. We read, for instance, of the prince's dislike of swearing and blasphemous language amongst the members of his household, a sentiment he shared with his younger brother, afterwards King Charles I.

It might have been well for England had the gifted and popular young man lived to reign as the second Stuart king—with the tolerant, humane and witty knight at his elbow as a foil to a too uncompromising rectitude. Then, perhaps, the country would have been saved from a civil war and nearly a dozen years of Puritan dictatorship. Unhappily both men were nearing their end, although neither can have guessed that death was so close at hand.

The prince was cut off by typhoid fever in 1612, the year in which death came to Sir John also. In the spring of that year Robert Cecil, who had become the first Earl of Salisbury, visited the merry poet whose application for the primacy of the Protestant Church in Ireland he had left unanswered. Merriment and poetry were alike ended for Sir John Harington. In middle age—he was only fifty-one—he had a stroke which reduced him to a state of helplessness. Cecil describes him as 'sick of a dead palsy'. That was in the middle of May. Neither the doctors nor dearest Mall could do anything for the stricken knight. He lingered on until the winter, and died in November. He was buried in Kelston Church, within the chancel. Mary survived him for more than a score of years. Until the latter part of the eighteenth century the house at Kelston was still occupied by Haringtons, descendants of the seven out of nine children who survived their father, a good record for an age of appalling infant mortality.

The snuffing-out at the age of fifty-one by a 'dead palsy' of the cheerful, humane, and tolerant knight appears tragic to us as we piece his story together from the fragments scattered through his various writings. He comes closer to ourselves in various ways than most of the Elizabethans. His care for personal cleanliness and his love of animals are of the twentieth rather than the sixteenth century. The picture of his domestic life in his Somersetshire home has a pleasing, eighteenth-century air about it. His was a time when the rack and the thumbscrew, burning alive, the executioner's rope and the disembowelling knife, were all accepted methods of dealing with what our age calls subversive activities. Deviations from *Cujus regio, ejus religio*, or, in other words, the Party Line, were treated to some or all of these barbarities. Harington, however, wished 'all rancour laid away on all sides' and, appealing to all the major parties who argued over the succession to the throne of his godmother, he wrote, 'I exhort therefore againe and againe all parties, to leave to persecute, and learne to perswade. Attempt by reason and not by rigour to wynne the adverse parte.'

When all has been said, however, the merry poet, although a late Elizabethan, was a genuine Renaissance Englishman. Into fifty-one years he crammed enough experience and enough activity, even in the pursuit of ease, to furnish careers for several Grand Old Men of later eras—the friendship and affection of England's Elizabeth I, happy family life and country squiredom, a successful writer's career, with at least one best-seller, the translation of *Orlando Furioso*, and a resounding *succès de scandale*, the *Ajax*, a term of military service marked by courage and endurance and rewarded with a knighthood, the tutorship of a brilliant and popular young prince, and, throughout it all, that zest for life which seems to be only a nostalgic memory for us of the atomic age.

Nihil obstat

CAROLUS DAVIS, S.T.L.
Censor deputatus.

Imprimatur

E. MORROGH BERNARD
Vic. Gen.

Westmonasterii, die 13a Junii, 1956.